FAHRENHEIT 451

Common Core
LitPlans

Teacher's Guide
& Student Workbook

Common Core Aligned
Differentiated Instruction Friendly

Meets and exceeds the Common Core Standards to give you the very best, most comprehensive resources for teaching literature, reading, writing, vocabulary, life lessons, and more to students on a variety of levels.

COPYRIGHT INFORMATION

This is copyrighted material.
It may not be copied or distributed in any way
without written permission from Teacher's Pet Publications.

The purchaser may copy the student materials
for his or her classroom use only.
No other portion may be copied or distributed in any way.

No portion may be posted on the Internet
without written permission from Teacher's Pet Publications.

Copyright violations are prosecuted to the fullest extent of the law
and are subject to a minimum of a $500.00 fine,
imposed by Teacher's Pet Publications,
in addition to any other legal judgments obtained.

Copyright questions?
Contact Teacher's Pet Publications
www.tpet.com

ISBN 978-1-60249-711-5
Copyright 2014
Mary B. Collins

Published by
Teacher's Pet Publications
www.tpet.com

TABLE OF CONTENTS
Common Core LitPlans: Fahrenheit 451

5	**STUDENT WORKBOOK**
7	Student Workbook Contents
149	**TEACHER'S GUIDE**
150	**How to Use This Guide**
151	**Lesson One**
152	Vocabulary Reading Assignment 1
156	**Lesson Two**
162	**Lesson Three**
163	Quiz Reading Assignment 1
165	Character Notes Reading Assignment 1
166	Events and Points of Interest Reading Assignment 1
167	**Lesson Four**
168	Study Questions Reading Assignment 1
171	Passages for Discussion Reading Assignment 1
172	**Lesson Five**
173	Vocabulary Reading Assignment 2
177	Writing Assignment 1
178	**Lesson Six**
179	Quiz Reading Assignment 2
181	Character Notes Reading Assignment 2
182	Events and Points of Interest Reading Assignment 2
183	Study Questions Reading Assignment 2
186	Passages for Discussion Reading Assignment 2
188	**Lesson Seven**
189	Vocabulary Reading Assignment 3
193	Oral Reading Evaluation
194	**Lesson Eight**
195	Quiz Reading Assignment 3
197	Character Notes Reading Assignment 3
198	Events and Points of Interest Reading Assignment 3
200	Study Questions Reading Assignment 3
204	Passages for Discussion Reading Assignment 3
207	**Lesson Nine**
208	Vocabulary Reading Assignment 4
212	Writing Assignment 2
213	**Lesson Ten**
214	Writing Evaluation
215	**Lesson Eleven**
216	Quiz Reading Assignment 4
218	Character Notes Reading Assignment 4
219	Events and Points of Interest Reading Assignment 4
220	Study Questions Reading Assignment 4
222	Passages for Discussion Reading Assignment 4

TABLE OF CONTENTS (Continued)
Common Core LitPlans: Fahrenheit 451

225	**Lessons Twelve Through End**
226	Lesson: Historical Context
229	Lesson: Point of View
231	Lesson: Setting and Conflict
233	Lesson: Character Development
243	Lesson: Symbolism
259	Lesson: Theme
267	Discussion Activity: Censorship
269	Activity: Exploration of Additional Themes
272	Lesson: Use of Language
279	**Additional Lessons, Activities, and Assignments**
281	Comic Strip Characters (Reading Assignment 1)
283	Clarisse's Poem (Reading Assignment 1)
285	Back In The Day (Reading Assignment 1)
288	Writing Technique (Reading Assignment 1)
289	Are You Happy? (Reading Assignment 1)
291	What's In Your Window? (Reading Assignment 1)
293	Play The Man, Master Ridley (Reading Assignment 2)
295	Books, Books, Books (Reading Assignment 2)
297	Dover Beach (Reading Assignment 3)
300	TV Favorites (Reading Assignment 3)
302	Judging A Candidate (Reading Assignment 3)
304	If I Were A Book (Reading Assignment 4)
305	The Things That Must Be Thought (Reading Assignment 4)
306	Ecclesiastes (Reading Assignment 4)
309	**Unit Tests**
335	**Additional Resources**

Note: In the Student Workbook, references to the exact title and publisher have been removed to try to make it harder for students to look on line to find the teacher's guide and answer keys.

FAHRENHEIT 451

Student Workbook
& Study Guide

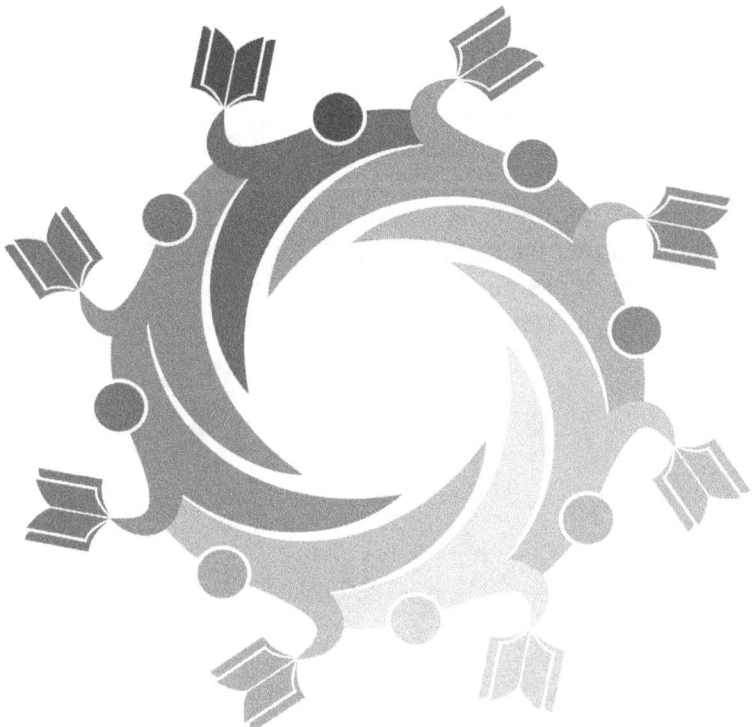

Study Questions
Vocabulary Worksheets
Elements Of Fiction
Writing Assignments

Get the most out of what you read with this comprehensive resource for studying literature.
Improve your reading, writing, vocabulary, and other essential skills.

© 2014

COPYRIGHT INFORMATION

This is copyrighted material.

The purchaser may copy the student materials
for his or her classroom use only.
It may not be copied or distributed for any other purpose
without written permission from the publisher.

No portion may be posted on the Internet
without written permission from the publisher.

Copyright violations are prosecuted to the fullest extent of the law
and are subject to a minimum of a $500.00 fine,
imposed by the publisher
in addition to any other legal judgments obtained.

ISBN 978-1-60249-712-2
Copyright 2014
All Rights Reserved

TABLE OF CONTENTS
STUDENT WORKBOOK
Fahrenheit 451

9	**How To Use This Workbook**
11	**Reading Assignment 1**
13	Character Notes Reading Assignment 1
14	Events and Points of Interest Reading Assignment 1
15	Vocabulary Reading Assignment 1
19	Study Questions Reading Assignment 1
22	Passages for Discussion Reading Assignment 1
23	Comic Strip Characters
24	Clarisse's Poem
25	Back In The Day
27	What's In Your Window?
28	Reader Response Reading Assignment 1
31	**Reading Assignment 2**
33	Character Notes Reading Assignment 2
34	Events and Points of Interest Reading Assignment 2
35	Vocabulary Reading Assignment 2
39	Study Questions Reading Assignment 2
42	Passages for Discussion Reading Assignment 2
43	Play The Man, Master Ridley
44	Books, Books, Books
45	KWL Reading Assignment 2
46	Reader Response Reading Assignment 2
47	**Reading Assignment 3**
49	Character Notes Reading Assignment 3
50	Events and Points of Interest Reading Assignment 3
51	Vocabulary Reading Assignment 3
55	Study Questions Reading Assignment 3
59	Passages for Discussion Reading Assignment 3
61	Dover Beach
62	TV Favorites
63	Judging A Candidate
64	KWL Reading Assignment 3
65	Reader Response Reading Assignment 3
67	**Reading Assignment 4**
69	Character Notes Reading Assignment 4
70	Events and Points of Interest Reading Assignment 4
71	Vocabulary Reading Assignment 4
75	Study Questions Reading Assignment 4
77	Passages for Discussion Reading Assignment 4
79	Ecclesiastes
80	KWL Reading Assignment 4
81	Reader Response Reading Assignment 4

TABLE OF CONTENTS (continued)
STUDENT WORKBOOK
Fahrenheit 451

- 83 **Writing Assignments**
- 91 **Whole Book Study**
- 93   Historical Context
- 95   Point of View
- 96   Story Map
- 97   Plot Diagram
- 98   Setting & Conflict
- 99   Character Development
- 108   Character Comparison
- 110   Character Traits
- 113   Symbolism & Imagery
- 118   Article Evaluation
- 127   Themes
- 134   Exploration of Additional Themes
- 136   Use of Language
- 142   Figurative Language
- 144   Unit Crossword
- 146   Vocabulary Crossword

HOW TO USE THIS STUDENT WORKBOOK
Fahrenheit 451

This workbook contains assignments, graphic organizers, study questions, vocabulary work, writing assignments, and more to help you get the most out of reading *Fahrenheit 451* by Ray Bradbury.

Before you begin a reading assignment:
- **Read through the materials in this workbook for that section of the novel.**
- **Complete the Vocabulary Work for that section of the novel.**

This will give you a "heads up" about what will be important in the reading assignment and alert your brain ahead of time to look for certain information and will help prepare you to understand what you are reading.

As you read:
- **Make notes on the AS YOU READ Character and Events and Points of Interest pages in your workbook.**

This will help you remember what you have read and give you notes to refer to and study. You might be able to do this as you read through the first time, but the best way to do this is to read through the assignment first, and then go back and make notes on the workbook pages. **You will be surprised how much more you will discover and remember if you take the time to read each assignment a second time.**

After you read the assignment:
- **Prepare answers for the STUDY & DISCUSSION QUESTIONS.**

These workbook pages point out important ideas presented in the text. Your teacher may have more specific directions about how and when these pages are to be completed.

Throughout this book study, you will have a variety of additional assignments. Your teacher will tell you which of the additional assignments in this workbook you will be responsible to complete and by when they must be completed.

A Final Note:
As with most things in life, you will get out of this unit what you put into it. If you do the assignments in a timely manner with care and your best efforts, you will be rewarded with knowledge and skills that will help you in life.

Relevance:
Most people who have heard anything about *Fahrenheit 451* think of it as "about book burning and censorship." But a careful reading of this novel reveals so much more. It is a book about what causes a society to degenerate and collapse. It is a warning to all generations about the dangers of giving up responsibility and active participation in life. It is a herald of the consequences of seeking happiness in the wrong places. And, like Clarisse subtly challenges Montag in the novel, this book challenges us to evaluate our own lives and our own society.

NOTES
Fahrenheit 451

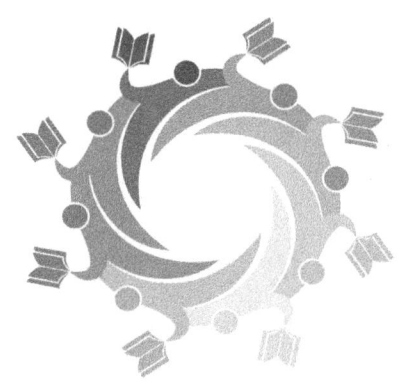

READING ASSIGNMENT 1
Fahrenheit 451

THIS ASSIGNMENT COVERS APPROXIMATELY
THE FIRST HALF OF CHAPTER ONE:
"THE HEARTH AND THE SALAMANDER"

START:
Beginning of chapter one

END:
Read through the end of the paragraph beginning
"And, then, Clarisse was gone."

NOTES
Fahrenheit 451

CHARACTER NOTES
Reading Assignment 1 Fahrenheit 451

As you read Assignment 1 use this graphic organizer to jot down information about characters.

MONTAG	CLARISSE

MILDRED	BEATTY

EVENTS & POINTS OF INTEREST
Reading Assignment 1 Fahrenheit 451

As you read Assignment 1 make notes of the series of main events that take place. Put them in the order that they are given in the text.

_____

_____

_____

_____

_____

_____

_____

OTHER POINTS OF INTEREST TO IDENTIFY OR KNOW THE SIGNIFICANCE OF:

Seashells

The sleeping pills

The parlor walls

The Hound

VOCABULARY WORK FOR ASSIGNMENT 1
Fahrenheit 451

PART I: Using Prior Knowledge And Contextual Clues
Use any clues you can find in the sentences from the text combined with your prior knowledge and write what you think the bold word means.

1. With his symbolic helmet number 451 on his **stolid** head...he flicked the igniter and the house jumped up in a gorging fire.
   _____

2. Impossible: for how many people did you know that **refracted** your own light to you.
   _____

3. And if the muscles of his jaws stretched **imperceptibly**, she would yawn long before he would.
   _____

4. He felt that the stars had been **pulverized** by the sound of the black jets and that in the morning the earth would be covered with their dust like a strange snow.
   _____

5. And the men with the cigarettes in their straight-lined mouths, the men with the eyes of puff adders, took up their load of machine and tube, their case of liquid **melancholy** and the slow dark sludge of nameless stuff, and strolled out the door.
   _____

6. Light flickered on bits of ruby glass and on sensitive **capillary** hairs in the nylon-brushed nostrils of the creature...
   _____

7. Below, the Hound had sunk back down upon its eight incredible insect legs and was humming to itself again, its **multifaceted** eyes at peace.
   _____

8. It's like a lesson in **ballistics**. It has a trajectory we decide on for it.
   _____

Vocabulary Work For Fahrenheit 451 Assignment 1, Page 2

PART II: Matching
Considering the usage in Part I, match the vocabulary words to their definitions.

_____ 1. stolid   A. Sadness; gloominess

_____ 2. refracted   B. The study of the dynamics of projectiles

_____ 3. imperceptibly   C. Having or revealing little emotion

_____ 4. pulverized   D. Having many faces, sides, or dimensions

_____ 5. melancholy   E. Deflected from a straight path

_____ 6. capillary   F. Without being detected by ordinary senses

_____ 7. multifaceted G. Fine; small in diameter

_____ 8. ballistics   H. Reduced to powder

Part III: Cloze Passage
Fill in the blanks with the appropriate vocabulary words from the list above.

The _____ colonel got ready for the testing of the latest army weapon. The missile with its _____ capabilities could not be _____ from a target no matter how an enemy might try to deflect it. The _____ behind the new invention were impressive, with the triggering mechanism being _____ in size. When fired, the missile would race _____ towards its target, which soon would be _____ upon impact. Though a complete success in design and function, a certain _____ fell over the observers as they thought how deadly such a weapon would be and how unsuspecting would be its victims.

Vocabulary Work For Fahrenheit 451 Assignment 1, Page 3

PART IV: Words In Practice
Answer the questions and be able to give short explanations to justify your answers.

1. If someone has a stolid reaction to what has happened, is that person excited about the results or unaffected by them?
   _____

2. If an object thrown at you is refracted, are you safe, or are you at risk?
   _____

3. If something is imperceptibly approaching you, do you know it's coming?
   _____

4. If an object has been pulverized, is it enhanced or has it most likely become useless?
   _____

5. If a person is melancholy, is that person ready to party or more likely to want to be left alone?
   _____

6. Do your capillary veins carry the bulk of your blood flow?
   _____

7. Give an example of something that is multifaceted.
   _____

8. Would someone be more likely to find expertise in ballistics at the FBI or among one's friends?
   _____

VOCABULARY CROSSWORD
Reading Assignment 1 Fahrenheit 451
Use the word list from Part II Matching

Deflected from a straight path (9)
Fine; small in diameter (9)
Having many faces or sides (12)
Having or revealing little emotion (6)
Impossible to detect by ordinary senses (13)
Reduced to powder (10)
Sadness; gloominess (10)
The study of the dynamics of projectiles (10)

STUDY & DISCUSSION QUESTIONS
Reading Assignment 1 Fahrenheit 451

1. What is Montag's occupation, and how is his job different from what we expect?

2. Of what is the number 451 on Montag's helmet symbolic?

3. What is a "minstrel man," and why does Bradbury choose this image?

4. What words and phrases does Bradbury use to give a feeling of mystery or anticipation just before Montag first meets Clarisse?

5. Why is Clarisse able to "get to" Montag in their first meetings?

Study & Discussion Questions: Fahrenheit 451 Reading Assignment 1, Page 2

6. Explain in what ways Clarisse and Mildred are different from each other.

7. Montag is thinking about Clarisse when he thinks, "...how many people did you know that refracted your own light back at you?" How does this thought apply to Clarisse and Montag?

8. One of the men who comes to pump Mildred's stomach says, "You don't need an M.D., case like this; all you need is two handymen, clean up the problem in half an hour." How does this statement aptly sum up the whole process described in the preceding paragraphs?

9. What does the Hound's reaction to Montag at the firehouse tell us?

10. Early in the first reading assignment, Montag's ventilator grill is mentioned twice. Review these two references and tell what you think is behind the ventilator grill.

Study & Discussion Questions: Fahrenheit 451 Reading Assignment 1, Page 3

11. Clarisse calls herself "crazy" and "a fool." Others call her "anti-social." Do you think Clarisse is crazy, a fool, or anti-social? Support your answer with logical reasoning and examples from the text.

12. About school, Clarisse says, "It's all a lot of funnels and water poured down the spout and out the bottom, and them telling us it's wine when it's not." What does she mean?

13. Beatty asks Montag if he has a guilty conscience. Montag glances up quickly. Then Beatty stares at him and begins to laugh softly. What do you make of this exchange?

14. How is the world Clarisse and Montag live in similar to our world today?

15. Is our world more like the "old days" Clarisse's uncle speaks of, or is it more like the world of Clarisse and Montag's time?

Study & Discussion Questions: Fahrenheit 451 Reading Assignment 1, Page 4

ADDITIONAL PASSAGES FOR DISCUSSION

1. Discuss the imagery in the passage beginning, "The autumn leaves blew over the moonlit pavement...."

2. "You laugh when I haven't been funny and you answer right off. You never stop to think what I've asked you."

3. They walked the rest of the way in silence, hers thoughtful, his a kind of clenching and uncomfortable silence in which he shot her accusing glances.

4. Go on, anyway, shove the bore down, slush up the emptiness, if such a thing could be brought out in the throb of the suction snake.

5. Only an hour, but the world had melted down and sprung up in a new and colorless form.

6. "What a shame," she said. "You're not in love with anyone."

7. He saw the silver needle extend upon the air an inch, pull back, extend, pull back. The growl simmered in the beast and it looked at him.

8. My uncle says his grandfather remembered when children didn't kill each other.

COMIC STRIP CHARACTERS
Fahrenheit 451

The first reading assignment has some great material for making comic-strip-style representations of the characters.

At the opening of the story, there's **Montag**, a larger-than-life fireman holding that python hose spewing venomous kerosene.

Later, a few pages from the end of the reading assignment section, **Beatty and the Mechanical Hound** provide excellent material for a cartoon artist to run with.

And then, there's **Clarisse**...dear, sweet Clarisse with all the images of nature associated with her. You can find 3 different scenes involving Clarisse in this section of the book, from which you can draw on for ideas.

Your assignment is to draw 3 comic strip cells, one for each of the three references above.
- You can make them any size you want, but no smaller than 3 x 3, so details can be included and seen.
- They should be done in color.
- Have fun exaggerating their qualities, as a comic strip artist would!

Here's how to go about doing it:
1. Go back to the text and re-read the parts relating to each character before you begin to draw, to get ideas and mental pictures to work from.
2. Jot down notes about what will be included in your images, notes for each of the three drawings. Consider things like: characters' facial expressions, body stance, other things in the image (like background images, things the character would be holding, etc.), colors that will be used, and size of the images, etc.
3. Look at some comic strip images to see how different artists draw within the individual cells and how they show faces and other elements--angles, perspectives, etc. Choose some cell layouts that you think might work well for your images, and use them as models as you do your own work.
4. Decide on the media you will use (markers, computer, paints) and gather your materials.
5. Make rough-draft sketches showing the layouts of each image.
6. Proceed with creating your masterpieces!

CLARISSE'S POEM (SONG)
Fahrenheit 451

Isn't it a nice time of night to walk? I like to smell things and look at things, and sometimes stay up all night, walking, and watch the sun rise.
--- Clarisse

She isn't physically present in any scenes after the first reading assignment section, yet her presence is felt throughout the novel. Have you ever met someone like that...someone whose personality sticks with you in a positive way long after he or she has left the room...someone like Clarisse?

Your assignment is to write a poem (or lyrics) entitled Clarisse's Poem (or Song), in which you convey the essence of Clarisse's character based on her scenes in the novel.

There is no specific length requirement, but it is highly unlikely you could do this assignment justice in just a few lines.

Here's how to go about doing it:
1. Skim through the text of Reading Assignment 1 to locate and reread the passages in which Clarisse participates.
2. Make notes about the things she does, what she says, how she is described. You can use words or phrases directly from the text.
3. Analyze what you have read and the notes you have made to construct in your own mind the key things that made Clarisse the person she was. What is the essence of her character?
4. Circle, jot down, or note what words or phrases would best convey "Clarisse."
5. Choose a form for your work: If you do a poem, what kind of a poem will you do? Free form? A poem with a strict rhyming pattern? A series of Haiku poems? If you do song lyrics, will they be in the form of rap? To the tune of a particular song you know or like or think would be appropriate for Clarisse?
6. Begin a rough draft of organizing words and phrases into your form. Don't be afraid to add your own words, not just words from the text. This is *your* work; you're not stuck with only Mr. Bradbury's words. Be descriptive. Make your readers *feel* who Clarisse was.
7. Rework, reword, rearrange, edit. Craft your poem (or song) about Clarisse carefully, to be the best you can make it.
8. Then, write a final draft. Decorate your final draft with appropriate illustrations if you are so inclined.

BACK IN THE DAY
Fahrenheit 451

Have you ever found an old coin, maybe dated 30 or 40 years ago, and wondered where all that coin had traveled in all those years...who else had it, what they bought with it? It's fun to imagine where it has been. The sad part is that you can never really *know*; it's not like the thing can tell its life's story.

Old *people*, on the other hand, can. They can tell you where they've been, what they've seen first-hand, what they remember about how things used to be, back in the day...like Clarisse's grandfather.

In terms of the message in Fahrenheit 451, people didn't *know* what had been done in the past; they just assumed that whatever they were being told was the truth. That often is a good assumption...but not always. If you don't know that firemen used to put out fires, and you see that they only start fires now...then it would be easy to assume that they never put out fires, if no one ever told you that they did. Did you know that all gas stations used to be full service and you never had to pump your own gas? The attendant did it--and he washed your windshield and checked your oil, too! ...Or did you just assume that everyone always pumped his or her own gas? A thing like that doesn't make a lot of difference, but some other things *do*.

If we don't talk to our grandfathers and grandmothers, our great-aunts and great-uncles, the old fella who lives down the street, or that old woman in the nursing home, we lose the passing-on of first-hand information. 30 or 40 years from now when your grandchild asks you how something was back in the 1900's, you may not have experienced it, but you can say, "My mother, my grandmother, or that old fella down the street once told me..." And *their* first-hand experience is passed on through several generations. You (thankfully) might never know what it was like to not be able to drink from the same water fountain as another person...but someone else can express to you the humiliation, the anger, the frustration he or she felt. And you know it was real. And because you know it was real, your grandchild will know it was real, too, when you tell her about it.

So *talk* with an old person...frequently. Listen to the stories of his life experiences, ask her about how things were different back in the day. What was it like when he came home from Vietnam? What did it mean to her to see the first man walk on the moon? What things did his grandfather tell *him* about why he came to America? Ask questions, listen, and remember. Then, some day in the future, if the history books say Americans never went to the moon; that's just an old story, you will recognize the lie, you will *know* what really happened.

Your assignment is to talk (and listen) to an old person. If you don't have old relatives, visit the American Legion or a nursing home, explain your assignment, and ask for some time to talk with someone there.

Fahrenheit 451: Back In The Day Activity, page 2

Some things to keep in mind:
- *Speak clearly and be patient.*
- *Be prepared with a list of questions.* If you really listen to what is said and if you think about it rather than just letting it go in one ear and out the other, you will probably also naturally have questions within the conversation.
- *Take notes so you can refer to them later.* If you have a recording device, ask the person you talk with if you may record the conversation rather than taking notes during it. Then go back later to make notes from the recording.
- *Be polite.* You may bump into a topic that the person is uncomfortable talking about. Just go on to something else. Your goal is not to upset anyone. Also, "please" and "thank you" are still appreciated by most people.

Here are some sample questions to get you started:
- What things from your childhood do you remember most vividly?
- What world events have had the most effect on you in your lifetime?
- What was your favorite thing to do when you were my age?
- Did you know your grandparents or great-aunts and uncles, and if so, what do you remember about them? What did they do for a living?
- What's the most important thing you have learned in your lifetime?

Add more of your own questions to this list. The point of the questions is to find out what really happened and what things were really like "back in the day," at a time before you can remember.

After you complete your interview, write a narrative telling about your experience with the interview. Here are some guidelines for this writing assignment:

Write an *introductory paragraph* in which you state the name and age of your interviewee and your relationship to that person. You could also mention how you felt about doing the interview. Were you nervous? Were you looking forward to it? Were you dreading it?

The body of your narrative should tell about the interview itself.
- You could organize the body of the narrative by making a paragraph for each of the questions you asked for which the interviewee had lengthy or interesting answers. Based on the first question above, the topic sentence for the paragraph might be something like this: "The thing [interviewee name] remembers most vividly about [his/her] childhood is...." And then your paragraph would include some of the details from the interviewee's reply.
- Another way to organize the body of the narrative would be by your reactions to the information you received in reply to your questions. For example, "I was surprised to find out that..." or "The most touching moment, for me, in the interview was..." or "It made me sad to find out that..." Think about how you felt about different parts of the interview conversation to come up with your own topic sentences. Then, fill out your paragraphs with details about what was said that made you feel that way, and why.

Write a concluding paragraph stating what you will remember most about this interviewing experience, and why.

WHAT'S IN YOUR WINDOW?
Fahrenheit 451

He stood outside the talking house in the shadows, thinking he might even tap on their door and whisper, "Let me come in. I won't say anything. I just want to listen. What is it you're saying?" --Guy Montag

Guy stood outside of Clarisse's home that evening, listening to the conversation. He wanted to hear more. If Montag were to stand outside your home, looking in your window, what would he see and hear on any typical evening?

Your assignment is to describe from Montag's point of view what he sees and hears while standing outside of your home one evening, looking in your window.

You may write this in any format you choose:
- as a descriptive essay
- as a play scene
- as a poem or song lyrics
- as a comic strip

Here's how to begin:
1. Choose the setting. In what room are things most likely to be going on at your house in the evening?
2. Make some notes describing the room--essential as well as unusual characteristics.
3. Make some notes about who will be in the room.
4. Make notes about what kind of conversation or activity that will typically be going on.
5. Go back and sketch in any dialogue that might be happening
6. Decide on the format for your description.
7. Begin writing a draft.

Think about and be prepared to state what Montag's reaction to what he sees and/or hears might be (and why you think he would feel that way).
- Would he want to come in just to listen?
- Would he be bored?
- Would he want to stay at the window watching?

READER RESPONSE
Fahrenheit 451

Complete a reader response journal entry for each reading assignment.
Here are some ideas of things you could write about in your entries!

CHECK YOUR UNDERSTANDING
Explain how the story is making sense to you.
Give examples & note page numbers.
Explain the setting, mood, point of view, conflicts, or character relationships.
Discuss the stated themes.

MAKE INFERENCES
Explain your thoughts about the feelings or motives of the characters.
Discuss implied themes.

MAKE AND REVISE PREDICTIONS
At the end of each assignment, make a prediction about what you think will happen next.
After you read, go back and check your predictions.
Tell if you had to revise them, and why.

ASK QUESTIONS
Ask questions about scenes or events that are confusing.
Record the answers when you discuss the questions in class or if you later find the answer in the story.

GIVE YOUR OPINION
Give your opinion about the literary quality of the work.
Discuss the author's style, use of language, and use of literary devices.
Tell why you do or do not like the story or a character.
Compare the book with others you have read.

MAKE CONNECTIONS
Think about ways the characters and events relate to your own life experiences. Put yourself in a character's place and discuss how you would feel or what you would do in that situation.

READER RESPONSE: Reading Assignment 1
Fahrenheit 451

Use this page to write down your reader response entry. Try to write a whole page of content.

General Topic _____

_____
_____
_____
_____
_____
_____
_____
_____
_____
_____
_____
_____
_____
_____
_____
_____
_____
_____
_____
_____
_____
_____
_____
_____
_____
_____

A Few Ideas (Pick one or create your own.)
- How would you have felt if you were Montag and came home to find Mildred in that condition?
- Do you think you would like to have Clarisse as a good friend? Why or why not?
- Clarisse gives her opinion of school. Do you agree with her? What's your opinion of school?
- Do you know people who just give automatic responses without thinking? How's it make you feel when you talk with them?

NOTES
Fahrenheit 451

READING ASSIGNMENT 2
Fahrenheit 451

THIS ASSIGNMENT COVERS APPROXIMATELY
THE LAST HALF OF CHAPTER ONE:
"THE HEARTH AND THE SALAMANDER"

START:
"The flutter of cards, motion of hands, of eyelids, the drone of the time-voice in the firehouse ceiling '. . . one thirty-five, Thursday morning, November 4th, . . . one thirty-six . . . one thirty-seven A.M. . . .'"

END:
End of chapter one

NOTES
Fahrenheit 451

CHARACTER NOTES
Reading Assignment 2 Fahrenheit 451

As you read Assignment 2 use this graphic organizer to jot down information about characters.

MONTAG	BEATTY

WOMAN WITH BOOKS	MILDRED

EVENTS & POINTS OF INTEREST
Reading Assignment 2 Fahrenheit 451

As you read Assignment 2 make notes of the series of main events that take place. Put them in the order that they are given in the text.

_____

_____

_____

_____

_____

_____

_____

_____

OTHER POINTS OF INTEREST TO IDENTIFY OR KNOW THE SIGNIFICANCE OF:

The ventilator grill

An ordinary kitchen match

Montag's sickness

The beetle

Montag's books

VOCABULARY WORK FOR ASSIGNMENT 2
Fahrenheit 451

PART I: Using Prior Knowledge And Contextual Clues
Use any clues you can find in the sentences from the text combined with your prior knowledge and write what you think the bold word means.

1. . . . all the sounds came to Montag, behind the barrier he had momentarily **erected**.

   _____

2. Were all firemen picked then for their looks as well as their **proclivities**?

   _____

3. Beatty, Stoneman, and Black ran up the sidewalk, suddenly **odious** and fat in their plump fireproof slickers.

   _____

4. He felt one hand and then the other work his coat free and let it slump to the floor. . . . His hands were **ravenous**. And his eyes were beginning to feel hunger, as if they must look at something, anything, everything.

   _____

5. "Life becomes one big **pratfall**, Montag; everything bang, boff, and wow!"

   _____

6. There was no **dictum**, no declaration, no censorship, to start with, no!

   _____

7. Cram them full of **noncombustible** data, chock them so damned full of 'facts' they feel stuffed, but absolutely 'brilliant' with information.

   _____

8. I'll think I'm responding to the play, when it's only a **tactile** reaction to vibration.

   _____

Vocabulary Work For Fahrenheit 451 Assignment 2, Page 2

PART II: Matching
Considering the usage in Part I, match the vocabulary words to their definitions.

_____ 1. erected   A. Humiliating failure; a fall on the buttocks

_____ 2. proclivities   B. Predispositions; tendencies

_____ 3. odious   C. Does not burn easily

_____ 4. ravenous   D. Arousing strong dislike or displeasure

_____ 5. pratfall   E. Extremely hungry; greedy for gratification

_____ 6. dictum   F. Authoritative pronouncement

_____ 7. noncombustible   G. Relating to the sense of touch

_____ 8. tactile   H. Set up; established

Part III: Cloze Passage
Fill in the blanks with the appropriate vocabulary words from the list above.

The scaffolding had been _____ by _____ of the patron who wished to paint the ceiling of his ancestral home. The project required a complete, _____, hands-on approach as the task was rather _____ due to the fact the ceiling was 100 feet high. The artist was _____ to finish, especially considering his _____ towards acrophobia. On the very first day he had a humiliating _____ sending him with a lamp in his hand into a bucket of chemicals. Fortunately they were _____.

Vocabulary Work For Fahrenheit 451 Assignment 2, Page 3

PART IV: Words In Practice
Answer the questions and be able to give short explanations to justify your answers.

1. When you erect a monument, do you build it up or tear it down?

2. Name something that would be a good proclivity.

3. If you are asked to do something you think is odious, are you happy to do it or would you rather not?

4. Who is someone who would be ravenous?

5. Give an example of a pratfall.

6. Who would create a dictum?

7. Which is noncombustible, a match or an asbestos tile?

8. What is something that is pleasant to the tactile senses?

VOCABULARY CROSSWORD
Reading Assignment 2 Fahrenheit 451
Use the word list from Part II Matching

Arousing strong dislike or displeasure (6)
Authoritative pronouncement (6)
Does not burn easily (14)
Extremely hungry; greedy for gratification (8)
Humiliating failure; a fall on the buttocks (8)
Predispositions; tendencies (12)
Relating to the sense of touch (7)
Set up; established (7)

STUDY & DISCUSSION QUESTIONS
Reading Assignment 2 Fahrenheit 451

1. When he goes to the firehouse, Montag realizes that all firemen look alike, and he wonders if they were chosen simply because they look that way. If that is true, what does it say about the society in which they live?

2. Early in the second reading assignment, Beatty states, "Any man's insane who thinks he can fool the government and us." Do you agree or disagree with that statement? Support your viewpoint.

3. When the firemen respond to the alarm at North Elm, the woman is still there. How does her presence "spoil the ritual" for the firemen?

4. Before the firemen burn her books, the woman says, "Play the man, Master Ridley; we shall this day light such a candle, by God's grace, in England, as I trust shall never be put out." Explain the significance of this quotation.

5. When Montag returns home after burning the woman's home, he describes his hands as "infected." What does he mean by this?

Study & Discussion Questions: Fahrenheit 451 Reading Assignment 2, Page 2

6. How does Millie break the news of Clarisse's death to Montag? Why is it important that she does it in that way?

7. What do you think Montag means when he says, "But that was another Mildred...so deep inside this one, and so bothered, really bothered, that the two women had never met." ?

8. Beatty says, "We must all be alike. Not everyone born free and equal, but everyone made equal. Each man the image of every other; then all are happy, for there are no mountains to make them cower, to judge themselves against." Do you agree with Beatty's vision of happiness? Why or why not?

9. In his speech, Beatty describes their world as being happy. Do you think he believes it? Support your answer with quotes from the text.

Study & Discussion Questions: Fahrenheit 451 Reading Assignment 2, Page 3

10. Why doesn't Mildred tell Beatty about the book she finds?

11. Toward the end of Part One, Montag wonders why the firemen were so afraid of people like Clarisse. Why do you think they might be?

12. Summarize Beatty's explanation of how and why society changed in the 20th Century.

Study & Discussion Questions: Fahrenheit 451 Reading Assignment 2, Page 4

ADDITIONAL PASSAGES FOR DISCUSSION

1. Discuss the imagery used in the paragraph beginning, "Books bombarded his shoulders..." (pg. 34 of the 60th Anniversary edition).

2. "Will you turn the parlor off?"
   "That's my family."

3. "We burned a thousand books. We burned a woman."
   "Well?"

4. "...this fire'll last me the rest of my life. God! I've been trying to put it out, in my mind, all night..."
   "You should have thought of that before becoming a fireman."

5. "We need not to be let alone. We need to be really bothered once in a while."

6. This time, Mildred ran. The yammering voices stopped yelling in the parlor.

7. "You ask Why to a lot of things and you wind up very unhappy indeed, if you keep at it. The poor girl's better off dead."

PLAY THE MAN, MASTER RIDLEY
Fahrenheit 451

The woman on North Elm decided she would rather die than live without her books. Perhaps she also had heard that people with books were sometimes sent to the insane asylum. At some point, though, she made up her mind to deliberately stay in her burning home with her burning books. No doubt she had thought about this before the alarm was ever called in. When you break the law, you usually think about the consequences and what you would do if you got caught.

We're going to diverge from the actual story of Fahrenheit 451 for a little bit. Suppose the North Elm woman knew ahead of time that the alarm was going to be called in, and she had already decided to go down with her books. After making this decision, she wrote a letter to her daughter, which she mailed when she found out the alarm had been called in. What would she have said to her daughter in that letter?

Your assignment is to write a letter from the North Elm woman to her daughter (or son, your choice) explaining why she refused to leave her home, and giving her daughter (or son) her parting words.

- Be thorough in your explanations
- Use a friendly letter format

Here's a way to go about doing this assignment:

1. Pretend you are the North Elm woman.
2. Think about why you would do what she did, knowing what you know about her world. Jot down any reasons you can think of as to why she would choose to do this.
3. Think about what you would say to your child, knowing you would soon be gone. What words of advice, what final words would you say? Jot down any ideas you have.
4. Look over your notes. Choose the best reasons and advice. Organize them in a logical way. Do any thoughts go together or naturally flow from one to another? Identify those kinds of things in your notes.
5. Write a rough draft of your letter. A few words of introduction, stating your intentions, would be appropriate. Follow that with your reasons. Follow that with any advice or final words you have.
6. Re-read, revise, have someone else read your letter and make suggestions. Edit and revise as necessary until you are happy with the final draft.

BOOKS, BOOKS, BOOKS
Fahrenheit 451

Find 10 different kinds of reading materials in your library or media center. Tell what kind each is, list the tiles, read the covers to see what they are about and fill in the About column, and then tell if each looks interesting to you or not. A few boxes are bigger in case you need more room for some titles

Kind	Title	About	Interesting To You?

KWL Reading Assignment 2
Fahrenheit 451

Write what you know and what you want to find out.
After you have read the next section, fill in what you learned.

K What I Know	**W** What I Want To Find Out	**L** What I Learned

READER RESPONSE: Reading Assignment 2
Fahrenheit 451

Use this page to write down your reader response entry. Try to write a whole page of content.

General Topic _____

_____
_____
_____
_____
_____
_____
_____
_____
_____
_____
_____
_____
_____
_____
_____
_____
_____
_____
_____
_____
_____
_____
_____

A Few Ideas (Pick one or create your own.)
- What do you think of the woman who lit the match to set her home and herself on fire? Is there anything you would be willing to do that for?
- If books were being banned, which books would you stash copies of? Tell why for each.
- Beatty talks about how society changed in the 20th century. In what kind of a society would you like to live? Tell a few main characteristics of it and say why those are important to you.
- Did you think Beatty would find out about the book under Montag's pillow? What would have been going through your mind if you were Montag?

READING ASSIGNMENT 3
Fahrenheit 451

THIS ASSIGNMENT COVERS
ALL OF CHAPTER TWO
"THE SAND AND THE SIEVE"

START:
Beginning of chapter two

END:
End of chapter two

NOTES
Fahrenheit 451

CHARACTER NOTES
Reading Assignment 3 Fahrenheit 451

As you read Assignment 3 use this graphic organizer to jot down information about characters.

MONTAG

FABER

MILDRED

BEATTY

MRS. PHELPS

EVENTS & POINTS OF INTEREST
Reading Assignment 3 Fahrenheit 451

As you read Assignment 3 make notes of the series of main events that take place. Put them in the order that they are given in the text.

_____

_____

_____

_____

_____

_____

_____

_____

OTHER POINTS OF INTEREST TO IDENTIFY OR KNOW THE SIGNIFICANCE OF:

The White Clown

The sieve and the sand

Denham's dental detergent

3 things that are missing

The green bullet

The Sea Of Faith

VOCABULARY WORK FOR ASSIGNMENT 3
Fahrenheit 451

PART I: Using Prior Knowledge And Contextual Clues
Use any clues you can find in the sentences from the text combined with your prior knowledge and write what you think the bold word means.

1. ...he talked in a **cadenced** voice...and when an hour had passed he said something to Montag and Montag sensed it was a rhymeless poem.

   _____

2. The train radio vomited upon Montag, in **retaliation**, a great tonload of music made of tin, copper, silver, chromium and brass.

   _____

3. Books were only one type of **receptacle** where we stored a lot of things we were afraid we might forget.

   _____

4. Proof of my terrible **cowardice**.

   _____

5. On one wall a woman smiled and drank orange juice **simultaneously**. How does she do both at once, thought Montag...

   _____

6. For these were the hands that had acted on their own, no part of him, here was where the conscience first **manifested** itself to snatch books, dart off with Job and Ruth and Willie Shakespeare, and now, in the firehouse, these hands seemed gloved with blood.

   _____

7. You towered with rage, yelled quotes at me, I calmly **parried** every thrust. Power, I said.

   _____

8. The folly of mistaking a metaphor for a proof, a torrent of **verbiage** for a spring of capital truths, and oneself as an oracle, is inborn in us, Mr. Valery once said.

   _____

Vocabulary Work For Fahrenheit 451 Assignment 3, Page 2

PART II: Matching
Considering the usage in Part I, match the vocabulary words to their definitions.

_____ 1. cadenced   A. Ignoble fear in the face of danger

_____ 2. retaliation   B. A container that holds matter

_____ 3. receptacle   C. At the same time

_____ 4. cowardice   D. Returning like for like

_____ 5. simultaneously   E. Wordiness

_____ 6. manifested   F. Showed; revealed

_____ 7. parried   G. Deflected; avoided

_____ 8. verbiage   H. With a rhythmic flow

Part III: Cloze Passage
Fill in the blanks with the appropriate vocabulary words from the list above.

The newscaster began his report with a _____ voice which _____ a _____ of unparalleled intensity. _____ was his motive, for he was accusing another station of _____ because of the underhanded way they were attacking his broadcasts. He had previously _____ their attacks, but now he was _____ responding to them openly and hitting back with his own assertions about their station. At the end of his broadcast, he threw his notes into a trash _____ to close with a dramatic flourish.

Vocabulary Work For Fahrenheit 451 Assignment 3, Page 3

PART IV: Words In Practice
Answer the questions and be able to give short explanations to justify your answers.

1. Does a cadenced march help keep soldiers in step together or make being in step difficult?
   _____

2. If someone came up and slapped you in the face, is it likely you would want to retaliate?
   _____

3. What is one common household receptacle?
   _____

4. Is cowardice on the battlefield usually considered to be heroic?
   _____

5. Name two things that often happen simultaneously.
   _____

6. In what ways does the flu manifest itself?
   _____

7. In what occupation is a lot of verbiage required?
   _____

8. What is something that can be parried?
   _____

VOCABULARY CROSSWORD
Reading Assignment 3 Fahrenheit 451
Use the word list from Part II Matching

A container that holds matter (10)
Deflected; avoided (7)
Happening at the same time (14)
Ignoble fear in the face of danger (9)
Returning like for like, especially evil (11)
Showed; revealed (10)
With a rhythmic flow (8)
Wordiness (8)

STUDY & DISCUSSION QUESTIONS
Reading Assignment 3 Fahrenheit 451

1. How do we know that the dog at the door is the mechanical hound?

2. Why is the event with the mechanical hound at the door significant?

3. The details in this book are important. There are only a few sentences about the door-voice in the incident with the dog at the door, but they are important:
    "Someone--the door--why doesn't the door-voice tell us---"
    "I shut it off."
   What do we learn about Montag and Mildred from these two lines?

4. Why does Montag insist on continuing to read the books?

5. From Mildred's point of view, explain why the parlor walls are better than books.

Study & Discussion Questions: Fahrenheit 451 Reading Assignment 3, Page 2

6. Mildred asks Montag, "Why should I read? What *for*?" Summarize Montag's answer by finishing his sentence, "An hour a day, two hours, with these books, and maybe . . ."

7. Compare and contrast Montag's first meeting with Faber in the park with his first meeting with Clarisse.

8. Montag asks Millie "Does the White Clown love you . . . does your 'family' love you?" What is the significance of Montag's questions?

9. What is the difference between talking "things" and talking "the meaning of things"?

10. "The train radio vomited upon Montag, in retaliation, a great tonload of music made of tin, copper, silver, chromium, and brass." What type of figure of speech is exemplified in this sentence? The music is in retaliation of what? Why is the music described as being made of metals?

Study & Discussion Questions: Fahrenheit 451 Reading Assignment 3, Page 3

11. Faber says that there are three things missing from the world. What are they?

12. Faber calls himself a coward for not speaking up against the bad changes in their society as they were happening, before it was too late. He later calls Montag "brave" after he learns that Montag stole the Bible. Do you think Faber is/was a coward and Montag is brave, or do you think their actions could be governed by something other than cowardice and/or bravery?

13. Montag and Faber hatch a plan to plant books in Firemen's houses to help bring down the system, while also setting up clandestine reading rooms. Do you think this is a good plan? Evaluate their chances for success.

14. Why are Millie and her friends made so nervous when Montag turns the TV walls off?

15. Describe Mrs. Bowles's parenting style and describe the type of children she is raising.

Study & Discussion Questions: Fahrenheit 451 Reading Assignment 3, Page 4

16. Compare Mrs. Phelps's responses and reactions to Montag with Montag's responses and reactions to Clarisse.

17. Earlier in the book, Beatty says "If you don't want a man unhappy politically, don't give him two sides of a question to worry him; give him one. Better yet, give him none." On what criteria do Millie and her friends judge the political candidates, and how does their political conversation between Millie and her friends relate to Beatty's statement?

18. Why does Mrs. Phelps start crying in response to the poem?

19. Chapter Two is entitled "The Sieve and the Sand." To what does this refer?

Study & Discussion Questions: Fahrenheit 451 Reading Assignment 3, Page 5

ADDITIONAL PASSAGES FOR DISCUSSION

1. Faber tells Montag "It's not the books you need, it's some of the things that once were in books. The same things could be in the 'parlor families' today." What do you think he means by this?

2. "We are living in a time when flowers are trying to live on flowers, instead of growing on good rain and black loam."

3. "We cannot tell the precise moment when friendship is formed. As in filling a vessel drop by drop, there is at last a drop which makes it run over; so in a series of kindnesses there is at least one which makes the heart run over."

4. Mildred kicked the book. "Books aren't people. You read and I look all around, but there isn't *anybody*!...my 'family' is people. They tell me things; *I* laugh, *they* laugh! and the colors!"

5. "Who's more important, me or that Bible?" She was beginning to shriek now, sitting there like a wax doll melting in its own heat."

6. "My wife's dying. A friend of mine's already dead. Someone who may have been a friend was burnt less than twenty-four hours ago. You're the only one I knew might help me. To see. To see . . ."

7. "Nobody listens anymore. I can't talk to the walls because they're yelling at *me*. I can't talk to my wife; she listens to the *walls*. I just want someone to hear what I have to say. And maybe if I talk long enough, it'll make sense. And I want you to teach me to understand what I read."

8. "And don't look to be saved in any *one* thing, person, machine, or library. Do your own bit of saving, and if you drown, at least die knowing you were headed for shore."

9. "Remember, the firemen are rarely necessary. The public itself stopped reading of its own accord. . . . People are having *fun*."

Study & Discussion Questions: Fahrenheit 451 Reading Assignment 3, Page 6

Additional Passages For Discussion, Continued

10. I remember the newspapers dying like huge moths. No one wanted them back. No one missed them. And then the Government, seeing how advantageous it was to have people reading only about passionate lips and the fist in the stomach, circled the situation with your fire-eaters."

11. "I don't want to change sides and just be *told* what to do. There's no reason to change if I do that."

12. "He is no wise man who will quit a certainty for an uncertainty."

13. "But remember the Captain belongs to the most dangerous enemy to truth and freedom, the solid unmoving cattle of the majority."

14. The men ran like cripples in their clumsy boots, as quietly as spiders.

DOVER BEACH
Fahrenheit 451

Dover Beach
BY MATTHEW ARNOLD

The sea is calm tonight.
The tide is full, the moon lies fair
Upon the straits; on the French coast the light
Gleams and is gone; the cliffs of England stand,
Glimmering and vast, out in the tranquil bay.
Come to the window, sweet is the night-air!
Only, from the long line of spray
Where the sea meets the moon-blanched land,
Listen! you hear the grating roar
Of pebbles which the waves draw back, and fling,
At their return, up the high strand,
Begin, and cease, and then again begin,
With tremulous cadence slow, and bring
The eternal note of sadness in.

Sophocles long ago
Heard it on the Ægean, and it brought
Into his mind the turbid ebb and flow
Of human misery; we
Find also in the sound a thought,
Hearing it by this distant northern sea.

The Sea of Faith
Was once, too, at the full, and round earth's shore
Lay like the folds of a bright girdle furled.
But now I only hear
Its melancholy, long, withdrawing roar,
Retreating, to the breath
Of the night-wind, down the vast edges drear
And naked shingles of the world.

Ah, love, let us be true
To one another! for the world, which seems
To lie before us like a land of dreams,
So various, so beautiful, so new,
Hath really neither joy, nor love, nor light,
Nor certitude, nor peace, nor help for pain;
And we are here as on a darkling plain
Swept with confused alarms of struggle and flight,
Where ignorant armies clash by night.

Notes:

tranquil = peaceful; calm

tremulous = trembling
cadence = rhythmic pace

Aegean = the Aegean Sea, part of the Mediterranean Sea
turbid = muddy; cloudy; not clear

The sound of the sea waves reminded Sophocles of the coming and going of good and bad times for humankind.

---

girdle = something that encircles or confines
furled = rolled tightly in upon itself

At one time, humankind had faith, but people no longer do.

---

certitude = certainty

Without faith, there is no certainty or peace in the world. All we have left is each other, so let's be true to one another in a confused world full of war.

TV FAVORITES
Fahrenheit 451

List your three most favorite television shows below.

1. _____
2. _____
3. _____

For each of the TV shows you listed, answer these questions:
What kind of a show is it (reality, sports, news, drama...)?

1. _____ 2. _____ 3. _____

What is the level of intellectual engagement or educational value of the show (on a scale of 1 to 10 with 10 being the highest level of intellectual engagement or educational value)?

1. _____ 2. _____ 3. _____

What values does the show promote?

1. _____
2. _____
3. _____

What kind of language is used on the show (common, vulgar, intellectual)?

1. _____ 2. _____ 3. _____

Is the show purely "entertainment," or does it have other value (if so, what)?

1. _____ 2. _____ 3. _____

Would it fit well into programming on the Parlor Walls (yes or no)?
1. _____ 2. _____ 3. _____

Has this program become your "family"? Do you schedule your activities around seeing it and talk a lot about it?

1. _____ 2. _____ 3. _____

Why do you like this show so much? What about it appeals to you?

1. _____
2. _____
3. _____

JUDGING A CANDIDATE
Fahrenheit 451

In Reading Assignment 3, Millie urges her friends to have a discussion about politics to please Guy. Review that section of the text and answer the following questions:

1. On what kinds of things do the women compare and contrast the candidates?

2. On what kinds of things should they compare and contrast the candidates?

3. Do you listen to what the candidates say? Why or why not?

4. What could happen if people would stop listening to what candidates say and would vote based on the criteria the women in the novel use?

5. Does what the candidates say always match up with the actions they take? Explain.

6. Why is it important to both listen to AND evaluate actions of a candidate?

7. Does the moral character of a candidate make a difference? Why or why not?

KWL Reading Assignment 3
Fahrenheit 451

Write what you know and what you want to find out.
After you have read the next section, fill in what you learned.

K What I Know	W What I Want To Find Out	L What I Learned

READER RESPONSE: Reading Assignment 3
Fahrenheit 451

Use this page to write down your reader response entry. Try to write a whole page of content.

General Topic _____

_____
_____
_____
_____
_____
_____
_____
_____
_____
_____
_____
_____
_____
_____
_____
_____
_____
_____
_____
_____
_____
_____
_____
_____
_____

A Few Ideas (Pick one or create your own.)
- What do you think of the parlor walls? Do you think having them would be awesome or terrible? Why?
- Do you like to have quiet time to think, or not? How do you feel about silence?
- Would your parenting style be like Mrs. Bowles's, or would you want to be with your children? Explain why.
- Has a poem, story, song, or movie touched you and made you cry? What about it made you have such strong feelings?

NOTES
Fahrenheit 451

READING ASSIGNMENT 4
Fahrenheit 451

THIS ASSIGNMENT COVERS
ALL OF CHAPTER THREE
"BURNING BRIGHT"

START:
Beginning Of Chapter Three

END:
End Of Chapter Three

NOTES
Fahrenheit 451

CHARACTER NOTES
Reading Assignment 4 Fahrenheit 451

As you read Assignment 4 use this graphic organizer to jot down information about characters.

MONTAG	BEATTY

FABER	MILDRED
	GRANGER

EVENTS & POINTS OF INTEREST
Reading Assignment 4 Fahrenheit 451

As you read Assignment 4 make notes of the series of main events that take place. Put them in the order that they are given in the text.

_____

_____

_____

_____

_____

_____

_____

OTHER POINTS OF INTEREST TO IDENTIFY OR KNOW THE SIGNIFICANCE OF:

The river

The railroad tracks

The Book of Ecclesiastes

Phoenix

VOCABULARY WORK FOR ASSIGNMENT 4
Fahrenheit 451

PART I: Using Prior Knowledge And Contextual Clues
Use any clues you can find in the sentences from the text combined with your prior knowledge and write what you think the bold word means.

1. The other firemen waited behind him, in the darkness, their faces illumined faintly by the **smoldering** foundation.

   _____

2. The other was like a chunk of burnt pinelog he was carrying along as penance for some **obscure** sin.

   _____

3. Two dozen of them flurried, wavering, **indecisive**, three miles off.

   _____

4. And there on the small screen was the burnt house, and the crowd and something with a sheet over it and out of the sky, fluttering, came the helicopter like a **grotesque** flower.

   _____

5. ...Montag might...see himself dramatized, described, made over, standing there, **limned** in the bright small television screen from outside....

   _____

6. He saw a great **juggernaut** of stars form in the sky and threaten to roll over and crush him.

   _____

7. He smelled the heavy musk like perfume mingled with blood and the gummed exhalation of the animal's breath, all **cardamon** and moss and ragweed odor in this huge night where the trees ran at him....

   _____

8. The most important single thing we had to pound into ourselves is that we were not important; we mustn't be **pedants**; we were not to feel superior to anyone else in the world.

   _____

9. There was a silly damn bird called a Phoenix back before Christ; every few hundred years he built a **pyre** and burned himself up.

   _____

Vocabulary Work For Fahrenheit 451 Assignment 4, Page 2

PART II: Matching
Considering the usage in Part I, match the vocabulary words to their definitions.

_____ 1. smoldering   A. Described; portrayed; delineated

_____ 2. obscure   B. Not able to make a decision

_____ 3. indecisive   C. A pile of combustible materials for burning a corpse

_____ 4. grotesque   D. Bizarre; distorted

_____ 5. limned   E. Burning with little smoke and no flame

_____ 6. juggernaut   F. Overwhelmingly advancing sight crushing all in its path

_____ 7. cardamon   G. Those who flaunt their knowledge

_____ 8. pedants   H. Not clear; partially hidden; remote

_____ 9. pyre   I. An Indian spice

Part III: Cloze Passage
Fill in the blanks with the appropriate vocabulary words from the list above.

The _____ predicted that a meteor would fall. An object initially appeared _____ in the sky, but suddenly the full _____ approached no longer leaving the skeptics _____ about the forecasted event. The rather _____ presence of this phenomenon in the night sky was now before them. When it hit, the meteor created a _____ crater that gave off smells of sulphur and a faint hint of _____, as it had landed in a field where this spice was grown. Depending on the conditions _____ in his insurance policy, the farmer might get reimbursed for the loss of his crops, but probably not for the cow that dropped dead at the shock of the event. The farmer would have to make a _____ and dispose of the poor animal.

Vocabulary Work For Fahrenheit 451 Assignment 4, Page 3

PART IV: Words In Practice
Answer the questions and be able to give short explanations to justify your answers.

1. Would a smoldering fire keep you very warm on a cold winter's night?
   _____

2. Name an obscure person in the field of sports, music, or movies.
   _____

3. In what occupation would it be bad to be indecisive?
   _____

4. At what holiday might you wear something grotesque?
   _____

5. What kind of a document might have conditions limned in its pages?
   _____

6. Is a juggernaut something to embrace or run from?
   _____

7. Would cardamon be more likely to be used by a chef or a mechanic?
   _____

8. What characteristics would someone who is a pedant have?
   _____

9. What foreign people from long ago are known for funeral pyres?
   _____

VOCABULARY CROSSWORD
Reading Assignment 4 Fahrenheit 451
Use the word list from Part II Matching

A pile of combustible materials for burning a corpse (4)
Bizarre; distorted (9)
Burning with little smoke and no flame (10)
Described (6)
Italian herb (8)
Not able to make a decision (10)
Not readily noticed or seen; not commonly known (7)
Overwhelming, advancing sight crushing all in its path (10)
Those who flaunt their knowledge (7)

STUDY & DISCUSSION QUESTIONS
Reading Assignment 4 Fahrenheit 451

1. Beatty confesses that he sent the Hound to Montag's home. Why did he send it?

2. Compare the Mildred we saw at the beginning of the book with the Mildred who flees the house and zooms off in a beetle.

3. What is the significance of the vacuum that occurs when Montag destroys the TV walls?

4. What motivates Montag to pull the trigger on the flame-thrower and set Beatty on fire?

5. Montag believes Beatty wanted to die. Explain why you agree or disagree with him.

6. Montag wonders if the teenagers who almost ran him over just for fun were the ones who ran over Clarisse. Is there any evidence to support this thought? Based on evidence in the book, would you say Clarisse's death was likely a random or a premeditated act?

7. Is what Montag does to Mrs. Black's house a just thing to do? Is it moral? Is it right? Explain why or why not.

8. Explain the symbolism of the things that Montag does in the river.

Study & Discussion Questions: Fahrenheit 451 Reading Assignment 4, Page 2

9. How is the fire in the countryside different from the fire Montag has experienced?

10. Montag listens to the silence and wonders how Millie would take it. What do you think Millie would do if she were with Montag? Do you think she could adapt?

11. Why does the search team find someone else to kill in place of Montag?

12. The men in the countryside have a plan for saving books. What is it, and do you think it is a good plan?

13. Explain Granger's metaphor of the Phoenix.

14. Explain why Granger misses his grandfather but Montag won't miss Millie.

15. Why did Ray Bradbury make Montag the Book of Ecclesiastes rather than some other book?

Study & Discussion Questions: Fahrenheit 451 Reading Assignment 4, Page 3

ADDITIONAL PASSAGES FOR DISCUSSION

1. "By the time the consequences catch up with you, it's too late, isn't it, Montag?"

2. "Now, Montag, you're a burden. And fire will lift you off of my shoulders, clean, quick, sure; nothing to rot later. Antibiotic, aesthetic, practical."

3. Beatty . . . twisted in on himself like a charred wax doll and lay silent.

4. [Montag] stood and he had only one leg. The other was like a chunk of burnt pine log he was carrying along as a penance for some obscure sin.

5. . . . simply a number of children out for a long night of roaring five or six hundred miles in a few moonlit hours, their faces icy with wind, and coming home or not coming at dawn, alive or not alive, that made the adventure.

6. They would have killed me, thought Montag. . . . For no reason at all in the world they would have killed me.

7. Mrs. Black, are you asleep in there? . . . The house did not reply.

8. He felt as if he had left a stage behind and many actors. He felt as if he had left the great seance and all the murmuring ghosts. He was moving from an unreality that was frightening into a reality that was unreal because it was new.

9. . . . the river was mild and leisurely, going away from the people who ate shadows for breakfast and steam for lunch and vapors for supper.

10. This was all he wanted now. Some sign that the immense world would accept him and give him the long time he needed to think all the things that must be thought.

Study & Discussion Questions: Fahrenheit 451 Reading Assignment 4, Page 4

Additional Passages For Discussion, Continued

11. Ane he was surprised to learn how certain he suddenly was of a single fact he could not prove. Once, long ago, Clarisse had walked here, where he was walking now."

12. . . . there was a foolish and yet delicious sense of knowing himself as an animal come from the forest, drawn by the fire.

13. But you can't *make* people listen. They have to come round in their own time, wondering what happened and why the world blew up under them.

14. ". . . shake the tree and knock the great sloth down on his ass."

15. Silently, Granger arose, felt of his arms and legs, swearing, swearing incessantly under his breath, tears dripping from his face.

16. In the trees, the birds that had flown away quickly now came back and settled down.

ECCLESIASTES
Fahrenheit 451

Montag "became" the Book of Ecclesiastes (from the Bible). Below is a passage from the beginning of the Book of Ecclesiastes (New International Version).

Your assignment is to read this passage and (in writing) respond to, discuss, or explain any one of the numbered verses.
- Several paragraphs would be an appropriate length for your written work.

3 What do people gain from all their labors
   at which they toil under the sun?
4 Generations come and generations go,
   but the earth remains forever.
5 The sun rises and the sun sets,
   and hurries back to where it rises.
6 The wind blows to the south
   and turns to the north;
   round and round it goes,
   ever returning on its course.
7 All streams flow into the sea,
   yet the sea is never full.
   To the place the streams come from,
   there they return again.
8 All things are wearisome,
   more than one can say.
   The eye never has enough of seeing,
   nor the ear its fill of hearing.
9 What has been will be again,
   what has been done will be done again;
   there is nothing new under the sun.
10 Is there anything of which one can say,
   "Look! This is something new"?
   It was here already, long ago;
   it was here before our time.
11 No one remembers the former generations,
   and even those yet to come
   will not be remembered
   by those who follow them.

One way to begin the writing portion of the assignment is to re-read each verse and see what ideas come to your mind. When you find one for which you have several ideas, focus on that one. Jot down your ideas. Expand upon them with additional notes. Begin to formulate them into complete thoughts and organize them so one idea will flow to the next. Use examples to help support and explain your statements.

KWL Reading Assignment 4
Fahrenheit 451

Write what you know and what you want to find out.
After you have read the next section, fill in what you learned.

K What I Know	**W** What I Want To Find Out	**L** What I Learned

READER RESPONSE: Reading Assignment 4
Fahrenheit 451

Use this page to write down your reader response entry. Try to write a whole page of content.

General Topic _____

_____

A Few Ideas (Pick one or create your own.)
- Would you prosecute Montag for killing Beatty? Why or why not?
- If you could "be" a book (like Montag is Ecclesiastes) what book would you be?
- Is there someone you miss like Granger misses his grandfather? Who? Why?
- Do you like being outdoors in nature? Camping, walking, looking at the stars at night? What?
- How likely do you think it is that a city you know will be destroyed like the city in the book?

NOTES
Fahrenheit 451

WRITING ASSIGNMENTS
Fahrenheit 451

WRITING ASSIGNMENT 1   DUE _____

WRITING ASSIGNMENT 2   DUE _____

WRITING ASSIGNMENT 3   DUE _____

Completed writing assignments can be stapled to the backs of the assignment pages.

NOTES
Fahrenheit 451

WRITING ASSIGNMENT 1
Fahrenheit 451
Fire Escape Plan

PROMPT
Fire has long been a fascinating thing for mankind. It can be useful; it can be pretty; it can keep us warm, but it can also be very dangerous. Every kid knows Smokey the Bear and has been advised how dangerous fire is to our wildlife friends. Everyone knows and fears the possibility of having a house fire while we are snuggled up in our beds at night. We are fortunate that modern technology has brought us sprinkling systems and fire alarms for our homes. The question then becomes, "What do we do when the smoke alarm goes off?"

Your assignment is to make and write down a fire escape plan for your family and your house. You must give written directions as well as make a map for occupants of each bedroom in your home.

PREWRITING
- First of all, draw a little diagram of your house or apartment. It doesn't have to be perfect for this prewriting exercise. Locate the main rooms of your home. Think for a minute. Where would a fire be most likely to start? Probably in the kitchen, near a heating source, or near an area with a lot of electrical wiring. Locate these and any other areas in your home that are areas where a fire might be likely to start. Put an X on each of those areas.
- Where are the bedrooms in your home in relation to the X marks? Find the best route of escape for the occupants of each of the bedrooms. Mark them on your diagram. If the X marks eliminate all routes of escape, deal with the X marks that are most likely to be trouble spots.
- Think for a minute and make a list of the things that will need to be done to get everyone out safely. Next to each job, write down the name of the person who should be responsible for that job.

DRAFTING
- Write an introductory paragraph telling the circumstances of the prospective fire.
- Write one paragraph for each member of your family, giving them simple, specific instructions as to what to do if there is a fire in your home while you are all in bed asleep. Each person should start from his or her own bedroom.
- Write a concluding paragraph in which you give miscellaneous details about what rooms in your home should have fire extinguishers, rope ladders, or other emergency equipment.
- Make a diagram of your house for each bedroom, and mark each bedroom's escape route on the diagram in a bright color so it can be easily seen.

When you finish the rough draft of your paper, ask a student who sits near you to read it. After reading your rough draft, he/she should tell you what he/she liked best about your work, which parts were difficult to understand, and ways in which your work could be improved. Reread your paper considering your critic's comments, and make the corrections you think are necessary.

PROOFREADING
Do a final proofreading of your paper, double-checking your grammar, spelling, organization, and the clarity of your ideas. Make a final, good copy to submit for grading.

NOTES
Fahrenheit 451

WRITING ASSIGNMENT 2
Fahrenheit 451
The Future World

PROMPT

Ray Bradbury wrote Fahrenheit back in 1951, yet his work is still very relevant today. It is amazing that he was able to foresee the progression of so many things so accurately. When he wrote this book, television had just been invented. There were no such things as "ear buds" or "ear phones." The world of micro-technology and computers had not yet been discovered.

No one really knows how things will be in the future, but at one time or another, we all think about it. What is your vision of the future? What do you think our world will be like 50 years from now?

Your assignment is to describe our world as you believe it will be 50 years from now.

PREWRITING
- Choose five major topics for your composition--five areas of our lives you will describe. Some areas to consider are government, ecology, business, lifestyle, transportation, jobs/workplaces, family, economy, food, shelter, clothing, music, architecture, agriculture, and entertainment, but don't feel limited by these; you may consider other areas as well.
- Make five columns on a piece of paper and title each with one of the five topics you have chosen. Under each topic, in the appropriate columns, jot down notes about how you think each will be in 50 years.

DRAFTING
- Write a paragraph in which you introduce the idea that you believe life will be different in 50 years, especially in the areas you have chosen to write about (your five topics).
- In the body of your composition, write one paragraph for each of your topics. Use a topic sentence to state exactly how you believe that topic will be different in 50 years, and then fill in your paragraph with specific examples from your column of notes. Do this for each of your five topics, one paragraph for each topic.
- Write a paragraph in which you summarize your ideas and conclude your composition.

When you finish the rough draft of your paper, ask a student who sits near you to read it. After reading your rough draft, he/she should tell you what he/she liked best about your work, which parts were difficult to understand, and ways in which your work could be improved. Reread your paper considering your critic's comments, and make the corrections you think are necessary.

PROOFREADING
Do a final proofreading of your paper, double-checking your grammar, spelling, organization, and the clarity of your ideas. Make a final, good copy to submit for grading.

NOTES
Fahrenheit 451

PERSUASIVE WRITING ASSIGNMENT
Fahrenheit 451
Which Is Better Now Or The Future?

PROMPT

Well, we know what it is like living in our world today. And now we have some ideas about how our future might be. Which one is better?

Your assignment is to convince me that either our world today is better than the future will be or that the future will be better than our world is today.

PREWRITING
- Decide for yourself which you think will be better: the present world or the world of the future.
- Write down three of the most important things that convinced you to make your decision.
- On a piece of paper, make two columns. Title one "Now" and title the other one "Future."
- Down the left-hand margin of your paper, leaving plenty of space in between, write down the three most important things that convinced you to make your decision in the paragraph above.
- Now fill in the little chart you have made. Consider the first thing. Write down how it is today in your "Now" column. Write down how it will be in the "Future" column.
- Do the same thing with each of the items in your far-left column.

DRAFTING
- Write a paragraph in which you introduce the idea that either today is better than the future or that the future is better than the present.
- In the body of your composition, write one paragraph for each of your main points. Take your first "most important thing that convinced you" and write a paragraph about that. Make a topic sentence in which you tell your reason why the "Now" or "Future" world will be better. Fill out your paragraph by comparing our world today with the future world on this point. (Use your chart.) Write one paragraph in this way for each of your three reasons.
- Write a concluding paragraph in which you summarize your ideas and conclude your composition.

When you finish the rough draft of your paper, ask a student who sits near you to read it. After reading your rough draft, he/she should tell you what he/she liked best about your work, which parts were difficult to understand, and ways in which your work could be improved. Reread your paper considering your critic's comments, and make the corrections you think are necessary.

PROOFREADING

Do a final proofreading of your paper double-checking your grammar, spelling, organization, and the clarity of your ideas. Revise to a final draft as necessary.

NOTES
Fahrenheit 451

WHOLE BOOK STUDY
Fahrenheit 451

ASSIGNMENTS AND ACTIVITIES
TO STUDY DIFFERENT ASPECTS
OF THE WHOLE BOOK

NOTES
Fahrenheit 451

HISTORICAL CONTEXT
Fahrenheit 451

In 1951 Ray Bradbury wrote a short story ("The Fireman") on which Fahrenheit 451 (published in 1953) was based. What was going on in Bradbury's world and in his mind to prompt him to create Montag's world? Take a few minutes to jot down some things that were going on between 1941-1953. Then, see which of these things you can make correlations to in Fahrenheit 451.

World Events:

_____
_____
_____
_____
_____
_____
_____
_____

Entertainment:

_____
_____
_____
_____
_____
_____
_____
_____

Science & Technology:

_____
_____
_____
_____
_____
_____
_____

Social:

_____
_____
_____
_____
_____

Other:

_____
_____

Historical Context: Fahrenheit 451 Page 2

EVENT	EFFECT IN FAHRENHEIT 451

POINT OF VIEW
Fahrenheit 451

Point Of View

Point of View is the lens through which the story is told.

There are several different kinds of Point of View:
- **First Person:** Told by a character in the story using "I"
- **Third Person Limited:** Told by a character in the story
- **Third Person Omniscient:** Told by the author through a character in the story; all-knowing

Based on these descriptions, which do you think fits Fahrenheit 451? Why?

_____
_____
_____
_____
_____

Why is it important that the story is told from Montag's point of view?

_____
_____
_____
_____
_____
_____

STORY MAP
Fahrenheit 451

Tell what happens at each part of the story.

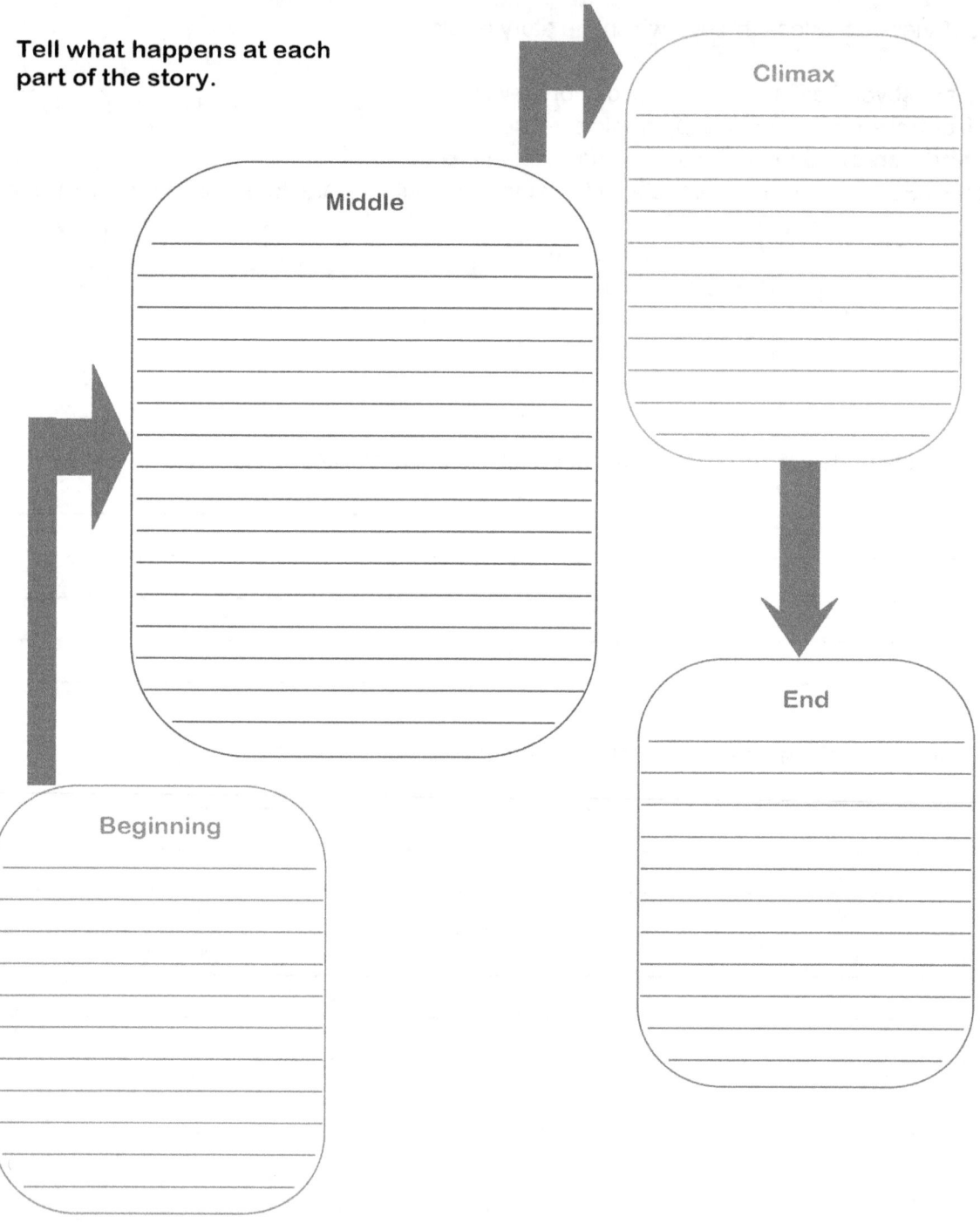

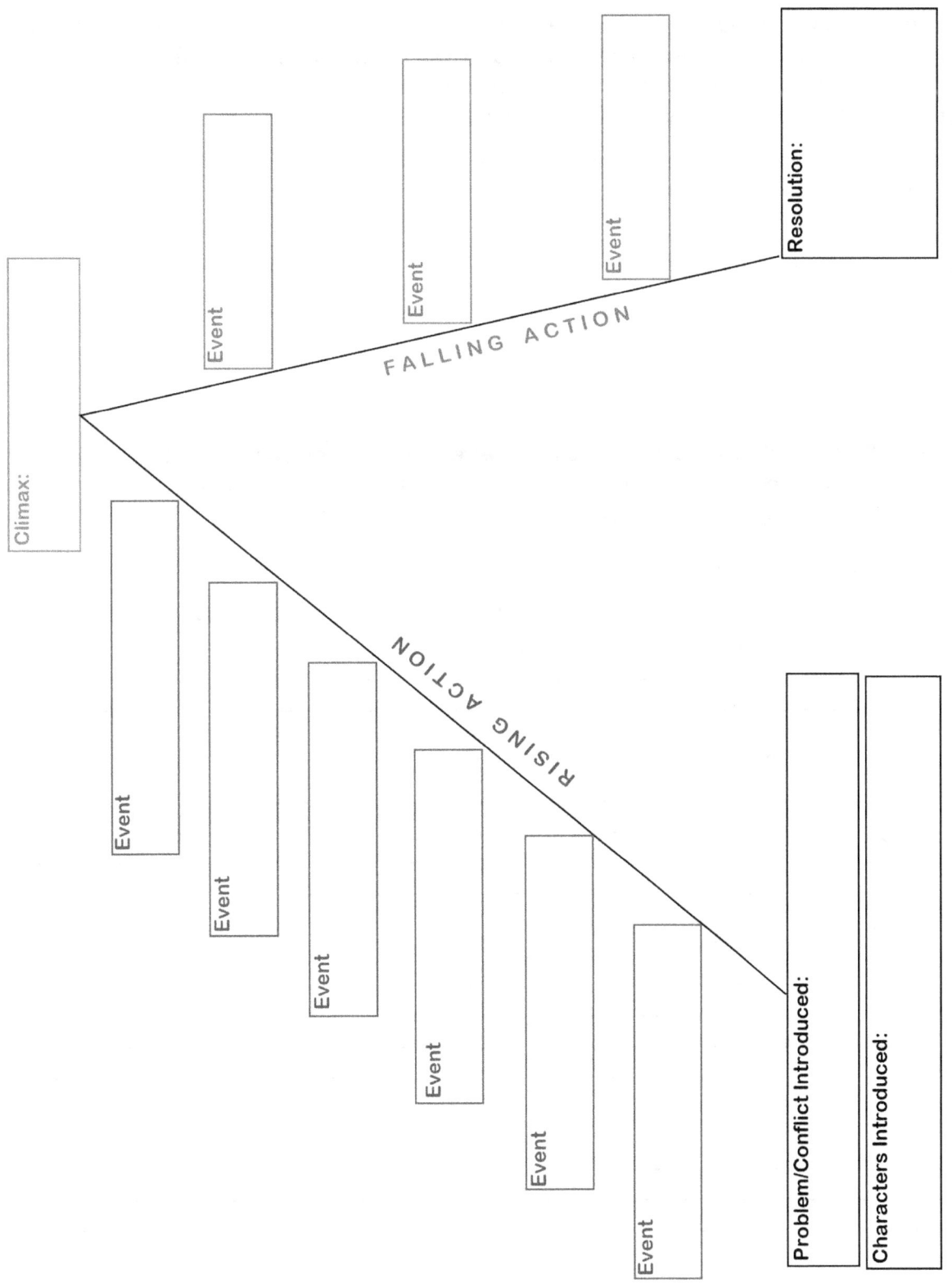

SETTING & CONFLICT
Fahrenheit 451

Setting

Though it is never stated, we assume the setting is in the United States, at some time in the future. Enough time has passed for two nuclear wars to have happened since the year 2022. Perhaps Bradbury set it 100 years into the future from 1950; it's never made completely clear, but it doesn't really matter what the exact year is. Why not?

_____

_____

Conflict

The basic types of conflict are:
- person vs. person
- person vs. self
- person vs. society
- person vs. nature

Main conflicts usually occur with the main character being the "person" against something. There can also be conflicts with other characters against the same elements. Think about Fahrenheit 451 and complete the exercise below with examples from Fahrenheit 451.

Examples of Person vs. Person

_____ vs _____
_____ vs _____
_____ vs _____
_____ vs _____

Examples of Person vs. Self

_____
_____
_____

Examples of Person vs. Society

_____
_____
_____

Examples of Person vs. Nature

_____
_____
_____

CHARACTER DEVELOPMENT
Fahrenheit 451

PART I: Character As An Element Of Fiction

1. Define "protagonist" _____

2. Define "antagonist" _____

3. The protagonist in Fahrenheit 451 is _____

4. The antagonist(s) in Fahrenheit 451 is/are _____

5. Define "dynamic character" _____

6. Define "static character" _____

7. What is a "stereotype"? _____

8. Which character in Fahrenheit 451 is dynamic? _____

9. Which characters in Fahrenheit 451 are static? _____

_____

10. Are any characters in Fahrenheit 451 stereotypes? If so, which ones?

_____

Below are the names of characters in Fahrenheit 451. On the blank to the left of each name, identify the person as having a major or minor role in the story. On the blank to the right of the name, identify the character

_____	Capt. Beatty	_____
_____	Clarisse McClellan	_____
_____	Granger	_____
_____	Guy Montag	_____
_____	Mildred	_____
_____	Mrs. Black	_____
_____	Elm St. Woman	_____
_____	Mrs. Bowles	_____
_____	Mrs. Phelps	_____
_____	Professor Faber	_____
_____	Stoneman and Black	_____

CHARACTER DEVELOPMENT
Fahrenheit 451

PART 2: Character Studies - Beatty, Clarisse, Mildred, Faber, Mrs. Phelps

Beatty

1. List some of Beatty's physical characteristics.

   _____   _____   _____

2. What is one habit Beatty has that is symbolically important?

   _____

3. Find & list 5 events in Fahrenheit 451 in which what Beatty does or says is important.

   _____
   _____
   _____
   _____
   _____

4. Is Beatty *for* or *against* Montag? Support your answer with evidence from the book.

5. Montag thinks Beatty wanted to die. Do you agree or disagree with him? Use evidence from the book to support your answer.

CHARACTER DEVELOPMENT
Fahrenheit 451

PART 2: Character Studies - Beatty, Clarisse, Mildred, Faber, Mrs. Phelps

Clarisse

1. List some of Clarisse's physical characteristics.

   _____   _____   _____

2. Give a few examples of the natural elements associated with Clarisse.

   _____   _____   _____

3. What is the single most important question Clarisse asks Montag?

   _____

   Why is that question important? What effect does it have on Montag?

   _____
   _____
   _____
   _____

4. What is the one thing about Clarisse that most attracts Montag to her? Tell *why* it attracts Montag to her.

   _____
   _____
   _____

5. Explain why Clarisse's death is important in Fahrenheit 451.

   _____
   _____
   _____
   _____
   _____
   _____
   _____

CHARACTER DEVELOPMENT
Fahrenheit 451

PART 2: Character Studies - Beatty, Clarisse, Mildred, Faber, Mrs. Phelps

Mildred

1. List some of Mildred's physical characteristics.

_____   _____   _____

2. Choose one word or phrase you believe best sums-up Mildred's personality. Support your choice with examples from the text.

_____
_____
_____
_____
_____
_____
_____
_____

3. What are 3 things Mildred routinely does?

_____
_____

What do these three things have in common, and what does that say about Millie?

_____
_____
_____
_____

4. Why does Mildred call in the alarm on her own house?

_____
_____
_____
_____
_____
_____

CHARACTER DEVELOPMENT
Fahrenheit 451

PART 2: Character Studies - Beatty, Clarisse, Mildred, Faber, Mrs. Phelps

Faber

1. List some of Faber's physical characteristics.

   _____   _____   _____

2. Faber is a relatively minor character in Fahrenheit 451, but he is important. What function does Faber's character have in the story?

   _____
   _____
   _____
   _____
   _____
   _____
   _____

3. Give a verbal snapshot of Faber before Montag solicits his help and afterwards.

   Before: _____
   _____

   After: _____
   _____

4. Did Faber live at the end of the story? What evidence is in the text? Does it matter if Faber lives or dies at the end of the story?

   _____
   _____
   _____
   _____
   _____
   _____

CHARACTER DEVELOPMENT
Fahrenheit 451

PART 2: Character Studies - Beatty, Clarisse, Mildred, Faber, Mrs. Phelps

Mrs. Phelps

1. List 5 of the most important things Mrs. Phelps says or does.

_____
_____
_____
_____
_____

2. Which of the 5 things you listed above gives us the most insight into Mrs. Phelps's character? Why?

_____
_____
_____
_____
_____

3. Compare and contrast Mrs. Phelps and Mildred.

Similarities: _____
_____
_____

Differences: _____
_____
_____
_____

4. What is Mrs. Phelps's use as a character in the story?

_____
_____
_____

CHARACTER DEVELOPMENT
Fahrenheit 451

PART 3: Montag's Development Through The Book

1. Montag goes through a number of events that transform him from the obedient Fireman Montag into the Book Of Ecclesiastes. Give a brief explanation of how or why each listed event changed him.

EVENT	EFFECT OF THE EVENT ON MONTAG
Montag meets Clarisse	
Mildred's stomach is pumped	
Montag realizes he is not happy	
Mrs. Blake lights the fire	
Clarisse dies	
Montag realizes he does not love Millie	
Faber agrees to help	
Montag burns down his own house	
Beatty verbally assaults Montag and threatens to get Faber	
Montag meets Granger	

CHARACTER DEVELOPMENT
Fahrenheit 451

PART 3: Montag's Development Through The Book, page 2

2. In a work of fiction, the author can simply tell you about the character. That's called **Direct Characterization**.

In fiction, as in real life, we can also learn about the character
- through the character's physical appearance
- through the character's own words, thoughts, and actions
- through the comments of other characters

This is called **Indirect Characterization.**

Look through the text and find examples of each of these kinds of indirect characterization as they apply to Montag. Include the words from the text and, if not evident, what we learn about Montag from the example given.

Physical Appearance _____
_____
_____
_____

Character's Own Words _____
_____
_____
_____
_____

Character's Own Thoughts _____
_____
_____
_____
_____

Character's Own Actions _____
_____
_____
_____
_____

Comments Of Other Characters _____
_____
_____
_____
_____

CHARACTER DEVELOPMENT
Fahrenheit 451

PART 3: Montag's Development Through The Book, page 3

3. A character who changes has to be motivated by something. What is Montag's motivation to change? What does he want more than anything else, enough to lose his home, his wife, and his job? Support your answer with textual evidence.

_____
_____
_____
_____
_____
_____
_____
_____
_____

4. Clarisse dies. Do you think Montag's development would have been different if Clarisse hadn't died? Explain.

_____
_____
_____
_____
_____
_____

5. Mildred is incapable of sharing Montag's journey. Do you think Montag's development would have been different if Millie had been able to share Montag's passion for finding a new life? Explain.

_____
_____
_____
_____
_____
_____

CHARACTER COMPARISON
Fahrenheit 451

Write Montag's traits on the top lines, Faber's on the bottom lines, and the traits the two characters have in common on the middle lines.

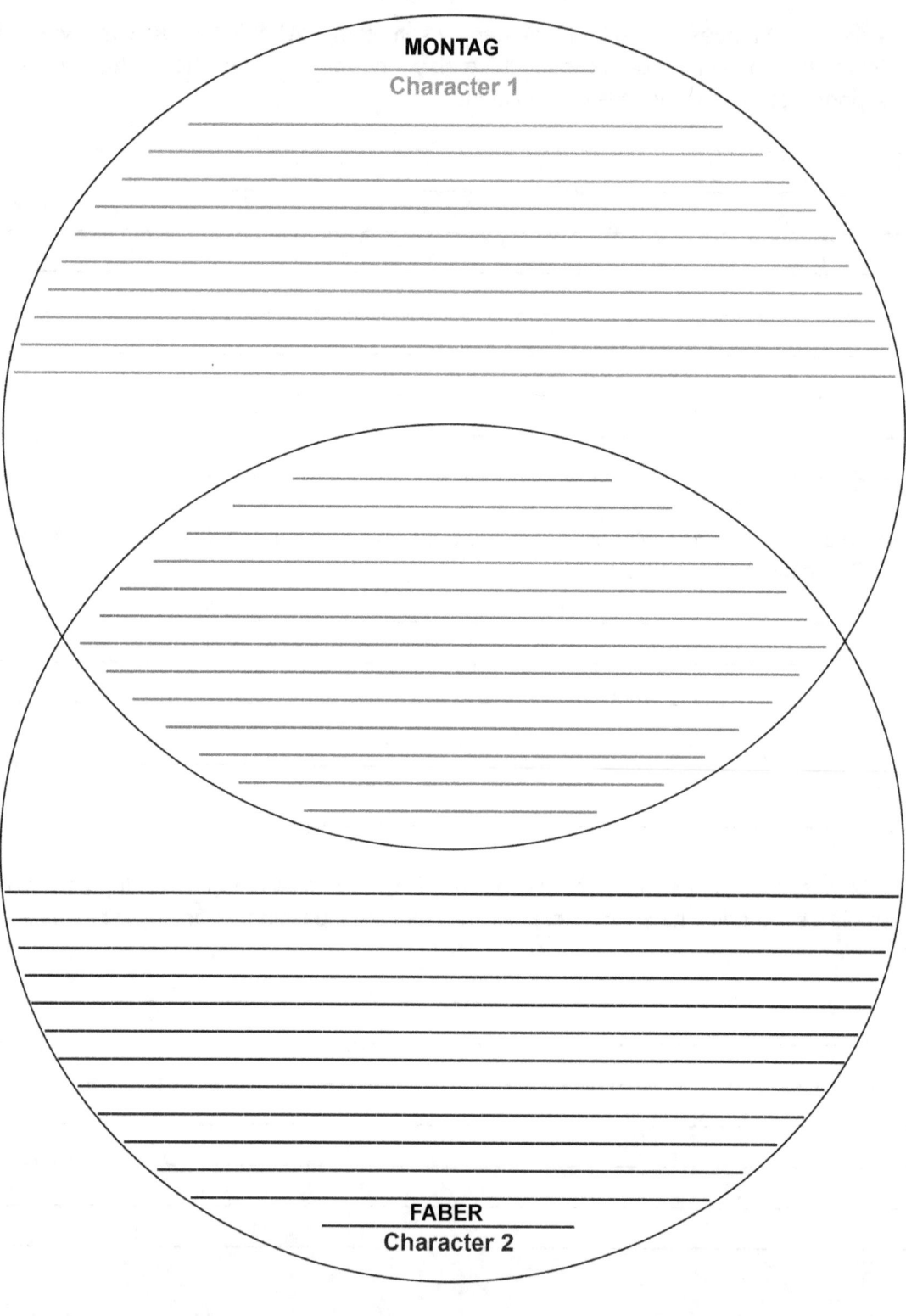

CHARACTER COMPARISON
Fahrenheit 451

Write Montag's traits on the top lines, Beatty's on the bottom lines, and the traits the two characters have in common on the middle lines.

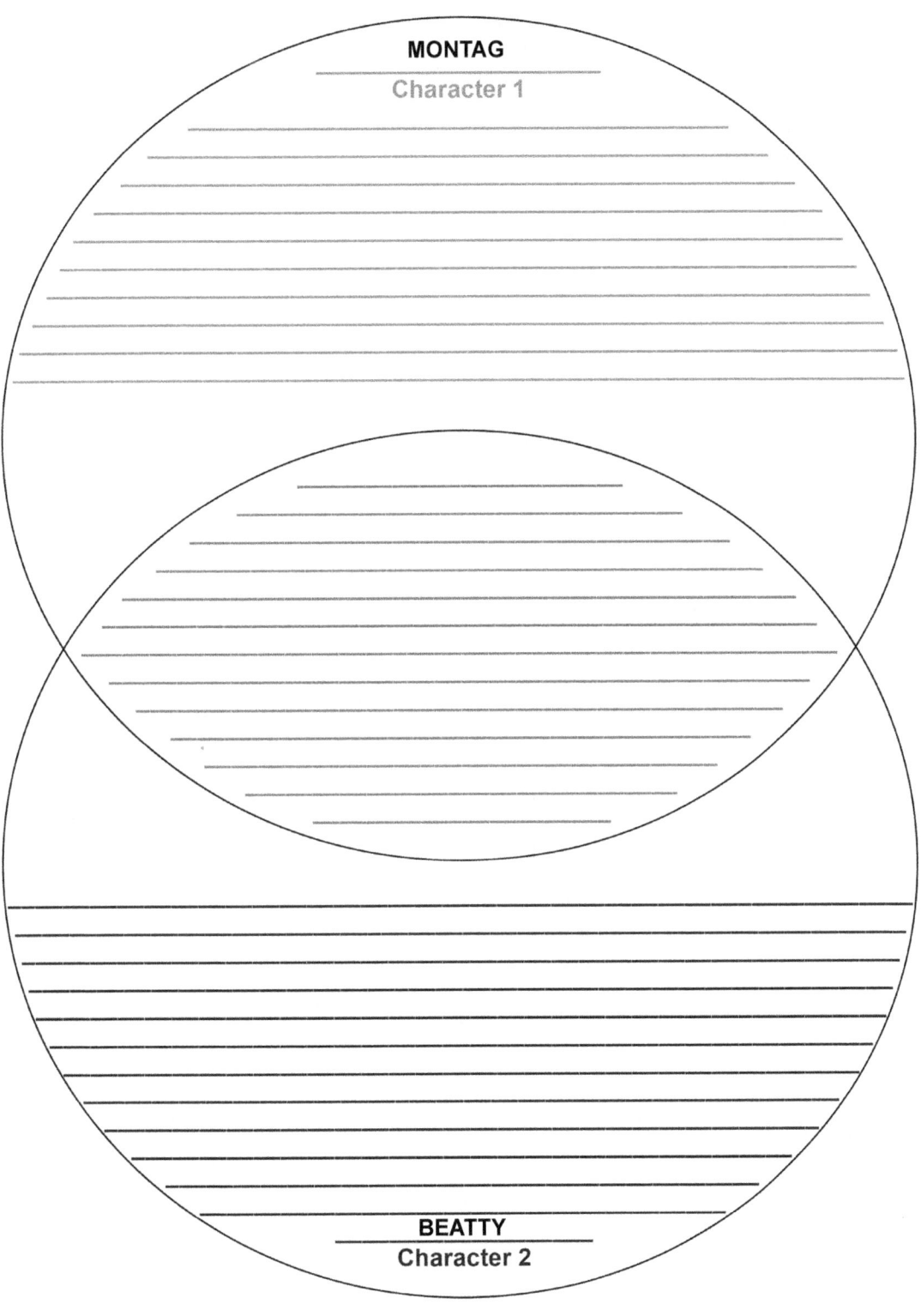

CHARACTER TRAITS: MONTAG
Fahrenheit 451

Choose 4 of Montag's character traits. Write one trait in each top box.
In the bottom boxes, note the evidence of that trait and the text page on which it is found.

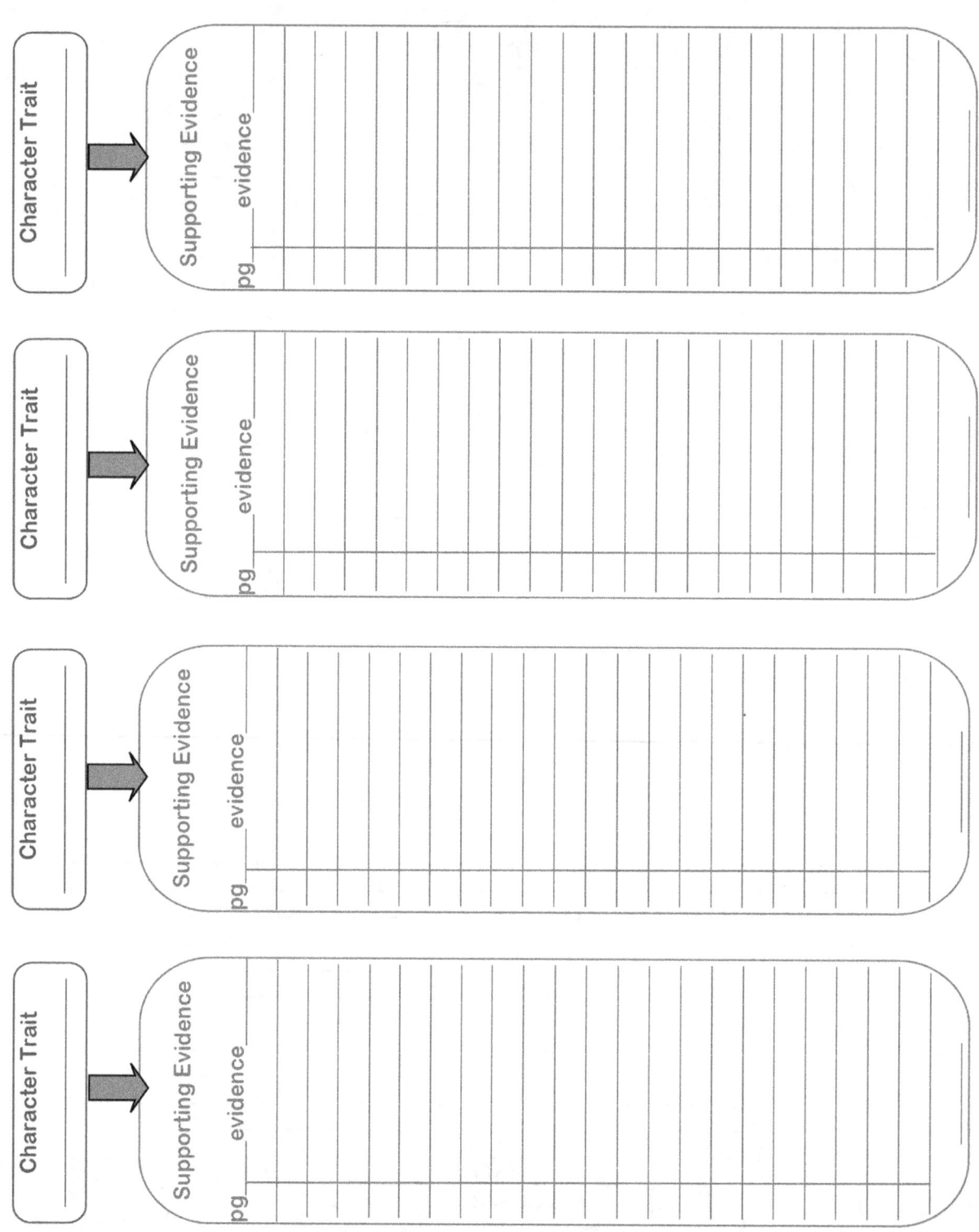

CHARACTER TRAITS: MILDRED
Fahrenheit 451
Choose 3 of Mildred's character traits. Write one trait in each top box.
In the bottom boxes, note the evidence of that trait and the text page on which it is found.

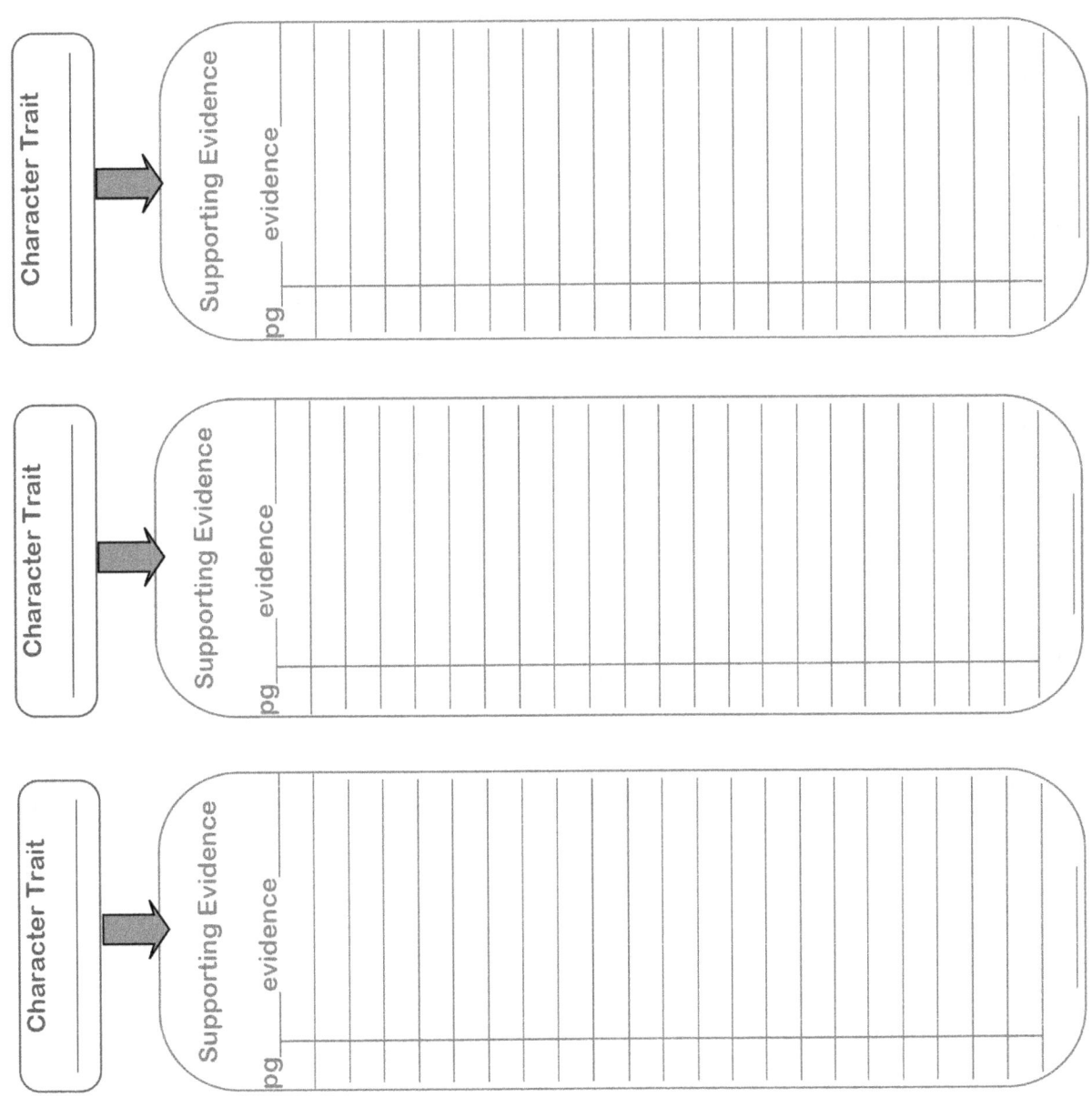

CHARACTER TRAITS: BEATTY
Fahrenheit 451

Choose 3 of Beatty's character traits. Write one trait in each top box.
In the bottom boxes, note the evidence of that trait and the text page on which it is found.

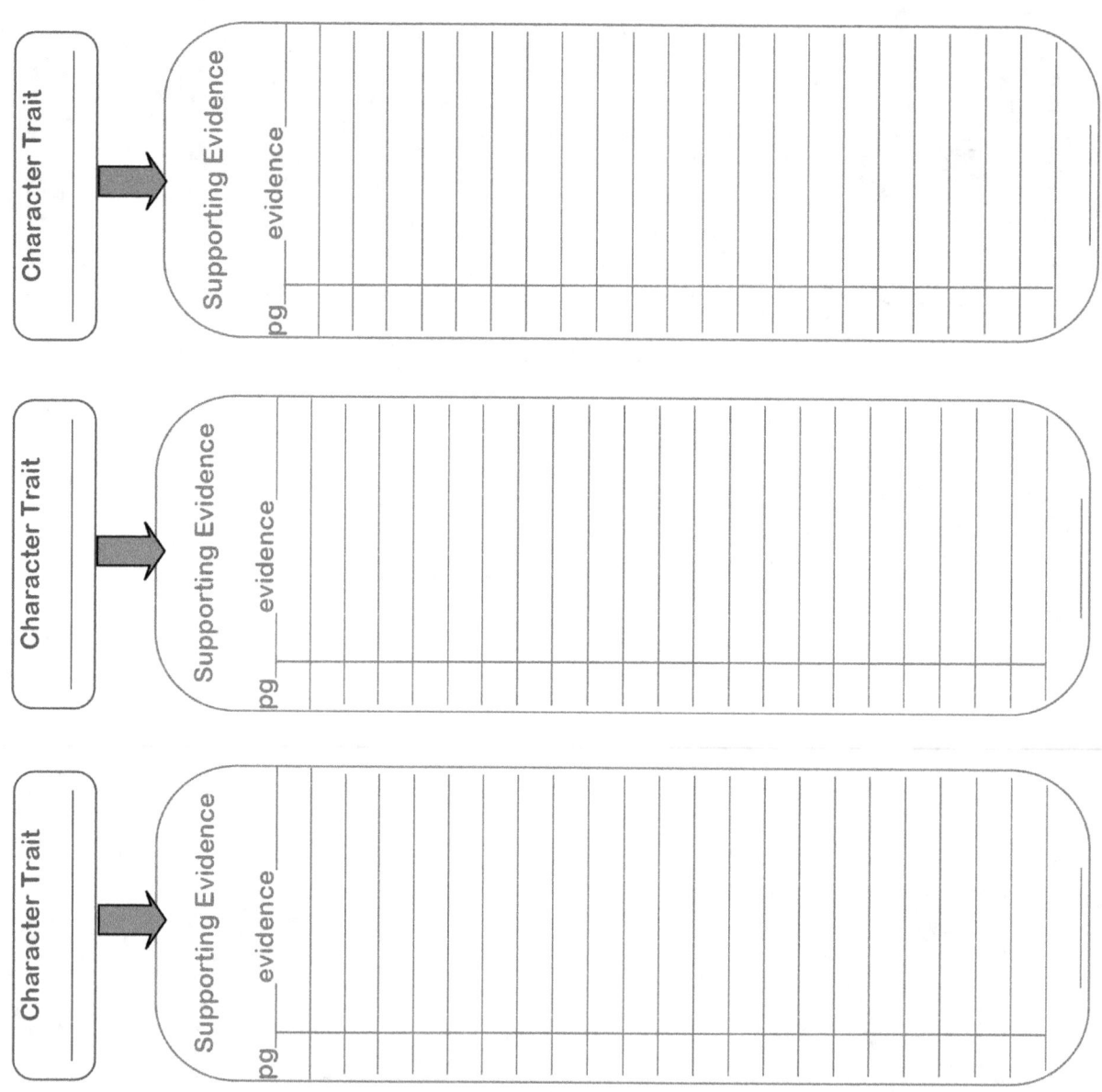

SYMBOLISM & IMAGERY
Fahrenheit 451

PART 1: The Chapter Titles

The passages below are about symbolism and the relevance of each chapter's title to the contents of the chapter and the book. Read these passages and answer the questions that follow.

The Hearth And The Salamander

A "hearth" is the brick or stone part of a fireplace that extends out into the room. Often the hearth is raised up from floor level, but it doesn't have to be. Sometimes "hearth" is used to refer to the fireplace as a whole.

In the days before other home heating methods and gas or electric stoves were available, big fireplaces with huge hearths were located in the kitchen or in the kitchen/living/dining room space. Family life centered around these hearths. Food would be cooked in kettles or pans that were heated by the fire. Dinner would be served at a table near the hearth, and after dinner family members would sit near the hearth to keep warm while reading, doing needlework, or conducting other activities. Because the hearth was so central to family life, it often is a symbol of "home."

Salamanders are amphibians. Like many frogs, they live in or near water or in other cool, damp places. In appearance, they resemble a lizard in form with skin more like a frog's in texture. Salamanders can be poisonous, so many are brightly colored to warn predators of their toxicity.

The important thing about salamanders, as far as their symbolic importance in Fahrenheit 451, is their association with fire. In ancient times, people thought salamanders were born from fire! Actually, they lived in rotten logs and when the logs were burned, the salamanders came out to escape the flames. For centuries people thought that salamander skin was fireproof and that salamanders could even put out fires.

In Fahrenheit 451 the fire trucks are called salamanders. Why? It's probably because of the ancient legends about salamanders coming from fire and being able to put out fires.

(continued on next page)

Symbols In Fahrenheit 451: Chapter Names, Page 2

But how do "hearth" and "salamander" go together to be an appropriate name for this chapter? Yes, the fire trucks are called salamanders but they carry firemen who start fires in homes; they don't put out fires. Consider that the salamander might represent something other than the firetrucks. To figure out what that might be, look at what the chapter is about.

Montag is the central character in this chapter, and he's a fireman. Therefore there's a good chance that he is somehow connected with this salamander symbolism. Salamanders were thought to be born from fire. Montag in his current occupation starts fires; fire is a big part of his life. Salamanders were thought to come out of the fire. Montag meets Clarisse and sees Mrs. Blake set fire to herself and her home--events which start to bring him away from (out of) his life of starting fires and into a state where he doesn't want to start fires anymore. In fact, he wants to stop the fires from being set. Hmmm. Salamanders were thought to put out fires. Are you seeing the connections? "Salamander" in the title refers to Montag. The new Montag comes from a life of fire and goes into a life of stopping fires, wanting the book and home burnings to stop.

So what does "hearth" have to do with any of this? Traditionally, as previously explained, "hearth" is a symbol of "home." Notice it isn't a symbol of "house." "Home" encompasses family, safety, warmth, and love; it is associated with tradition and roots, wholeness and togetherness.

In this chapter, Montag burns homes along with the books. Montag's own home is not "homey" at all; in fact, it is cold, almost sterile in nature. There's no warmth, no hearth, no good smells, no love, no togetherness, no sharing. Our salamander Montag sees the contrast between his own house and Clarisse's home, his own lifestyle and Clarisse's lifestyle--and realizes how empty his life is. He begins to want the emptiness of his life to be filled up.

So, The Hearth And The Salamander is a very appropriate name for this chapter. Montag, the salamander, is born from a life of fire. He is brought out of this life of fire through meeting Clarisse and realizing how empty his life is. He sees his own house is not a home and he begins looking for something that will satisfy his yearnings. He thinks books hold the answer. Burning books, burning homes, burning people becomes directly opposed to what Montag most wants; in fact, he wants the burning of books, homes, and people to stop. He becomes a catalyst, a force for the goal of stopping the fires.

(continued on next page)

The Sand And The Sieve

A sieve is a device, usually shaped like a shallow bowl or a tall cup, with holes punched in the bottom. The purpose of a sieve is to let smaller particles through the holes while retaining the larger parts, to separate the larger particles from the smaller ones.

The title of this chapter comes from Montag's remembering that as a child at the beach, a cousin offered him a dime if he would fill a sieve up with sand. The sand, of course, went right through the holes in the sieve. He tried and tried to fill it up, but he just couldn't do it. He sat there and cried.

What basically happens in chapter two? Montag remembers Faber, finds his address, and takes a book to him. While on the train, Montag realizes he'll have to give the book to Beatty very soon, so he tries to memorize it on the train ride to Faber's house. But he can't. The PA system on the bus is busy blaring an advertisement for Denham's Dentifrice, Denham's Dandy Dental Detergent. It's impossible to concentrate, to think, to remember with the ad blaring. He gets really frustrated and finally bursts out yelling for the thing to shut up. He tries to retain the words, but they slip through his mind like sand through a sieve.

That's one connection. But is it enough to name a whole chapter for it? What else goes on in the chapter? At this point in the novel, Montag has some knowledge: he knows he is unhappy; he has discovered some things that seem like a better way of life; he believes books hold the information he needs to find happiness and fulfillment. This is a great discovery, and he wants to share it with someone. He tries to share it with Millie and then with Millie and her friends, but they don't "get it." No matter how hard he tries to make them enlightened in the way he has become enlightened, they just don't "get it." He tries and tries to fill them up with these wonderful, new ideas but Millie and her friends are incapable of understanding or retaining the ideas he is trying to share with them, just like the sieve was incapable of holding the sand he tried to put in it.

Symbols In Fahrenheit 451: Chapter Names, Page 4

Burning Bright
The title of this chapter is a reference to a poem called "The Tyger" by William Blake:

> Tyger Tyger, burning bright,
> In the forests of the night;
> What immortal hand or eye,
> Could frame thy fearful symmetry?
>
> In what distant deeps or skies.
> Burnt the fire of thine eyes?
> On what wings dare he aspire?
> What the hand, dare seize the fire?
>
> And what shoulder, & what art,
> Could twist the sinews of thy heart?
> And when thy heart began to beat,
> What dread hand? & what dread feet?
>
> What the hammer? what the chain,
> In what furnace was thy brain?
> What the anvil? what dread grasp,
> Dare its deadly terrors clasp!
>
> When the stars threw down their spears
> And water'd heaven with their tears:
> Did he smile his work to see?
> Did he who made the Lamb make thee?
>
> Tyger Tyger burning bright,
> In the forests of the night:
> What immortal hand or eye,
> Dare frame thy fearful symmetry?

The idea is, "Who made the tiger, so beautiful on the outside, yet with such a fierce heart? And, was the maker pleased with his creation?" The connection to Fahrenheit 451 is "Who made mankind, so beautiful on the outside but so prone to all the things that lead to self destruction and war? And is the maker pleased with his creation?" Notice, too, that tigers' coats are orange and black and white--important colors in Fahrenheit 451: fire, evil, purity.

The chapter title is also appropriate literally: Montag's house is burned and Mildred leaves, freeing him from his past. Beatty and the Mechanical Hound are burned, in a sense freeing Montag from nagging and fear...and possibly foreshadowing the end of the society. The city burns in a bright flash of light, ending all mankind built into it and clearing the slate for a new beginning. As Beatty said, "Burn all, burn everything. Fire is bright and fire is clean."

SYMBOLISM & IMAGERY
Fahrenheit 451

PART 1: The Chapter Titles
Questions To Answer

1. The hearth is usually a symbol of _____.

2. People used to think that salamanders were born from _____ and were _____.

3. The title Burning Bright is a reference to _____.

4. Four things burn brightly in chapter three:
   _____
   _____
   _____
   _____

5. The _____ is a good symbol for Montag because _____
   _____
   _____
   _____

6. Mildred and her friends are like a _____ because they _____
   _____

7. While on the train, Montag yelled, "Shut up!" because _____
   _____
   _____

8. Montag's house is not a home because _____
   _____
   _____

ARTICLE EVALUATION
Fahrenheit 451

Reading & Evaluating Informational Texts

1. What is the purpose of the article? How well did it achieve this purpose?

___

2. What is the central idea of the article?

___

2. Are the points that are made logical; is the reasoning sound? Give an example or two.

___

3. Are the points well developed? Explain why you think so or not.

___

4. Do you think this article is well-done as-written, or do you think it should be revised to be better? What would make it better?

___

SYMBOLISM & IMAGERY
Fahrenheit 451

PART 2: Symbols & Imagery Within The Text

There are many symbols within the text of Fahrenheit 451. Read about some of them below and then complete the exercise that follows.

Fahrenheit 451

Paper burns around 451 degrees Fahrenheit. This number isn't exact because the actual number depends on the chemical composition of the paper, moisture content, and so on. However, for the purposes of this novel, 451 is symbolic of the temperature at which book paper burns.

Snake Imagery

Here are some passages where the snake imagery is found:
- "One of them [the machines] slid down into your stomach like a black cobra down an echoing well...."
- "...a silly empty man near a silly empty woman, while the hungry snake made her still more empty."
- "There's a Phoenix car just drove up and a man in a black shirt with an orange snake stitched on his arm coming up the front walk."
- "I saw the damnedest snake in the world the other night. It was dead but it was alive. It could see but it couldn't see."
- "A voice drifted after him, 'Denham's Denham's Denham's,' the train hissed like a snake. The train vanished in its hole."

Traditionally, snakes are the bad guys--evil incarnate. This started with the story of Adam and Eve in the Garden of Eden in the Bible, when the Devil, disguised as a snake, tempted Eve to eat the forbidden fruit from the Tree of Knowledge.

In the passages above, the stomach-pumping machine is like a snake, Beatty has the symbol of a snake on his arm, and the train hisses like a snake. The need for stomach-pumping (and having it done in such a cold, uncaring manner like a janitorial mop-up), and the train's PA system's pounding noise and advertising at the occupants so they could think of nothing else are bad things in and for people, signs of an unhealthy society.

In the other three references noted, the snake represents whomever is creating the rules and pushing for this kind of lifestyle. Beatty is Captain of the firemen, definitely an enforcer of the rules. The hungry snake that "made her still more empty" is the society that has so emptied its citizens. And the snake that was dead but was alive--the stomach-pumping apparatus that looked inside Mildred to suck out all the junk--also could represent the seemingly intangible yet ever-present forces that created Montag's society. Rules and laws are not living things, yet they can suck the life out of the living by stripping people of the ability to think for themselves, by eroding freedom and choices, and by taking all the fun, creativity, and "meat" out of daily life.

Fahrenheit 451 Symbols & Imagery Within The Text, Page 2

Book Burning

Books are the traditional method of recording knowledge. Therefore, books represent knowledge and are the record of all the things people have thought, done, and imagined for all of recorded time. When there is no written record of something, it is easy to forget (as well as to modify) the facts. "Oh, that never *really* happened. Someone just made it up." "Firemen never put out fires; that's an old tale." In this sense, the burning of the books is symbolic of the new regime getting rid of the past so it can indoctrinate the people into believing what it wants them to believe.

Books hold ideas. Ideas spark imagination and creativity. They inspire people to think, to suppose, to wonder, and to want to find truth in life. If a regime wants to control people, to make people fall in line and do what they are told, books are the enemy and must be destroyed. Creativity, thinking, and questioning go against being controlled. Burning books can therefore also represent the destruction of creativity and thought as well as the emergence of the dominance of a regime attempting to control a population.

You might also note that in Fahrenheit 451, the firemen not only burn the books, they also burn the houses and relocate the residents to asylums or elsewhere. It isn't just about removing the books; it's about totally eliminating any opposition, anyone who might disagree or want things to be different.

Phoenix

Granger tells the story of the Phoenix, the bird that every few hundred years built a pyre and burned himself up and then rose again from the ashes to start anew. The image of the Phoenix is visible on Montag's chest when he meets Clarisse as well as on the Captain's hat and car. It is often a part of the symbology for firemen because of the Phoenix's destruction by fire.

When Granger tells about the Phoenix, he says it "must have been first cousin to Man....it looks like we're doing the same thing." This not only speaks to Mankind's past, it foreshadows the bombing of the city and the renewal that will occur afterwards.

Parlor Walls

In the past, homes often had rooms called parlors. These rooms were like a formal living room where family and guests would gather, often after dinner. Men would discuss politics, business, or other intellectual matters. A wife might do needlework or read; children were either not present or would sit and read or quietly play a game. At some point in the evening, a child or the wife might play the piano or provide some other kind of entertainment such as reciting, singing, or acting. Parlors were before television. If no guests were present, spouses might discuss family matters, neighborhood news, church or social club events, or the like.

In contrast, the Parlor Walls in Fahrenheit 451 are television on steroids; opposite in almost every way to the old-fashioned parlor. The walls are loud, colorful, and bright. Mildred is passive except for a few scripted lines she may have as "interaction." She takes in and is entertained by the sights and sounds on the big screens, but she never has to do or think anything. So it's ironic that Bradbury named them the "parlor" walls. One could make a case that Mildred meets her "family" and interacts with them in her Parlor Walls, but the "family" isn't real, and the shows don't have any substance.

This kind of mindless entertainment for hours on end is one part of the erosion of Mildred to emptiness. During the time of the Roman Empire, the politicians devised (and carried out) a plan to give the people cheap food and lots of entertainment so they would be happy and distracted from the political issues of the day, making their rise to power easier and practically uncontested. No one cared. "Give them bread and circuses" is the often-used phrase coined by Roman satirist and poet Juvenal. In the same way, Mildred and her friends don't really care about politics or much of anything except their shows. They don't even know or care why their country is at war.

The Parlor Walls, therefore, become symbolic of the ignorance and shallowness developed and encouraged by those in power to keep the masses of people happy and unconcerned with what the politicians are doing. It is also part of the metaphoric "hungry snake" that "made her [Mildred] still more empty."

Finally, Parlor Walls are also a means of escape for Mildred and her friends. Being entertained with happy and shallow programming, they can avoid facing the reality of their lives.

Seashells

Think of the "Seashells" as modern day ear buds. When Mildred isn't absorbed by the Parlor Walls, she is plugged in to her Seashells, being entertained by music or the radio. Before going to bed, she takes sleeping pills and plugs in her Seashells to drown out any thoughts of the day that will keep her awake. Like the Parlor Walls, they are a means of escape that promote lack of thought, and they are symbolic of the ignorance and shallowness encouraged by those in power.

The Green Bullet

So what about the Green Bullet, then? It's like a Seashell, isn't it? In form, yes, it is. It is a small, green, and bullet-shaped radio that fits into Montag's ear, as a Seashell would. But in substance it is quite different. Let's look at the name. What is green? Natural, living things like plants are green. But then there's that word "bullet," which usually is associated with killing, bringing death. What does the Green Bullet do? It provides a communications link between Faber and Montag, so Montag can have some help in responding to Beatty and others. Faber is a part of those with a green, "living" lifestyle--full of life, full of thoughts, real emotions, ideas, and creativity. Faber and Montag want to deliver a verbal bullet, a response that stops Beatty. In a larger sense, the Green Bullet becomes symbolic of finding a way to stop the erosion of humanity.

Fahrenheit 451 Symbols & Imagery Within The Text, Page 4

Mirrors

Look for a minute at the places where mirrors are used in the text:

- "He [Montag] knew that when he returned to the firehouse, he might wink at himself, a minstrel man, burnt-corked, in the mirror."
- "How like a mirror, too, her [Clarisse's] face. Impossible; for how many people did you know that refracted your own light back to you?"
- "These men [the firemen] were all mirror images of himself!"
- "There was a crash like the falling parts of a dream fashioned out of warped glass, mirrors, and crystal prisms." (as Mildred left the house in the beetle)
- "The look of you is enough. You haven't seen yourself in a mirror lately." (Granger to Montag)
- "...because in the millionth part of time left, she [Millie] saw her own face reflected there, in a mirror instead of a crystal ball, and it was such a wildly empty face, all by itself in the room, touching nothing, starved and eating of itself...."
- "Come on now, we're going to go build a mirror factory first and put out nothing but mirrors for the next year and take a long look in them."

That which is seen in a mirror is not real; it is a reflection of that which is real. Also, we cannot see ourselves without a mirror. We cannot see what we really look like without examining our own reflections. Go back and re-read the quotes above considering these ideas.

This whole book is filled with things that are real but not real, living but not living, seeming to be real but...not. The Mechanical Hound is mechanical, but it seems alive to Montag. The door-voice is not real, but it is personified. The "family" is not real, but Mildred treats them as if they are. The war is very real, but seems like it is not (until it's too late). History is real but is made into a fairy tale, a made-up story. These are just a few examples. Mirrors, reflections, distortions, and ironies abound in a close reading of Fahrenheit 451.

Think about this again: We cannot see what we really look like without examining our own reflections. This is physically true, but it also applies to our character. Without looking at our own actions, reflecting on the things we do, thinking about the effects of what we do and the meaning of what we do, we cannot know ourselves as individuals or as a society.

The Mechanical Hound

The Hound, like Beatty is a symbol of the establishment. In addition, the Hound represents the blurring of the non-living and living in Montag's world.

SYMBOLISM & IMAGERY
Fahrenheit 451

Part 2 Symbols & Images In The Text
Questions For Review

1. List 9 things that are important images or symbols in Fahrenheit 451:

   _____   _____   _____

   _____   _____   _____

   _____   _____   _____

2. Name three things or people that represent the establishment, those in control:

   _____   _____   _____

3. Name three things that are a means of "escape" for Mildred:

   _____   _____   _____

4. Years after people read Fahrenheit 451, the thing they remember is that it is about book burning. What does the book burning actually symbolize?

   _____

   _____

   _____

   _____

   _____

5. Why are the Parlor Walls important in Fahrenheit 451?

   _____

   _____

6. Explain how the story of the Phoenix relates to the city.

   _____

   _____

   _____

   _____

SYMBOLISM & IMAGERY
Fahrenheit 451

PART 3: Analyzing And Evaluating The Symbolic Use Of Rain: Assignment

Your assignment is to analyze and evaluate the symbolic use of rain in Fahrenheit 451.

- Find the passages where rain is mentioned and write them down (with page numbers). (Hint: If you have access to a digital form of the book, you can search "rain" to find passages then look them up in your book.)
- Skim before and after the passages to see what is happening in that part of the story.
- Look at the possible symbolic meaning rain might have in each passage & make notes about it.
- Review your notes about each passage and see what is in common.
- Draw conclusions based on your passage analysis.
- Write an analysis of the symbolic use of rain in Fahrenheit 451

A few observations about rain:
    Rain can be cleansing or renewing.
    Rainy/stormy weather can foreshadow bad things happening.
    Rain helps things grow.
    Rain is water, which is life-giving.

SYMBOLISM & IMAGERY
Fahrenheit 451

PART 3: Analyzing And Evaluating The Symbolic Use Of Rain: Notes

Page	Passage	Notes

SYMBOLISM & IMAGERY
Fahrenheit 451

PART 3: Analyzing And Evaluating The Symbolic Use Of Rain: Written Analysis

THEMES
Fahrenheit 451

There are many ways to approach studying the themes of Fahrenheit 451, but any approach has to start with the text, for it is through the text that the themes are developed.

You have already read the text from beginning to end. You may have looked at specific passages to consider the symbols within the story or to study character development. Let's pull out some things now that will help us understand the larger themes of the work.

Our study will be based on:
- Montag's Realizations
- Words & Actions Of Mildred And Her Friends
- Beatty's Commentaries
- Clarisse, Faber, & Granger's Contributions
- The Ending

Montag's Realizations
We all get pretty used to our own daily routines and our own way of life. We accept that what we do is how life *is*. That's how Montag is...until Clarisse slips into his world that evening on his way home from work. Her world is very different from his. It seems interesting to him. And she asks a simple question--almost as an afterthought before parting: "Are you happy?".

Montag goes home to find his wife in bed with her Seashells plugged into her ears. Motionless. Pale. Dull. None of which is unusual. In fact, he doesn't realize she has overdosed on sleeping pills until he kicks the empty bottle. The men come to pump out her stomach and fix her up, but their casual attitude toward this "clean up job" is annoying and upsetting to Montag. It doesn't take Montag long in the beginning of the novel to realize that he is *not* happy.

Then there's Clarisse. What is it about her that intrigues him? He likes talking with her. Unlike his wife, she is responsive and thoughtful, a breath of fresh air in his stale life. Again, it doesn't take Montag long to realize that he wants *that* kind of a life...one of conversation and thought and genuine interaction rather than thoughtless, automatic responses.

On top of all that, Montag witnesses a woman who is willing to die rather than live her life without her books. That's pretty powerful. Even more powerful is Montag's witnessing her light the match that starts the fire--and realizing that what he does for a living has real consequences for real people.

Montag realizes he is unhappy, realizes what kind of a lifestyle he wants, realizes that books have something that is important enough to die for, and realizes what he has been doing as a fireman is not such a great thing.

There's one more important realization. He can't share his new life quest with Millie. She's just not capable of understanding what he has discovered.

Fahrenheit 451: Themes, page 2

Words And Actions Of Millie And Her Friends
"Why?" we must ask, "Why is Mildred incapable of understanding and sharing Montag's quest for a new life?" The answer is pretty simple, really: she's just too shallow of a person. Montag reads to her, but the words have no meaning, they're just words. "It doesn't mean anything! The Captain was right!" she says. Then she is relieved to pick up the ringing telephone, to talk with her friend about the White Clown show.

Millie spends all of her time watching mindless shows on the Parlor Walls, listening to the radio through her Seashells, and talking with her friends about nothing in particular, the way her Parlor Wall "family" talks but says nothing of substance.

Children are a bother. No one in their right mind would want them. So ship them off to school to be taken care of by others. When they're home, plunk them in front of the Parlor Walls. There's a war, but no one knows why; it doesn't really matter. It happens somewhere else. Husbands go off to war and are expected back with no consequences. Elections are won on looks alone. Nothing that is troublesome or unpleasant is allowed in. Millie and her friends haven't a care in the world. In fact, Mildred says, "I am happy...and proud of it!"

How do Millie and her friends cope when things come into life that aren't so pleasant? They run away; escape to the Parlor Walls, the Seashells, the pills. They have no coping skills whatsoever. They are totally unprepared to meet real life. It overwhelms them. After the firetruck arrives at Montag's house, Mildred comes out...ignores Montag, like he is a stranger...talks to herself about the house as if it is someone else's...gets into the beetle and rides away.

Beatty's Commentaries
How did people become like Mildred...incapable of coping with reality? Ah, let's look back at Captain Beatty's commentaries and consider his words. Ironically, here is a condensed version of what Beatty says, with a whole bunch of stuff left out:

> "Whirl man's mind around about so fast under the pumping hands of publishers, exploiters, broadcasters that the centrifuge flings off all unnecessary, time-wasting thought! ... School is shortened, discipline relaxed, philosophies, histories, languages dropped....Life is immediate, the job counts, pleasure lies all about after work. ... Empty the theaters save for clowns and furnish the rooms with glass walls and pretty colors running up and down the walls.... More sports for everyone, group spirit, fun, and you don't have to think, eh? ... More pictures. The mind drinks less and less. Impatience. Highways full of crowds going somewhere, somewhere, somewhere, nowhere. ... Don't step on the toes of the dog-lovers, the cat-lovers, doctors, lawyers, merchants, ... There was no dictum, no declaration, no censorship, to start with, no! Technology, mass exploitation, and minority pressure carried the trick.... Today, thanks to them, you can stay happy all the time...."

> "We must all be alike. Not everyone born free and equal, as the Constitution says, but everyone made equal. Each man the image of every other; then all are happy, for there are no mountains to make them cower, to judge themselves against. ... A book is a loaded gun in the house next door. ... Who knows who might be the target of the well-read man?"

Fahrenheit 451: Themes, page 3

> "... Ask yourself, What do we want in this country, above all? People want to be happy....Well, aren't they? Don't we keep them moving, don't we give them fun? That's all we live for, isn't it? For pleasure, for titillation? ..."

> "Colored people don't like *Little Black Sambo*. Burn it. White people don't feel good about *Uncle Tom's Cabin*. Burn it. Someone's written a book on tobacco and cancer of the lungs? The cigarette people are weeping? Burn the book. ... Funerals are unhappy and pagan? Eliminate them, too. ... Burn all, burn everything. Fire is bright and fire is clean."

> "...So bring on your clubs and parties, your acrobats and magicians, your daredevils, jet cars, motorcycle helicopters, your sex and heroin, more of everything to do with automatic reflex."

And there you have it. That's basically how Beatty says the Mildreds and their friends came to be.

Clarisse, Faber, & Granger's Contributions
But the figurative door is left open, you see, because of Clarisse, Faber, Granger, and folks like them. Not *everyone* fell into the automatic reflex, always-happy trap. There are still people who like to have conversations and stand around, kicking leaves and thinking (Clarisse). There are still people who know that what has happened isn't a good thing, though they don't have the courage or the wherewithal to take action to change things on their own (Faber). There are still people who know, appreciate, and try to save that which has been burned, that which has been lost (Granger). And there are still people like Montag who say, "Hey! I want something more than this shallow, pretend-happy life."

The End
And in the end of the book, what happens? The shallow life Mankind acquiesced to over time brought itself down--and the outcasts, the thinkers, the do-ers, the people who could cope with reality, stepped in to start civilization anew.

Fahrenheit 451: Themes, page 4

Theme Notes

Use this page to jot down notes about theme in Fahrenheit 451.

1. Montag makes these important realizations:

- _____
- _____
- _____
- _____
- _____

2. Mildred is incapable of being a part of Montag's quest for a new lifestyle because

_____

3. Mildred and her friends can't cope with unpleasant realities. When they are faced with such things, their response is to _____ by turning to _____, _____, or _____.

4. Beatty gives a long speech stating how he thinks their society came to be as it is. Towards the end he says: "...So bring on your clubs and parties, your acrobats and magicians, your daredevils, jet cars, motorcycle helicopters, your sex and heroin, more of everything to do with _____ _____."

5. Not *everyone* fell into the automatic reflex, always-happy trap. There are still people who like to have conversations and stand around, kicking leaves and thinking (_____).

There are still people who know that what has happened isn't a good thing, though they don't have the courage or the wherewithal to take action to change things on their own (_____).

There are still people who know, appreciate, and try to save that which has been burned, that which has been lost (_____).

And there are still people like _____ who say, "Hey! I want something more than this shallow, pretend-happy life."

6. At the end of the book, the shallow life Mankind acquiesced to over time _____--and the outcasts, the thinkers, the do-ers, the people who could cope with reality, stepped in to _____.

Fahrenheit 451: Themes, page 5

From Text To Theme

We have looked at the text in a "big picture" way. Now, how do we get from this to that elusive thing called "theme"?

First we need to know what "theme" is.
Theme is the central idea of the book. It is the comment the book makes about life.
- Theme addresses the nature of humanity
- Theme addresses the nature of society
- Theme addresses the nature of humankind's relationship to the world
  and/or
- Theme addresses the nature of our ethical responsibilities

What is the nature of humanity as set forth in Fahrenheit 451?

_____

What is the nature of society as set forth in Fahrenheit 451?

_____

What is the nature of humankind's relationship to the world in Fahrenheit 451?

_____

What is the nature of our ethical responsibilities as set forth in Fahrenheit 451?

_____

All of that being said, and considering the "big picture" of the text that we have just examined, write one phrase or sentence that best states the main theme of Fahrenheit 451.

_____
_____

Are there other themes that are not the main theme? Did you have to choose among several things to determine the main theme? What other themes are in Fahrenheit 451?

_____
_____
_____

Fahrenheit 451: Themes, page 6

Theme In Context
You've read the book and by studying it and getting to the theme, you know what it is really about, not just the story line. The next question to ask is, "Why?". Why would Ray Bradbury back in 1950 put pen to paper to write this book? And what did he intend for his readers to get from it? In a sense, the "theme" is what we get from the book, but until we turn that into his advice for us, his efforts are in vain, worthless.

Why Did He Write It?
Think about Ray Bradbury's lifetime. (He was born in 1920 and died in 2012.) His childhood took place in the Roaring Twenties, followed by the Great Depression, WWII, the rise of Communism, and the Korean War. In his lifetime, technological advances were astounding. Any thoughtful person would look at the world and wonder where all this would lead, as did Ray Bradbury.

Bradbury's book is a cautionary story, warning people of the possible consequences of the direction he saw the country going.

What Would Ray Bradbury's Advice Be To Us, His Readers?
Think about Fahrenheit 451 and all that is in it. Think about the characters, the themes, the ideas presented and discussed. Make a list of items of advice Ray Bradbury would give to you.

Do These Things:

_____
_____
_____
_____
_____
_____
_____
_____
_____

Don't Do These Things:

_____
_____
_____
_____
_____
_____
_____
_____
_____

Fahrenheit 451: Themes, page 7

Now you have a decision to make: you need to decide if this is good advice or not. It might all be good advice, some might be good and some not so good, or it all could be bad advice. What do you think? Is Bradbury's advice good or not? Answer completely below, explaining your answer fully.

_____
_____
_____
_____
_____
_____
_____
_____
_____
_____
_____
_____

It is wise to take good advice, and we usually benefit from that in the long run. If you believe any of Mr. Bradbury's advice is good, think for a few minutes how that might apply to you. Make a list of things you should probably stop doing and things you should probably start doing to act upon the advice given.

Start Doing These Things:

Stop Doing/Do Less Of These Things:

Anytime someone gives you advice, you have to evaluate it. Decide if it is good advice or not, and then act accordingly. Consider the source, think about the consequences of following the advice, and evaluate what that might mean for you.

ACTIVITY: EXPLORATION OF ADDITIONAL THEMES
Fahrenheit 451

The idea of total governmental control over an apathetic people and the censorship that goes along with that are not the only two themes in Fahrenheit 451. Some of the others include:

- knowledge versus ignorance
- the natural order & elements of the world versus a man-made world
- the blurring of the lines between animate and inanimate objects
- religion, religious imagery, and scriptural references
- conscious versus subconscious, often shown by hands acting on their own

This is not an exhaustive list, but it does hit many of the highlights of themes and motifs in the novel.

Your assignment is to fully explore one of these themes in Fahrenheit 451.

Here's to go about doing this assignment:
You will scan the text for references to this theme and note the references on the chart on the following page. Your group should assign each person in the group one of the reading assignment sections to scan for references to your theme.

When you finish noting references, you should come back together as a group to discuss each of the references you have found and try to draw some conclusions about the cumulative meaning of the references. Write these down in a few sentences at the bottom of the Notes page.

When all groups have completed these tasks, the class will come back together as a whole to share information and discuss each theme/motif that has been explored. Be prepared to share your information with the whole class.

After your textual research is over, you should find and read at least two articles written by others about your assigned theme or motif in the novel.

Finally, each group member should write a summary about your theme or motif, clearly stating what your theme or motif is and explaining its use in the novel, using specific examples from the text to support your statements and including (and citing) any appropriate information from the additional articles you read.

THEME/MOTIF NOTES
Fahrenheit 451

Theme/Motif _____

PAGE	REFERENCE

Use an additional sheet of notebook paper if needed for more references.

Notes About Cumulative Meaning Of The References:

_____
_____
_____
_____
_____
_____
_____

USE OF LANGUAGE
Fahrenheit 451

Writing is often referred to as a "craft." You may hear authors say they've spent years working on their craft. Well, a "craft" is an occupation that requires special skills or particular attention to details. A woodworker, for example, may craft a fine piece of furniture, taking great time and effort to make every joint, every angle, every carved detail perfect. The same is true with writing: authors take a great deal of time and effort to make every word, every sentence, every chapter fit the purposes of their book perfectly. Ray Bradbury was a master at this.

We can't look at every passage in the whole book; there just isn't enough time. But we can look at a few passages that show Mr. Bradbury's mastery very well, then you can go on to look at other passages on your own to truly appreciate his finely crafted work. At some point you should go back and reread the novel from start to end after completing this study. You will see so many things you missed the first time around.

Let's take a look at the beginning of the book.

Passage	Commentary
It was a pleasure to burn.	What? A *pleasure* to burn? How odd! It grabs our attention, lets us know something unusual is going on, & lets us know this person *likes* burning things. It introduces a main element of the book: burning.
It was a special pleasure to see things eaten, to see things blackened and *changed*.	Why "eaten" instead of "burned"? "Eaten" is much more graphic; it personifies the fire, right away giving lifelike qualities to an inanimate thing, introducing the theme of "living but not living, inanimate but perceived as alive" paradox in the book. "Changed" is in italics; this whole book is about change of one kind or another.
With the brass nozzle in his fists, with this great python spitting its venomous kerosene upon the world, the blood pounded in his head, and his hands were the hands of some amazing conductor playing all the symphonies of blazing and burning to bring down the tatters and charcoal ruins of history.	Calling the hose a python brings it to life & begins the snake imagery often used in the book. "Blood pounding in his head" graphically tells us he's excited, working hard, energized. The element of "hands" often used throughout the book is introduced. Who would think to liken using a fire hose to conducting a symphony? What are tatters? They are torn pieces; bits of shredded clothing. What does "to bring down the tatters and charcoal ruins of history" mean? It brings a mental image of old charred buildings falling down but we know it's more than that. How do you "bring down" or destroy history?! Yet, that is also an important element in the book. Remember how Montag was told firemen never put out fires; that was just an old tale? That is shredding history, turning history into charcoal ruins. And here it is at the very start of the book!

Fahrenheit 451: Use Of Language, page 2

Passage	Commentary
With his symbolic helmet numbered 451 on his stolid head, and his eyes all orange flame with the thought of what came next, he flicked the igniter and the house jumped up in a gorging fire that burned the evening sky red and yellow and black.	Bradbury *tells* us 451 is symbolic; he leaves no doubt. Montag's head is "stolid": not easily stirred or moved mentally; unemotional. One word introduces the unemotional, lethargic, passive nature of people in this society. When you look at someone's eyes, you can tell a lot about them. Montag's are all orange flame. Orange is a bright color, a warning color, as in a yellow/orange light of a traffic light or "road work ahead" signs--fire. Danger. The house "jumped up." That's personification (giving inanimate objects human qualities). Again, very graphic. It's a "gorging" fire; "gorging," as in gorging on a meal--feasting; overeating (which brings back the eating image from the previous paragraph). The fire "burned the evening sky red and yellow and black"--the sky (nature) is being burned (destroyed), another subtheme in the book...humankind's unnatural existence in the city. Red and yellow and black--colors of danger and evil.
He strode in a swarm of fireflies. He wanted above all, like the old joke, to shove a marshmallow on a stick in the furnace, while the flapping pigeon-winged books died on the porch and lawn of the house. While the books went up in sparkling whirls and blew away on a wind turned dark with burning.	"Fireflies" gives a living quality to the bits of glowing embers in the air, which are not alive. The idea of shoving a marshmallow on a stick in the furnace refers to toasting a marshmallow on a stick over a fire, but the idea has degenerated through the years. People no longer have campfires, so they relate to doing it via the furnace, which is something they *do* have. And, it's an old joke now, not something that people really used to do. History has been changed, and it makes no sense, so it's a joke. Again, there's more personification with the flapping pigeon-winged books dying on the porch and lawn, as if they had life and they were being killed. Why pigeon-winged instead of some other bird? Carrier pigeons carry messages, as books do. The book sparks blow away on a "wind turned dark," ...wind (nature) turned dark (perverted) with burning.
Montag grinned the fierce grin of all men singed and driven back by flame.	Why does Montag "grin," and why is it a "fierce" grin? A "grin" is a broad smile, usually to show pleasure. "Fierce," in this case, is as in a *fierce* competition: furiously eager or intense. He's loving what he does and is right in there giving it his all. Notice, too, that he is the same as "all men singed..." and later in the book he realizes he looks like all the other firemen.

Fahrenheit 451: Use Of Language, page 3

Passage	Commentary
He knew that when he returned to the firehouse, he might wink at himself, a minstrel man, burnt-corked, in the mirror. Later, going to sleep, he would feel the fiery smile still gripped by his face muscles, in the dark. It never went away, that smile, it never ever went away, as long as he remembered.	Winking at oneself is usually an indication of happy self-congratulations. The minstrel-man image is one of being someone other than who you appear to be, doubly appropriate because minstrel-men often performed in "black face," with their white faces artificially blackened--and the firemen have sooty, blackened faces. The mirror introduces the idea of self-examination, mirrors, reflections, and crystals that appear throughout the book. His smile never went away. He, like others in his society, are perpetually happy, and he can't remember not having that smile. Remember, though, that he laughs when he doesn't know how to respond to Clarisse--and that is an auto-response laugh, not because she says anything funny. Perhaps this perpetual smile is an auto-response, too...just always there. And, finally, it says, "as long as he remembered," not "as long as he could remember." We usually say we've been doing something as long as we can remember. One reading of this last line could beg the question, "As long as he remembered *what*?".

And yet, when we read these passages for the first time, it just seems like a regular beginning of a story. Little do we suspect that Mr. Bradbury has given us such a thorough introduction to the book and has packed all of this symbolism and imagery into a few short paragraphs. *That* is use of language, professionally crafted.

Ray Bradbury doesn't just tell a story. He manipulates us, his readers, by careful use of language to tap into our emotions and to bring images to mind. This is what brings the story to life; we see things in our mind. We can *see* Montag holding a python hose and those poor little books flapping as they die on the porch.

Fahrenheit 451: Use Of Language, page 4

Now it's your turn. Read the passage in the left column then create a commentary about the use of language in the passage, as was done above.

Passage	Commentary
The autumn leaves blew over the moonlit pavement in such a way as to make the girl who was moving there seem fixed to a sliding walk, letting the motion of the wind and the leaves carry her forward. Her head was half-bent to watch her shoes stir the circling leaves. Her face was slender and milk-white, and in it was a kind of gentle hunger that touched over everything with tireless curiosity. It was a look, almost, of pale surprise; the dark eyes were so fixed to the world that no move escaped them. Her dress was white and it whispered. He almost thought he heard the motion of her hands as she walked, and the infinitely small sound now, the white stir of her face turning when she discovered she was a moment away from a man who stood in the middle of the pavement waiting.	

Fahrenheit 451: Use Of Language, page 5

Figurative Language

In the passages above, some inanimate objects were given qualities of living things--the python (hose) spitting its venomous kerosene upon the world, for example. This is an example of figurative language called *personification*. There are many kinds of figurative language an author can use to craft his work. Here are a few:

Personification: Giving inanimate objects qualities of living things

Hyperbole: Exaggerating or making an overstatement

Metaphor: Comparing two unlike things without using *as* or *like*

Simile: Comparing two unlike things using *as* or *like*

Understatement: Opposite of hyperbole; emphasizing something by significantly lessening its degree

Here are some examples from Fahrenheit 451:

Personification:
- ...the flapping pigeon-winged books died on the porch...
- A fountain of books sprang down upon Montag...

Hyperbole:
- He felt his chest chopped down and split apart.
- I don't know anything anymore...

Metaphor:
- ...her eyes were two miraculous bits of violet amber...
- People were more often...torches, blazing away until they whiffed out. (This is sort-of a trick one. In the book it says "he searched for a simile" but what he actually used was a metaphor. If he had said "People were more often...*like* torches..." it would have been a simile.)
- The woman on the bed was no more than a hard stratum of marble...

Simile:
- How like a mirror, too, her face.
- ...she was like the eager watcher of a marionette show...
- Her face was like a snow-covered island upon which rain might fall...
- [The Mechanical Hound] was like a great bee come home from some field where the honey is full of poison wildness...

Understatement:
- The breath coming out the nostrils was so faint it stirred only the furthest fringes of life, a small leaf, a black feather, a single fiber of hair.
- A fountain of books sprang down upon Montag as he climbed shuddering up the sheer stairwell. How inconvenient!

Fahrenheit 451: Use Of Language, page 6

Figurative Language Exercise

How many examples of figurative language can you find in Fahrenheit 451? Jot them down and identify the type of figurative language for each (as well as the page number in the text) in the chart below.

Type = personification, hyperbole, metaphor, simile, or understatement

Type	Page	Example

FIGURATIVE LANGUAGE
Fahrenheit 451

This page tells you about different kinds of figurative language and gives examples. On the second page, write in an example of each kind that you can find in the text of Fahrenheit 451.

Kinds Of Figurative Language

irony — Use of words to express something different from and often opposite to their literal meaning
Sitting in school on a lovely spring day is my favorite thing to do.

onomatopoeia — Use of words that imitate the sounds associated with the things they refer to
buzz, splash, pop

simile — A comparison using the words "like" or "as"
smart like a fox growing like a weed as pretty as a picture

hyperbole — Extreme exaggeration used to describe a person or thing
She had as many pairs of shoes as there are stars in the sky.

metonymy — One word or phrase is substituted for another with which it is closely associated
Using "the sword" to indicate military power

personification — Attributing human qualities to inanimate objects, animals, or ideas
The wind howled. The trees nodded in agreement.

cliché — An expression that has been used repeatedly and has lost its appeal
as white as snow eat like a bird

metaphor — A comparison without the words *like* or *as*
The cat is a bag of bones.

paradox — A seemingly self-contradictory statement that has some truth to it
Standing is more tiring than walking.

142
© 2014

FIGURATIVE LANGUAGE
Fahrenheit 451

Write in an example of each kind of figurative language that you can find in the text of Fahrenheit 451.

UNIT CROSSWORD
Fahrenheit 451

144

UNIT CROSSWORD CLUES
Fahrenheit 451

ACROSS
1. Condensed version of a book
5. Remains after burning
7. Small communications device used by Montag & Faber
9. Clarisse was killed by one
10. It smelled like perfume to Montag
12. What we do with books
15. Flames
18. Where Montag went after fleeing Faber's house
19. She liked to think and talk
22. Rising from the ashes
24. Destroy with flames
25. He wanted a more meaningful lifestyle
26. Faber's destination: St. ____
27. Time when most fires were set
28. To get away

DOWN
1. Stop living
2. Place where radio transmitter was put for use
3. Place where Montag met Faber
4. Rain tasted like this beverage
6. Mechanical ____
8. He helped Montag
11. Montag's path to safety
13. Not bound
14. ____ Hound
16. Flame starter
17. Mildred took an overdose of sleeping ___
20. Montag took a book from the Elm woman's ___
21. Ear thimbles
23. They memorized literature
24. Captain of the firemen

VOCABULARY CROSSWORD
Fahrenheit 451

VOCABULARY CROSSWORD CLUES
Fahrenheit 451

ACROSS
1. With a rhythmic flow
6. A pile of combustible materials for burning a corpse
7. The study of the dynamics of projectiles
12. Arousing strong dislike or displeasure
14. Returning like for like, especially evil
17. Having many faces or sides
18. Those who flaunt their knowledge
19. Sadness; gloominess

DOWN
2. Fine; small in diameter
3. Authoritative pronouncement
4. Bizarre; distorted
5. Not readily noticed or seen; not commonly known
8. Described
9. Italian herb
10. Ignoble fear in the face of danger
11. Apparatus consisting of a compartment spun around a central axis
13. Having or revealing little emotion
15. Relating to the sense of touch
16. Set up; established

NOTES
Fahrenheit 451

TEACHER'S GUIDE DIVIDER
Fahrenheit 451

TEACHER'S GUIDE BEGINS HERE

HOW TO USE THIS GUIDE
Fahrenheit 451

This guide comes as two documents in one. It has a Student Workbook followed by a Teacher's Guide.

Student Workbook
- The purchaser may reproduce by Xerox copying (from the printed document) or printing out (from the digital document) pages (any or all) from the Student Workbook for use by students in his/her own classroom.
- **You may NOT post any Student Workbook pages on the Internet.** That is a violation of copyrights and will result in at least a $500 fine imposed by the publisher plus any court judgments awarded. Current law allows for up to $10,000 per instance.
- Professionally printed Student Workbooks are available from Teacher's Pet Publications.

Teacher's Guide
- The Teacher's Guide includes lesson instructions, CCSS correlations, and answer keys.
- It is set up so you can use any or all of the materials provided, at your own discretion.
- **You may NOT post any part of the Teacher's Guide on the Internet.** That is a violation of copyrights and will result in at least a $500 fine imposed by the publisher plus any court judgments awarded. Current law allows for up to $10,000 per instance.
- You may not reproduce any portion of the Teacher Guide for any reason without written permission from the author.
- **The lessons are arranged in 3 groups:**

    The first lessons take you through each reading assignment (groups of pages or chapters). They focus on vocabulary, reading comprehension, and a basic understanding of the most important elements in each reading assignment.

    The next set of lessons are based on the Elements of Fiction. Each lesson focuses on a different element as it relates to the whole book.

    Finally, there are additional activities for each reading assignment. You should look at these in advance and decide if you want to use any as your students read through the book. They could also be used after completing the reading.

Assessment
- There are a variety of types of assessments throughout the materials: worksheets, graphic organizers, written assignments, oral work, and quizzes.
- Following the lessons, there is a section of **test materials** including matching, short answer, extended answer, quotations, and vocabulary. There are at least 3 different versions of each type. The test pages are designed to be mix-and-match so you can choose from any of the pages of materials to put together a test.

A Word Of Explanation From The Format Author

I redesigned the LitPlans in response to comments made by you, the users, over the years AND in response to the literally thousands of copyright violations I have had to deal with. The intent is to provide you with in-depth materials and to safeguard answer keys. Putting the Student Workbook in front also enables us to use Google Book Previews (1st 15% of the book) without making answer keys visible. **I welcome your comments about the new format.**

                                        Mary mcollins@tpet.com

LESSON ONE
Fahrenheit 451

CCSS: SL.9-10.1 SL 9-10.1a SL 9-10.1c SL 9-10.1d SL 9-10.3
L.9-10.4 L.9-10.4a L.9-10.4b L.9-10.4c L.9-10.4d

Objectives:
- Students will find and bring images of "ways people escape from or cope with stress" to class.
- Students will participate in a class discussion about coping with stress, the ways people deal with stress, and the dangers associated with certain coping devices.
- Students will be given and be shown how to use the materials for the Fahrenheit 451 unit.

Purpose: To introduce Fahrenheit 451 and the materials to be used in the unit

Note: Prior to this class, students should each have found a picture of something which represents a way people escape from or cope with the stresses of life. Post their pictures on the board or wall as you do the discussion for Activity #1. This is a good way to get your bulletin board done if you are short on time, and it also gives students a physical way to contribute to your classroom. Something they have contributed will be on display.

Activity #1
Start by talking about the stresses people have in our society. Perhaps ask students what stresses they have in their own lives. Ask students to get out the pictures they have brought showing ways people escape from or cope with the pressures of life. Have each student explain the relevance of his or her picture, and post it on the bulletin board. After all the examples have been given, take a few minutes to discuss ways advertisers take advantage of our need to relax, our need to "escape." Follow up by asking what happens when people go too far in their escapes--when their minds and/or bodies go "on holiday" too long. Use this as a transition to briefly introduce *Fahrenheit 451*.

Activity #2
Distribute the Student Workbooks and Fahrenheit 451 novels.

Activity #3
Review the workbook page entitled HOW TO USE THIS WORKBOOK. Make any additions or changes that suit your needs.

Activity #4
Show students how to preview the Reading Assignment 1 materials by leading their preview. Reading the HOW TO USE THIS WORKBOOK section will help you lead this preview.

- Show them the CHARACTERS and EVENTS & POINTS OF INTEREST worksheets and explain how to use them.
- <u>Do the VOCABULARY WORKSHEETS for Reading Assignment 1 together in class.</u>
- Read through the STUDY AND DISCUSSION QUESTIONS

After this, students will know how to do the previewing for the other assignments.

VOCABULARY WORK FOR ASSIGNMENT 1 ANSWER KEY
Fahrenheit 451

PART I: Using Prior Knowledge And Contextual Clues
Use any clues you can find in the sentences from the text combined with your prior knowledge and write what you think the bold word means.

1. With his symbolic helmet number 451 on his **stolid** head...he flicked the igniter and the house jumped up in a gorging fire.

    Having or revealing little emotion

2. Impossible: for how many people did you know that **refracted** your own light to you.

    Deflected from a straight path

3. And if the muscles of his jaws stretched **imperceptibly**, she would yawn long before he would.

    Without being detected by ordinary senses

4. He felt that the stars had been **pulverized** by the sound of the black jets and that in the morning the earth would be covered with their dust like a strange snow.

    Reduced to powder

5. And the men with the cigarettes in their straight-lined mouths, the men with the eyes of puff adders, took up their load of machine and tube, their case of liquid **melancholy** and the slow dark sludge of nameless stuff, and strolled out the door.

    Sadness; gloominess

6. Light flickered on bits of ruby glass and on sensitive **capillary** hairs in the nylon-brushed nostrils of the creature...

    Fine; small in diameter

7. Below, the Hound had sunk back down upon its eight incredible insect legs and was humming to itself again, its **multifaceted** eyes at peace.

    Having many faces or sides

8. It's like a lesson in **ballistics**. It has a trajectory we decide on for it.

    The study of the dynamics of projectiles

Vocabulary Work For Fahrenheit 451 Assignment 1, Page 2

PART II: Matching
Considering the usage in Part I, match the vocabulary words to their definitions.

C 1. stolid   A. Sadness; gloominess

E 2. refracted   B. The study of the dynamics of projectiles

F 3. imperceptibly   C. Having or revealing little emotion

H 4. pulverized   D. Having many faces, sides, or dimensions

A 5. melancholy   E. Deflected from a straight path

G 6. capillary   F. Without being detected by ordinary senses

D 7. multifaceted   G. Fine; small in diameter

B 8. ballistics   H. Reduced to powder

Part III: Cloze Passage
Fill in the blanks with the appropriate vocabulary words from the list above.

The STOLID colonel got ready for the testing of the latest army weapon. The missile with its MULTIFACETED capabilities could not be REFRACTED from a target no matter how an enemy might try to deflect it. The BALLISTICS behind the new invention were impressive, with the triggering mechanism being CAPILLARY in size. When fired, the missile would race IMPERCEPTIBLY towards its target, which soon would be PULVERIZED upon impact. Though a complete success in design and function, a certain MELANCHOLY fell over the observers as they thought how deadly such a weapon would be and how unsuspecting would be its victims.

Vocabulary Work For Fahrenheit 451 Assignment 1, Page 3

PART IV: Words In Practice
Answer the questions and be able to give short explanations to justify your answers.

1. If someone has a stolid reaction to what has happened, is that person excited about the results or unaffected by them?

    Unaffected

2. If an object thrown at you is refracted, are you safe, or are you at risk?

    Safe

3. If something is imperceptibly approaching you, do you know it's coming?

    No

4. If an object has been pulverized, is it enhanced or has it most likely become useless?

    Likely become useless

5. If a person is melancholy, is that person ready to party or more likely to want to be left alone?

    Likely to want to be left alone

6. Do your capillary veins carry the bulk of your blood flow?

    No; they are small

7. Give an example of something that is multifaceted.

    Answers will vary. Some examples are: diamonds, people with many talents, polygons

8. Would someone be more likely to find expertise in ballistics at the FBI or among one's friends?

    FBI

VOCABULARY CROSSWORD KEY
READING ASSIGNMENT 1
Fahrenheit 451

```
        I           C
      M E L A N C H O L Y
        P           P
        E           I
        R           L
        C           L
R E F R A C T E D         P
        P           R     U
        T           Y     L
        I                 V
                          E
      B A L L I S T I C S R
        L         T       I
        Y         O       Z
              M U L T I F A C E T E D
                  I       D
                  D
```

Deflected from a straight path (9)
Fine; small in diameter (9)
Having many faces or sides (12)
Having or revealing little emotion (6)
Impossible to detect by ordinary senses (13)
Reduced to powder (10)
Sadness; gloominess (10)
The study of the dynamics of projectiles (10)

LESSON TWO
Fahrenheit 451

CCSS: SL.9-10.1 SL.9-10.6 RL.9-10.10

Objectives:
- Students will memorize short passages from the first reading assignment
- Students will recite their passages in the order in which they appear in the novel

Purpose:
The purpose of this lesson is to give students a frame of reference and appreciation for later in the book when Montag tries to memorize the Book of Ecclesiastes and others are introduced as having memorized whole books. This is a unique way to begin reading the book, which can get students drawn in, wondering what happens before and after their own passages.

Option: You can let students have their Passage Assignments available for referencing when they truly get stuck.

Prior To This Lesson: Print out (or photocopy) the Passage Assignments on the following pages and cut them apart so you can give one to each student. It doesn't matter if all the given passages are not assigned. After this lesson, students will pick up reading after the last assigned passage.

Activity #1
Give each student a Passage Assignment. Explain to students that they will be given a short time to memorize their passages, then they will be asked to recite their passages to begin Reading Assignment 1.

Share with students a few tricks to help them memorize their lines:
- read the whole passage silently, then aloud
- memorize short chunks at a time by reading and speaking the words
- writing the words will also help
- say the chunk you have learned aloud
- then say the passage from the beginning, adding each short chunk to the chunk(s) previously learned

Give students ample time to memorize their lines, then have students recite their lines in numerical order.

Activity #2
Discuss with students how easy or difficult it was to do this activity. What do students think helped them learn the lines the most? Even after the lines were learned, did having to recite them in front of the class make a difference in their ability to remember? Why was this activity easy/difficult?

Activity #3
Tell students that prior to the next class period, they should complete reading Reading Assignment 1.

PASSAGE 1
It was a pleasure to burn.
It was a special pleasure to see things eaten, to see things blackened and *changed*. With the brass nozzle in his fists, with this great python spitting its venomous kerosene upon the world, the blood pounded in his head, and his hands were the hands of some amazing conductor playing all the symphonies of blazing and burning to bring down the tatters and charcoal ruins of history.

PASSAGE 2
With his symbolic helmet numbered 451 on his stolid head, and his eyes all orange flame with the thought of what came next, he flicked the igniter and the house jumped up in a gorging fire that burned the evening sky red and yellow and black. He strode in a swarm of fireflies.

PASSAGE 3
He wanted above all, like the old joke, to shove a marshmallow on a stick in the furnace, while the flapping pigeon-winged books died on the porch and lawn of the house. While the books went up in sparkling whirls and blew away on a wind turned dark with burning.

PASSAGE 4
Montag grinned the fierce grin of all men singed and driven back by flame.

PASSAGE 5
He knew that when he returned to the firehouse, he might wink at himself, a minstrel man, burnt-corked, in the mirror. Later, going to sleep, he would feel the fiery smile still gripped by his face muscles, in the dark. It never went away, that smile, it never ever went away, as long as he remembered.

PASSAGE 6
He hung up his black beetle-colored helmet and shined it; he hung his flameproof jacket neatly; he showered luxuriously, and then, whistling, hands in pockets, walked across the upper floor of the fire station and fell down the hole.

PASSAGE 7
At the last moment, when disaster seemed positive, he pulled his hands from his pockets and broke his fall by grasping the golden pole. He slid to a squeaking halt, the heels one inch from the concrete floor downstairs.

PASSAGE 8
He walked out of the fire station and along the midnight street toward the subway where the silent air-propelled train slid soundlessly down his lubricated flue in the earth and let him out with a great puff of warm air onto the cream-tiled escalator rising to the suburb.

PASSAGE 9
Whistling, he let the escalator waft him into the still night air. He walked toward the corner, thinking little at all about nothing in particular.

PASSAGE 10
Before he reached the corner, however, he slowed as if a wind had spring up from nowhere, as if someone had called his name.

PASSAGE 11
The last few nights he had had the most uncertain feelings about the sidewalk just around the corner here, moving in the starlight toward his house.

PASSAGE 12
He had felt that a moment prior to his making the turn, someone had been there. The air seemed charged with a special calm as if someone had waited there, quietly, and only a moment before he came simply turned to a shadow and let him through.

PASSAGE 13
Perhaps his nose detected a faint perfume, perhaps the skin on the back of his hands, on his face, felt the temperature rise at this one spot where a person's standing might raise the immediate atmosphere ten degrees for an instant.

PASSAGE 14
There was no understanding it. Each time he made the turn, he saw only the white, unused, buckling sidewalk, with perhaps, on one night, something vanishing swiftly across a lawn before he could focus his eyes or speak.

PASSAGE 15
But now, tonight, he slowed almost to a stop. His inner mind, reaching out to turn the corner for him, had heard the faintest whisper. Breathing?

PASSAGE 16
Or was the atmosphere compressed merely by someone standing very quietly there, waiting?
He turned the corner.

PASSAGE 17
The autumn leaves blew over the moonlit pavement in such a way as to make the girl who was moving there seem fixed to a sliding walk, letting the motion of the wind and the leaves carry her forward.

PASSAGE 18
Her head was half bent to watch her shoes stir the circling leaves. Her face was slender and milk-white, and in it was a kind of gentle hunger that touched over everything with tireless curiosity.

PASSAGE 19
It was a look, almost, of pale surprise; the dark eyes were so fixed to the world that no move escaped them. Her dress was white and it whispered.

PASSAGE 20
He almost thought he heard the motion of her hands as she walked, and the infinitely small sound now, the white stir of her face turning when she discovered she was a moment away from a man who stood in the middle of the pavement waiting.

PASSAGE 21
The trees overhead made a great sound of letting down their dry rain. The girl stopped and looked as if she might pull back in surprise, but instead stood regarding Montag with eyes so dark and shining and alive, that he felt he had said something quite wonderful.

PASSAGE 22
But he knew his mouth had only moved to say hello, and then when she seemed hypnotized by the salamander on his arm and the phoenix-disc on his chest, he spoke again.

PASSAGE 23
"Of course," he said, "you're our new neighbor, aren't you?"
"And you must be--" she raised her eyes from his professional symbols "--the fireman." Her voice trailed off.
"How oddly you say that."

PASSAGE 24
"I'd--I'd have known it with my eyes shut," she said slowly.
"What--the smell of kerosene? My wife always complains," he laughed. "You never wash it off completely."
"No, you don't," she said, in awe.

PASSAGE 25
He felt she was walking in a circle about him, turning him end for end, shaking him quietly, and emptying his pockets, without once moving herself.

PASSAGE 26
"Kerosene," he said, because the silence had lengthened, "is nothing but perfume to me."
"Does it seem like that, really?"
"Of course. Why not?"

PASSAGE 27
She gave herself time to think of it. "I don't know." She turned to face the sidewalk going toward their homes. "Do you mind if I walk back with you? I'm Clarisse McClellan."
"Clarisse. Guy Montag. Come along. What are you doing out so late wandering around? How old are you?"

PASSAGE 28
They walked in the warm-cool blowing night on the silvered pavement and there was the faintest breath of fresh apricots and strawberries in the air, and he looked around and realized this was quite impossible, so late in the year.

PASSAGE 29
There was only the girl walking with him now, her face bright as snow in the moonlight, and he knew she was working his questions around, seeking the best answers she could possibly give.

PASSAGE 30
"Well," she said, "I'm seventeen and I'm crazy. My uncle says the two always go together. When people ask your age, he said, always say seventeen and insane. . . ."

PASSAGE 31
". . .Isn't this a nice time of night to walk? I like to smell things and look at things, and sometimes stay up all night, walking, and watch the sun rise."

PASSAGE 32
They walked on again in silence and finally she said, thoughtfully, "You know, I'm not afraid of you at all."
He was surprised. "Why should you be?"
"So many people are. Afraid of firemen, I mean. But you're just a man, after all. . . ."

LESSON THREE
Fahrenheit 451

CCSS: RL.9-10.1; RL.9-10.3; RL.9-10.10; W.9-10.10; SL.9-10.1; SL.9-10.1c; SL.9-10.1d SL,9-10.4

Objectives:
- Students will take a quiz on Reading Assignment 1 to check their reading comprehension.
- Students will re-read Reading Assignment 1, skimming for information to fill in the CHARACTERS and EVENTS & POINTS OF INTEREST graphic organizers
- Students will discuss the main characters, events, and points of interest in RA 1

Purposes:
The purposes of this lesson are:
- to check students' reading comprehension & make sure they did the reading assignment
- to make sure students understand how to do the graphic organizers
- to help students start noticing and tracking character traits and development
- to review the main events of the story to help students retain that knowledge
- to introduce main themes and ideas and get students thinking about them
- to engage students in thoughtful discussions

Prior To This Lesson: You need to have enough copies of the Multiple Choice: Reading Assignment 1 pages for each student to have a set. These questions are all fact-based. They will be used as a reading comprehension quiz and to make sure students have actually read the assignment. They are not included in the Student Workbook.

Activity #1
Distribute the Multiple Choice: Reading Assignment1 pages to each student. [These are not labeled as "quiz" in case you want to use them in a different way.] Give students ample time to answer the questions. Then, have student swap papers to check each others' work. Briefly discuss the answers as the papers are corrected. Collect the papers to review and/or record the grades after the work is checked. After reviewing/recording, return these to the students for study purposes.

Multiple Choice: Reading Assignment 1 Answer Key:
1.D 2.C 3.B 4.C 5.A 6.B 7.C 8.D 9.A 10.C 11.A 12.A 13.C 14.D

Activity #2
Do the CHARACTERS and EVENTS & POINTS OF INTEREST graphic organizers together as a whole class. This will show students how to do them as well as reviewing the material called for on the organizers.

For the CHARACTERS organizer, you might ask, "What have we learned about [character] in this part of the book? Jot down answers students give, and try to guide the discussion to incorporate all important information about the character in this reading assignment.

Skim through the first reading assignment with students to develop the list of main events. Discuss the Points of Interest and show students how to jot down notes about each.

MULTIPLE CHOICE: READING ASSIGNMENT 1
Fahrenheit 451

1. Who is Guy Montag?
    A. He is a librarian.
    B. He is the mayor.
    C. He is a doctor.
    D. He is a fireman.

2. Describe Montag's job.
    A. He maintains information files for the city.
    B. He teaches school.
    C. He burns books.
    D. He is a curator in a museum.

3. Describe Clarisse McClellan.
    A. She is shy and slightly handicapped.
    B. She is a young woman who likes to think and talk.
    C. She is extremely rigid and law-abiding.
    D. She is a flirt whose only concern is getting men to like her.

4. What smells like perfume to Montag?
    A. The printer's ink
    B. Cooking fumes from the restaurant
    C. Kerosene
    D. Smoke

5. Clarisse asks Montag a question. He discovers the answer is, "No." What is the question?
    A. Are you happy?
    B. Can you read?
    C. Do you want to get married?
    D. Have you ever committed a crime?

6. Who is Mildred?
    A. Clarisse's mother
    B. Montag's wife
    C. An Emergency Hospital doctor
    D. A writer who has gone underground

7. What dangerous event happens to Mildred?
    A. She is found with books and is sent to a prison camp.
    B. She contracts a fatal, contagious disease and has to be quarantined.
    C. She takes an overdose of sleeping pills and has to have her stomach pumped.
    D. She discovers Montag is having an affair with Clarisse.

Multiple Choice: Fahrenheit 451 Reading Assignment 1, Page 2

8. Why does the Emergency Hospital send technicians instead of a doctor to treat the patient?
    A. The patient doesn't have enough insurance coverage to pay for a doctor.
    B. Doctors only treat men.
    C. There aren't enough doctors to see everyone.
    D. The patient's common medical issue only requires technicians to handle it.

9. What are parlor walls?
    A. They are a kind of surround television with which the audience can interact.
    B. They are portable partitions that can be repositioned to create a variety of living spaces.
    C. They are hidden microphones that can monitor conversations.
    D. They are barricades that separate one neighborhood from another.

10. What is the Hound?
    A. It is Montag's dog.
    B. It is a dog that hangs out at the firehouse.
    C. It is a robotic animal programmed to hunt and kill.
    D. It is a dog trained to find books.

11. What does Montag believe has been done to the Hound?
    A. It has been programmed to act against Montag.
    B. It has been killed in the "entertaining" fights at the firehouse.
    C. It has been abused and malnourished.
    D. It has been deactivated.

12. How is Clarisse viewed by others in society?
    A. She is considered anti-social.
    B. She is tolerated with amusement.
    C. She is revered as a holy one because she knows about books.
    D. She is accepted as just another person.

13. Where does Clarisse get most of her information about the way life used to be?
    A. She gets information from old videos.
    B. She gets information from history class.
    C. She gets information from her uncle.
    D. She gets information from her grandmother's diaries.

14. What effect does Clarisse have on Montag?
    A. She has no effect on him.
    B. She affirms his beliefs that theirs is a great society.
    C. She makes him appreciate his wife.
    D. She makes him question his life.

CHARACTERS SUGGESTED NOTES
Reading Assignment 1 Fahrenheit 451

As you read Assignment 1 use this graphic organizer to jot down information about characters.

MONTAG
-- fireman
-- meets Clarisse & is intrigued by her
-- Clarisse makes him uneasy
-- wonders if he is happy
-- is married to Mildred
-- realizes Mildred took too many sleeping pills and calls for medical help
-- the idea of talking interests him
-- talking with Clarisse and the incident with Mildred confuse him
-- the mechanical Hound worries Montag
-- has no children

CLARISSE
-- teenager, neighbor of Montag
-- meets Montag as he walks to/from work
-- people say she is crazy & anti-social
-- loves being in nature and talking
-- has an uncle who remembers how it used to be
-- says Montag doesn't seem like a fireman
-- loves to watch people
-- notices details, smells, man in the moon
-- asks Montag if he is happy
-- sees a psychiatrist
-- is afraid of kids her own age

MILDRED
-- Montag's wife
-- plugged into seashell radio
-- overdosed on sleeping pills
-- doesn't remember or refuses to admit taking too many pills
-- likes the Parlor Walls

BEATTY
-- Captain of firefighters
-- Montag's boss
-- thinks the Hound is good
-- laughs at Montag's guilty look

EVENTS & POINTS OF INTEREST SUGGESTED NOTES
Reading Assignment 1 Fahrenheit 451

As you read Assignment 1 make notes of the series of main events that take place. Put them in the order that they are given in the text.

Montag obviously enjoys putting out a fire and being a fireman.

Montag meets Clarisse who intrigues him and asks him if he is happy.

Montag goes home, discovers Mildred has overdosed, and the men come to pump out Mildred's stomach.

The next morning, Mildred doesn't remember overdosing and denies taking too many pills.

Montag meets with Clarisse again, walking to work. She tells him he's not in love with anyone and asks how he came to be a fireman.

At the firehouse, the mechanical Hound threatens Montag. Captain Beatty thinks the Hound is a good machine, and he seems to suspect Montag has something to hide.

OTHER POINTS OF INTEREST TO IDENTIFY OR KNOW THE SIGNIFICANCE OF:

Seashells Seashells are little ear-sized radios. Mildred uses them a lot, especially to help her fall asleep at night. It's constant, meaningless noise that takes the place of meaningful conversation or quiet time for reflection and thought.

The sleeping pills Inevitably, one needs to ask WHY Mildred took the sleeping pills. WHY can't she sleep? ...and was the overdose intentional or an accident? The sleeping pills and the answers to these questions are the key to Mildred.

The parlor walls The parlor walls are huge, interactive television screens which entertain Mildred and occupy most of her time. Like the seashells in her ears, the screens fill her time with shallow and meaningless (but pretty and entertaining) drama and comedy. Again, spending all her time being entertained leaves no time for thought or interaction with real people. In addition, what Mildred sees on the walls becomes her reality--whether it is true or not and whether it makes any sense or not.

The Hound The Mechanical Hound is programmed to track down and kill by lethal injection anyone its programmers want eliminated. Montag fears it has started to dislike him (even though it is not alive and cannot have feelings). The Hound worries Montag. In essence, the Hound becomes symbolic of those who control it; the government that eliminates anyone who opposes its control and becomes troublesome.

LESSON FOUR
Fahrenheit 451

CCSS: SL.9-10.1a-d; SL.9-10.4; RL.9-10.1; RL.9-10.2; RL.9-10.3; RL.9-10.4; L.9-10.4

Objectives:
- Students will participate in a group discussion of Reading Assignment 1
- Students will cite textual evidence to support their answers to discussion questions
- Students will analyze the characters and their relationships
- Students will consider the written details of the text and their effect on the story
- Students will complete the pre-reading vocabulary worksheet for Reading Assignment 2

Purposes:
The purposes of this lesson are:
- To review the main events and ideas in Reading Assignment 1
- To understand characters and their motivations
- To look for parallels to draw from the story into students' current lives
- To examine details for meaning and apply the meaning to the larger themes of the text
- To become familiar with selected vocabulary words, their definitions, and usage for the end purpose of assimilating the words into students' own vocabularies as well as providing for a better understanding of the text.

Teacher's Note: How you handle the discussion of the questions is up to you, based on your own classroom situation and your own students. A few options you might consider would be:
- Break your class into small groups of 2-3 students and assign each group a few questions to consider prior to a whole-class discussion.
- Assign all students to individually compose answers to all the questions or specific ones prior to the whole-class discussion.
- Ask students to preview the questions and then volunteer to lead a class discussion on the question of their choice.
- Assign each student one question, then have them interview the other students in the class for their opinions as to the answers.

Each reading assignment has discussion questions. Varying the way in which the questions are approached each time will keep the class fresh and add interest. **Whichever method you choose should end or be followed up with a whole-class discussion of each of the questions.**

Directions for future discussion sessions for other reading assignments will simply say, "Discuss the questions for this reading assignment. See Lesson Four for additional notes."

Activity #1
Discuss the questions for Reading Assignment 1 in whatever way you choose.
See Teacher's Note above.

Activity #2
Tell students that prior to your next class meeting, they should preview the discussion questions and complete the vocabulary worksheets for Reading Assignment 2.

STUDY & DISCUSSION QUESTIONS SUGGESTED ANSWERS
Reading Assignment 1 Fahrenheit 451

1. What is Montag's occupation, and how is his job different from what we expect?
   Montag is a fireman. We expect a fireman to put out fires, but his hoses are full of kerosene, not water, and he starts fires instead of putting them out.

2. Of what is the number 451 on Montag's helmet symbolic?
   451 degrees Fahrenheit symbolically represents the temperature at which paper burns.

3. What is a "minstrel man," and why does Bradbury choose this image?
   Montag's face is covered by soot and ashes from the fire, making his face appear blackened. A minstrel man was a white man who blackened his face and performed a comic variety show that often made fun of African Americans. This uniquely American form of theatre was most popular in the late 1800's. the image of the minstrel man is appropriate not only because of Montag's blackened face but also because he is lighthearted, laughing, and having fun burning the homes and books- something we don't view as humorous just like we don't find making fun of African American's funny anymore.

4. What words and phrases does Bradbury use to give a feeling of mystery or anticipation just before Montag first meets Clarisse?
   "...he had the most uncertain feelings about the sidewalk just around the corner..."
   "The air seemed charged with a special calm..."
   "...something vanishing swiftly across a lawn..."
   "His inner mind, reaching out to turn the corner for him, had heard the faintest whisper..."

5. Why is Clarisse able to "get to" Montag in their first meetings?
   Montag is not like the other firemen; he has a sense of curiosity about the old and forbidden ways. Clarisse is fresh and interesting; he finds what she says to be thought-provoking and fascinating. She touches the part of him that is like her.

Study & Discussion Questions Suggested Answers: Fahrenheit 451 RA 1, Page 2

6. Explain in what ways Clarisse and Mildred are different from each other.

    Clarisse spends her time talking and listening, being out in nature, doing things, and thinking. She's very alive in the real world. Mildred spends her time plugged in to music or screens. She doesn't listen to Montag or carry on intelligent conversation. She doesn't even know she overdosed on sleeping pills -- even after Montag tells her. She is "out of it" to the point of almost not being human. Montag didn't seem to even notice anything was wrong with her until he found the empty pill jar and looked more closely at her.

7. Montag is thinking about Clarisse when he thinks, "...how many people did you know that refracted your own light back at you?" How does this thought apply to Clarisse and Montag?

    Clarisse makes comments that cause Montag to think abut himself and his own life -- to see himself and his own life in a more objective way than he had on his own, in a way as if he is shown his own life in a mirror. For example, she simply asks the question "are you happy?" and Montag soon comes to realize that he is not happy.

8. One of the men who comes to pump Mildred's stomach says, "You don't need an M.D., case like this; all you need is two handymen, clean up the problem in half an hour." How does this statement aptly sum up the whole process described in the preceding paragraphs?

    The men treated Mildred like two handymen might treat a clogged drainpipe. They pulled out their machines, cleaned her out and packed up to move on to the next job. They spoke to Montag about Mildred as if she were a thing, not a person. They had no sense of compassion, no special concern, no apparent feelings about this woman whose life is so bad or so empty that she overdosed on pills. They don't respond to Mildred and Montag with any human compassion.

9. What does the Hound's reaction to Montag at the firehouse tell us?

    The Hound seems to sense that Montag is different from the other firemen, and that he might not be as true blue and law-abiding as the others are. The Hound senses that Montag might be someone who should be eliminated.

10. Early in the first reading assignment, Montag's ventilator grill is mentioned twice. Review these two references and tell what you think is behind the ventilator grill.

    Answers will vary. We later learn that Montag has books. For now, though, students should have the idea that something illegal or bad is behind the grill.

Study & Discussion Questions Suggested Answers: Fahrenheit 451 RA 1, Page 3

11. Clarisse calls herself "crazy" and "a fool." Others call her "anti-social." Do you think Clarisse is crazy, a fool, or anti-social? Support your answer with logical reasoning and examples from the text.

    Answers will vary. The important thing is to get students thinking and evaluating Clarisse's statements and digging in the text for support of their answers.

12. About school, Clarisse says, "It's all a lot of funnels and water poured down the spout and out the bottom, and them telling us it's wine when it's not." What does she mean?

    Answers will vary. Basically Clarisse sees no real value in school. It lacks substance and truth. Note this image of water pouring down the spout and out the bottom is similar to the scene later in the book when Montag thinks back to a time when he was told to fill a sieve with sand.

13. Beatty asks Montag if he has a guilty conscience. Montag glances up quickly. Then Beatty stares at him and begins to laugh softly. What do you make of this exchange?

    Montag's quick glance up indicates to us and to Beatty that he might have something to hide. Beatty's *soft* laugh may indicate he suspects Montag of something and may indicate he will be against Montag at some point later. Villains in literature and movies tend to stare and laugh softly.

14. How is the world Clarisse and Montag live in similar to our world today?

    Many people today are "plugged in" like Mildred is- to our smartphones, iPads, and giant TV screens. Many people who provide medical or other services today don't really care, they just do their job treating everyone as just the next customer number to deal with. People who don't participate in sports or social media or who don't care about reality TV and pop culture are seen as anti-social or odd. Fewer people today engage in serious conversations about things other than themselves or popular culture. Our students (and others in our country) are killing each other and committing suicide at a much higher rate than even a few decades ago.

15. Is our world more like the "old days" Clarisse's uncle speaks of, or is it more like the world of Clarisse and Montag's time?

    Opinions will vary.

Study & Discussion Questions Discussion Guide: Fahrenheit 451 RA 1, Page 4

Enjoy discussing these passages with your students and see how many different ideas and responses your group can generate for each!

ADDITIONAL PASSAGES FOR DISCUSSION

1. Discuss the imagery in the passage beginning, "The autumn leaves blew over the moonlit pavement...."

    Clarisse is associated with natural things (leaves, wind) and curiosity. She wears a white dress (purity, innocence) that "whispered." Her hands are mentioned, one of many references to hands in the text. The language of this paragraph is beautiful and full of meaning.

2. "You laugh when I haven't been funny and you answer right off. You never stop to think what I've asked you."

    Is it important to think before we speak? How many times do we give "automatic" responses instead of really considering the questions and giving thoughtful answers. Are thoughtful answers always preferable? What is laughing a response to? Why do people sometimes laugh when the thing said isn't funny?

3. They walked the rest of the way in silence, hers thoughtful, his a kind of clenching and uncomfortable silence in which he shot her accusing glances.

    Note the contrast in how each handles the silence. Why is he shooting her accusing glances?

4. Go on, anyway, shove the bore down, slush up the emptiness, if such a thing could be brought out in the throb of the suction snake.

    This sentence is so graphic! What images and emotions it evokes. How does it do that? What emptiness is being slushed up? Why is the snake imagery appropriate and important?

5. Only an hour, but the world had melted down and sprung up in a new and colorless form.

    How quickly Montag's life has changed! What has happened in the last hour that changed Montag's world? Notice the fireman's world has appropriately *melted* down, playing on the images of fire and heat. We usually think of things springing up as being green and colorful. Why could it be important that Montag's world sprang up in a colorless form?

6. "What a shame," she said. "You're not in love with anyone."

    Is Montag, in fact, in love with anyone? Did Clarisse know this and just use the dandelion as a way of approaching the subject? Does Montag know he's not in love?

7. He saw the silver needle extend upon the air an inch, pull back, extend, pull back. The growl simmered in the beast and it looked at him.

    What effect does this sentence have on you as a reader? What effect did the Hound's actions have on Montag?

8. My uncle says his grandfather remembered when children didn't kill each other.

    How are children dying in Clarisse's world? How are they dying in ours? Are teen deaths increasing or decreasing today? Why?

LESSON FIVE
Fahrenheit 451

CCSS: L.9-10.1; L.9-10.2; L.9-10.4; L.9-10.4a; L.9-10.5;
W.9-10.2; W.9-10.2a; W.9-10.2c; W.9-10.2e; W.9-10.2f; W.9-10.4; W.9-10.5;

Objectives:
- Students will review and discuss the vocabulary work for Reading Assignment 2
- Students will create a fire escape plan for their own homes with both written and graphic elements
- Students will read Reading Assignment 2

Purposes:
The purposes of this lesson are:
- To make sure students have the correct understanding of the vocabulary words for RA 2
- To provide a practical connection to the work of literature
- To give students the opportunity to practice writing to inform, specifically to practice writing directions in both verbal and graphic formats
- To have students practice logical thinking, chronological sequencing, and organization as well as writing conventions

Activity #1
Students were supposed to have done the vocabulary pages for Reading Assignment 2. Take a few minutes to review the answers to those pages with students so you're sure they're on the right track. Do this in whatever way suits your teaching style.

Activity #2
Distribute Writing Assignment 1 (located in Writing Assignments section of the Student Workbook as well as on page 177 for your convenience). Discuss the directions in detail, advise students as to when the assignment will be collected for grading. Talk with students about what kinds of things will need to be in their assignments, including things like appropriate headings for quick reference, clear instructions, drawings showing the fire escape route from each room, and any other requirements you may have.

Activity #3
Tell students that prior to the next class meeting they should complete the reading of Reading Assignment 3.

Students should use the remainder of this class time to work on the writing assignment and/or the reading assignment.

VOCABULARY WORK FOR ASSIGNMENT 2

PART I: Using Prior Knowledge And Contextual Clues
Use any clues you can find in the sentences from the text combined with your prior knowledge and write what you think the bold word means.

1. . . . all the sounds came to Montag, behind the barrier he had momentarily **erected**.

    Set up; established; built

2. Were all firemen picked then for their looks as well as their **proclivities**?

    Predispositions; tendencies

3. Beatty, Stoneman, and Black ran up the sidewalk, suddenly **odious** and fat in their plump fireproof slickers.

    Arousing strong dislike or displeasure

4. He felt one hand and then the other work his coat free and let it slump to the floor. . . . His hands were **ravenous**. And his eyes were beginning to feel hunger, as if they must look at something, anything, everything.

    Extremely hungry; greedy for gratification

5. "Life becomes one big **pratfall**, Montag; everything bang, boff, and wow!"

    Humiliating failure; a fall on the buttocks

6. There was no **dictum**, no declaration, no censorship, to start with, no!

    Authoritative pronouncement

7. Cram them full of **noncombustible** data, chock them so damned full of 'facts' they feel stuffed, but absolutely 'brilliant' with information.

    Does not burn easily

8. I'll think I'm responding to the play, when it's only a **tactile** reaction to vibration.

    Relating to the sense of touch

Vocabulary Work For Fahrenheit 451 Assignment 2, Page 2

PART II: Matching
Considering the usage in Part I, match the vocabulary words to their definitions.

H 1. erected   A. Humiliating failure; a fall on the buttocks

B 2. proclivities   B. Predispositions; tendencies

D 3. odious   C. Does not burn easily

E 4. ravenous   D. Arousing strong dislike or displeasure

A 5. pratfall   E. Extremely hungry; greedy for gratification

F 6. dictum   F. Authoritative pronouncement

C 7. noncombustible   G. Relating to the sense of touch

G 8. tactile   H. Set up; established

Part III: Cloze Passage
Fill in the blanks with the appropriate vocabulary words from the list above.

The scaffolding had been ERECTED by DICTUM of the patron who wished to paint the ceiling of his ancestral home. The project required a complete, TACTILE, hands-on approach as the task was rather ODIOUS due to the fact the ceiling was 100 feet high. The artist was RAVENOUS to finish, especially considering his PROCLIVITIES towards acrophobia. On the very first day he had a humiliating PRATFALL sending him with a lamp in his hand into a bucket of chemicals. Fortunately they were NONCOMBUSTIBLE.

Vocabulary Work For Fahrenheit 451 Assignment 2, Page 3

PART IV: Words In Practice
Answer the questions and be able to give short explanations to justify your answers.

1. When you erect a monument, do you build it up or tear it down?

    Build it up

2. Name something that would be a good proclivity.

    Honesty, being helpful, any appropriate answer

3. If you are asked to do something you think is odious, are you happy to do it or would you rather not?

    Rather not

4. Who is someone who would be ravenous?

    Someone who skips lunch would be ravenous by dinner time, any appropriate answer

5. Give an example of a pratfall.

    Running the wrong way down the field with the football; any appropriate answer

6. Who would create a dictum?

    A king, a CEO, any appropriate answer

7. Which is noncombustible, a match or an asbestos tile?

    Asbestos tile

8. What is something that is pleasant to the tactile senses?

    Silk; warm water, any appropriate answer

VOCABULARY CROSSWORD KEY
READING ASSIGNMENT 2
Fahrenheit 451

```
                    O
                    D I C T U M
              N     I     A
              O     O     C
    E         N     U S   T
    R A V E N O U S       T
    E         C     S     I
    C         O           L
    T         M           E
    E         B
    D         U
              S
        P R A T F A L L
              I
              B
    P R O C L I V I T I E S
              E
```

Arousing strong dislike or displeasure (6)
Authoritative pronouncement (6)
Does not burn easily (14)
Extremely hungry; greedy for gratification (8)
Humiliating failure; a fall on the buttocks (8)
Predispositions; tendencies (12)
Relating to the sense of touch (7)
Set up; established (7)

WRITING ASSIGNMENT 1
Fahrenheit 451

PROMPT

Fire has long been a fascinating thing for mankind. It can be useful; it can be pretty; it can keep us warm, but it can also be very dangerous. Every kid knows Smokey the Bear and has been advised how dangerous fire is to our wildlife friends. Everyone knows and fears the possibility of having a house fire while we are snuggled up in our beds at night. We are fortunate that modern technology has brought us sprinkling systems and fire alarms for our homes. The question then becomes, "What do we do when the smoke alarm goes off?"

Your assignment is to make and write down a fire escape plan for your family and your house. You must give written directions as well as make a map for occupants of each bedroom in your home.

PREWRITING

- First of all, draw a little diagram of your house or apartment. It doesn't have to be perfect for this prewriting exercise. Locate the main rooms of your home. Think for a minute. Where would a fire be most likely to start? Probably in the kitchen, near a heating source, or near an area with a lot of electrical wiring. Locate these and any other areas in your home that are areas where a fire might be likely to start. Put an X on each of those areas.
- Where are the bedrooms in your home in relation to the X marks? Find the best route of escape for the occupants of each of the bedrooms. Mark them on your diagram. If the X marks eliminate all routes of escape, deal with the X marks that are most likely to be trouble spots.
- Think for a minute and make a list of the things that will need to be done to get everyone out safely. Next to each job, write down the name of the person who should be responsible for that job.

DRAFTING

- Write an introductory paragraph telling the circumstances of the prospective fire.
- Write one paragraph for each member of your family, giving them simple, specific instructions as to what to do if there is a fire in your home while you are all in bed asleep. Each person should start from his or her own bedroom.
- Write a concluding paragraph in which you give miscellaneous details about what rooms in your home should have fire extinguishers, rope ladders, or other emergency equipment.
- Make a diagram of your house for each bedroom, and mark each bedroom's escape route on the diagram in a bright color so it can be easily seen.

PROOFREADING

When you finish the rough draft of your paper, ask a student who sits near you to read it. After reading your rough draft, he/she should tell you what he/she liked best about your work, which parts were difficult to understand, and ways in which your work could be improved. Reread your paper considering your critic's comments, and make the corrections you think are necessary.

LESSON SIX
Fahrenheit 451

CCSS: SL.9-10.1a-d; SL.9-10.4; RL.9-10.1; RL.9-10.2; RL.9-10.3; RL.9-10.4; L.9-10.4

Objectives:
- Students will participate in a group discussion of Reading Assignment 2
- Students will cite textual evidence to support their answers to discussion questions
- Students will analyze the characters and their relationships
- Students will consider the written details of the text and their effect on the story
- Students will complete the pre-reading vocabulary worksheet for Reading Assignment 3

Purposes:
The purposes of this lesson are:
- To review the main events and ideas in Reading Assignment 2
- To understand characters and their motivations
- To look for parallels to draw from the story into students' current lives
- To examine details for meaning and apply the meaning to the larger themes of the text
- To become familiar with selected vocabulary words, their definitions, and usage for the end purpose of assimilating the words into students' own vocabularies as well as providing for a better understanding of the text.

Activity #1 (Optional)
If you want to check to see that students have read the assignment, you can use the Multiple Choice questions for RA 2. Distribute copies (not in the student workbook), give students time to complete the quiz, and check the papers in your usual method.

Answer Key For Multiple Choice: Reading Assignment 2:
1. A 2. B 3. D 4. A 5. C 6. D 7. A 8. C 9. B 10. D

Activity #2
Work through the Characters, and Events and Points of Interest graphic organizers together as a class. Students should have taken some notes as they were reading. This review will help complete their notes for study purposes and serve as a review of the main events in the reading assignment.

Activity #3
Discuss the Discussion Questions for Reading Assignment 2. See Lesson Four for additional notes.

Activity #4
Prior to the next class meeting, students should do the vocabulary work and preview the study and discussion questions for Reading Assignment 3.

MULTIPLE CHOICE: READING ASSIGNMENT 2
Fahrenheit 451

1. Who is Captain Beatty?
    A. Montag's boss
    B. A retired naval officer who tells stories
    C. The mayor
    D. Clarisse's uncle

2. How do the firemen know which houses have books?
    A. The books all have barcodes which could be read from up to a mile away by a special barcode device.
    B. Neighbors, family members, and friends inform the authorities when they suspect someone has books.
    C. Firemen conduct random searches for books.
    D. The Hounds find the books and transmit the information to the firehouses.

3. What lie does Captain Beatty tell Montag?
    A. Beatty tells Montag that authors have never been appreciated.
    B. Beatty tells Montag that women are too delicate for firemen's work.
    C. Beatty tells Montag that Montag is next in line for a promotion at work.
    D. Beatty tells Montag that firemen had never been used to put out fires, only to start them.

4. What does Montag do in the No. Elm woman's attic?
    A. He takes a book.
    B. He sits and cries.
    C. He destroys all of her family pictures.
    D. He takes a nap.

5. Why are most of the firemen's calls at night?
    A. People are at home then to let the firemen in.
    B. That is when people are most relaxed and vulnerable.
    C. Having the fires at night makes them prettier and more visible for everyone to see.
    D. Most firemen have day jobs elsewhere.

6. Mrs. Blake does something the firemen don't expect. What?
    A. She locks herself in her apartment and refuses to watch them burn the books.
    B. She dances and throws more books on the fire.
    C. She dresses in black, kneels before the fire, prays, and cries.
    D. She lights the fire and commits suicide.

Multiple Choice: Fahrenheit 451 Reading Assignment 2, Page 2

7. What happens to Clarisse?
    A. She is hit by a car and killed.
    B. She is hypnotized and forced to change her thinking.
    C. She is attacked by the Hound.
    D. She escapes to the wilderness to join the rebels.

8. What is Montag afraid will happen when Captain Beatty comes to visit?
    A. He is afraid Beatty will fire him.
    B. He is afraid Beatty will see how well he lives and cut his pay.
    C. He is afraid Beatty will find his books.
    D. He is afraid Beatty will stay a long time, causing him to miss his favorite show.

9. Which of these statements is something Captain Beatty appears to believe?
    A. All people should be masters of their own destinies.
    B. Books put upsetting thoughts into people's minds and keep them from being happy.
    C. Firemen should be the highest paid workers because they do the most important job.
    D. People who read books are stupid.

10. What does Montag do after Captain Beatty leaves his house?
    A. He sits and cries.
    B. He disinfects everything the captain has touched.
    C. He goes for a long drive.
    D. He shows Mildred the books he's been hiding.

CHARACTERS SUGGESTED NOTES
Reading Assignment 2 Fahrenheit 451

As you read Assignment 2 use this graphic organizer to jot down information about characters.

MONTAG

-- notices all the firemen look alike
-- begins to ask questions and wonder what it would be like to be the victim rather than the fireman
-- stole a book from Mrs. Blake's house
-- went home and cried over Mrs. Blake's death
-- neither he nor Millie could remember where they met
--Millie tells him Clarisse is dead, run over by a car
-- is so upset over Mrs. Blake and Clarisse and Millie that he's literally sick. Doesn't want to be a fireman anymore
-- confesses to Millie that he has books
-- says he's going to do "something big"
-- had begun to cry, not at death but at the thought of not crying at death

BEATTY

-- tries to get Mrs. Black to leave the house
-- knows the Master Ridley quote & it's context
-- knows Montag is going to call out sick
-- has "seen it all"
-- talks about how things came to be the way they are
-- calls himself and Montag the Happiness Boys
-- gives Montag 24 hours to turn in his book
-- tries to give Montag the answers he's looking for, tries to get Montag to accept society as it is rather than questioning and going against it

WOMAN ON ELM ST

-- refuses to leave her home and books
-- lights the kitchen match to start the fire herself
-- dies in the fire with her home and books
-- courage to stand for her convictions or perhaps just not liking the alternative?
-- makes Montag realize how much his setting fires affected people, not just things

MILDRED

-- doesn't remember where she & Montag met
-- remarks it's funny they can't remember where they met then goes and takes sleeping pills
--Millie's life is seashells in her ears, the parlor walls, speed in the car, sleeping pills. No meat; all surface. All things that fill time and space but have no meaning. All things that are entertaining. All things that keep her from feeling unhappy.
-- turns off the parlor walls immediately when Beatty tells her to, didn't when Montag told her earlier

EVENTS & POINTS OF INTEREST SUGGESTED NOTES
Reading Assignment 2 Fahrenheit 451

As you read Assignment 2 make notes of the series of main events that take place. Put them in the order that they are given in the text.

Montag plays cards at the firehouse, realizes all the firemen look like himself, asks what happened to the man whose house they burned, tries to imagine how it would feel "to have firemen burn *our* houses and *our* books." Asks if "once upon a time" things were different.

The firemen respond to an alarm on North Elm. Montag takes a book for himself. The woman there starts the fire herself saying, "Play the man, Master Ridley..." She refuses to leave and is burned with her home and books. This upsets Montag. He goes home and cries.

Montag realizes he and Mildred are strangers to one another and can't even remember where and when they met.

Montag becomes aware of the emptiness of the parlor wall shows, the emptiness of Mildred's fast driving, the emptiness of the seashells in her ears.

We learn via Millie that Clarisse was run over and is dead and that her family has moved away.

Montag is sick and wants to call out from work. Beatty comes to visit, knowing Montag is upset and suspecting he is wavering in his duty. Beatty explains how things have come to be the way they are, and he lets Montag know he understands firemen get "an itch" to find out what the books they are burning say. He lets Montag know Montag has to destroy the book he has and continue to be one of the Happiness Boys.

Mildred realizes Montag is unhappy and suggests he go for a drive. Montag refuses saying he wants to "hold onto this funny thing" even though he is unhappy. Mildred announces that she is proud of being happy and is tired of listening to "this junk."

Montag tells Millie he has books and shows them to her. She tries to burn them but stops fighting Montag and relents. Beatty returns but they don't answer the door. Montag starts reading the books to Millie.

OTHER POINTS OF INTEREST TO IDENTIFY OR KNOW THE SIGNIFICANCE OF:
The ventilator grill hides Montag's books.

An ordinary kitchen match is what the No. Elm woman uses to start the fire at her own home, destroying her home, her books, and herself.

Montag's sickness is a result of the realizations he is having about his society and his own life. It literally makes him sick, and he doesn't want to go to work and continue with his life the way it was.

The beetle is the car, a means of escape.

Montag's books have been accumulating in the ventilator shaft, indicating he has been saving them and stealing them for quite a while. His current feelings have accumulated over time.

STUDY & DISCUSSION QUESTIONS SUGGESTED ANSWERS
Reading Assignment 2 Fahrenheit 451

1. When he goes to the firehouse, Montag realizes that all firemen look alike, and he wonders if they were chosen simply because they look that way. If that is true, what does it say about the society in which they live?

    It says that it is a society built on forms without substance, caring more about theatricality rather than about life. Things are simply what they look like they are. They are recognizable by a certain physical appearance. You can judge a book by its cover.

2. Early in the second reading assignment, Beatty states, "Any man's insane who thinks he can fool the government and us." Do you agree or disagree with that statement? Support your viewpoint.

    Answers will vary. Accept any answer as long as the viewpoint is supported.

3. When the firemen respond to the alarm at Mrs. Blake's house, she is still there. How does her presence "spoil the ritual" for the firemen?

    Normally the firemen are in and out quickly, "...simply cleaning up. Janitorial work essentially." Mrs. Blake's presence makes Montag feel guilty as he is forced to see that he is actually hurting people by doing his job.

4. Before the firemen burn her books, the No. Elm woman says, "Play the man, Master Ridley; we shall this day light such a candle, by God's grace, in England, as I trust shall never be put out." Explain the significance of this quotation.

    Beatty later reveals that this was said by a man named Latimer, who was about to be burned to death for heresy. It is significant because it parallels the woman's situation; she is about to burn for going against the government's policies/beliefs. It is also significant in that it shows she planned her death as a statement, saying that books, or the ideas within them--or the right to own and read them--are worth dying for.

5. When Montag returns home after burning the No. Elm home, he describes his hands as "infected." What does he mean by this?

    Montag disassociates his hands from himself when he first steals the book. The infection he describes is the manifestation of his desire for more substance in the world and his displeasure with how things are.

Study & Discussion Questions Suggested Answers: Fahrenheit 451 RA 2, Page 2

6. How does Millie break the news of Clarisse's death to Montag? Why is it important that she does it in that way?

    Millie treats Clarisse's death in a very off-handed manner, having heard about her neighbor's death four days ago and forgotten. It underscores how numb she is to the real world and how distanced she is from Montag.

7. What do you think Montag means when he says, "But that was another Mildred...so deep inside this one, and so bothered, really bothered, that the two women had never met." ?

    Montag is implying that, on some level, Mildred took the pills as a deliberate suicide attempt. He indicates that there is a part of her that is very unhappy, but she is so much a part of their world that she cannot admit this to herself.

8. Beatty says, "We must all be alike. Not everyone born free and equal, but everyone made equal. Each man the image of every other; then all are happy, for there are no mountains to make them cower, to judge themselves against." Do you agree with Beatty's vision of happiness? Why or why not?

    Answers will vary. Accept any well-supported response.

9. In his speech, Beatty describes their world as being happy. Do you think he believes it? Support your answer with quotes from the text.

    Answers will vary.

Students who think Beatty *doesn't* believe that the world is happy might use some of these quotes:

   "Films and radios, magazines, books leveled down to a sort of past pudding norm."

   "Out of the nursery into college and back to the nursery; there's your intellectual pattern for the past five centuries or more."

   "More cartoons in books. More pictures. The mind drinks less and less."

Students who think Beatty *does* believe the world is happy might point to:

   "...the word 'intellectual,' of course, became the swear word it deserved to be."

   "Who knows who might be the target of the well-read man? Me? I won't stomach them for a minute."

   "Any man who can take a TV wall apart and put it back together again...is happier than any man who tries to slide-rule, measure, and equate the universe, which just won't be measured or equated without making man feel bestial and lonely. I know, I've tried it; to hell with it."

Study & Discussion Questions Suggested Answers: Fahrenheit 451 RA 2, Page 3

10. Why doesn't Mildred tell Beatty about the book she finds?

Answers will vary. Some might point to the lingering affection between Millie and Montag. Others may say that she was afraid she might get in trouble for it as well. Still others may point out that she might not have recognized the shape of the book, crying out, "What is this?" genuinely.

11. Toward the end of Part One, Montag wonders why the firemen were so afraid of people like Clarisse. Why do you think they might be?

Clarisse was different, and as Beatty says, we are often afraid of people who are different. More than that, Clarisse showed that the society they lived in was hollow, and if more people would follow her example, the society might collapse--not something those in power would want.

12. Summarize Beatty's explanation of how and why society changed in the 20th Century.

Students will give different amounts of details in their explanations. The amount of details you will require of them will depend on their abilities and your own standards.

Basically, their answers should have something to do with the pace of life speeding up. Inventions made doing necessary things faster, so people filled up their leisure time with more "fun" things to do (like sports)--and taking less time to do things in depth. Life became about quantity rather than quality...doing more rather than taking time to think and savor experiences.

Those in power (advertisers and government) used this trend to their own advantages, utilizing the media to indoctrinate the masses of people to their way of thinking and to create masses of people who were only concerned with themselves and their own entertainment, people who believed whatever was shown to them in the media, without really caring about it, much less questioning it.

Teacher's Note: You might take the opportunity here to have students analyze our society regarding these points...and to point out that in-depth discussions like the ones you are having in class ARE valuable, to learn to question, to think, to have opinions, and to be able to recognize both personal and societal flaws which can be improved upon to make us better people and a better society. This IS the point, the purpose of reading books like Fahrenheit 451 in school.

Study & Discussion Questions Discussion Guide: Fahrenheit 451 RA 2, Page 4

ADDITIONAL PASSAGES FOR DISCUSSION

1. Discuss the imagery used in the paragraph beginning, "Books bombarded his shoulders..." (pg. 34 of the 60th Anniversary edition).

    The pigeon imagery is interesting, perhaps alluding to books being carrier pigeons of knowledge. It's beautiful use of language, almost poetic. The dim, wavering light could be knowledge lingering, about to die, as the books are one-by-one snuffed out by firemen. The line Montag read "blazed in his mind...as if stamped there with fiery steel." This takes full advantage of the fire imagery, but ironically used for the good of remembering something worthwhile. "Time had fallen asleep in the afternoon sunshine" is like the people falling asleep to knowledge, thinking, and reality in the afternoon sunshine of entertainment. Then he drops the book, yet... another one falls into his arms. Fate will not let Montag surrender. He is destined to follow his feelings, to get to the root of the problem.

2. "Will you turn the parlor off?"
    "That's my family."

    Poor Mildred. The people on the parlor walls have become like family to her. How sad is that? They are empty people who say nothing and accomplish nothing; they are all emotion and entertainment. They give nothing back to Millie for all the hours of time she spends devoted to them. Good books, in contrast, give us food for thought, help us improve ourselves, and help us gain knowledge and understanding...like *Fahrenheit 451*.

3. "We burned a thousand books. We burned a woman."
    "Well?"

    Millie doesn't see what the big deal is, burning books or burning a woman. It's just data, facts without any meaning to her, and there is no differentiation between burning books and burning a woman in Millie's mind. She can't or doesn't think about what Montag is saying actually means.

4. "...this fire'll last me the rest of my life. God! I've been trying to put it out, in my mind, all night..."
    "You should have thought of that before becoming a fireman."

    This fire *will* last Montag the rest of his life; it is the turning point of his life, the event that makes him realize what he has been doing all this time actually affects people, not just things-- and the No. Elm woman's willingness to die for her books and the right to read them makes him think about what is IN the books and why books are so important to some people.

    Millie's cold retort shows she has no understanding of Montag or what he is experiencing. Moreover, she does not show any compassion for Montag. What Montag needs is a wife who shows she loves him by giving him comfort or at least showing some indication that she wants to help him. Instead, she throws out this cold, verbal slap in the face.

    What she says is true; perhaps he should have thought about that before becoming a fireman, but it's ironic coming from Mildred (who clearly does everything she can to keep from thinking about anything) and doubly ironic because Montag was raised in a place where he really had no chance to think about what it meant to be a fireman before he undertook it as a profession.

Study & Discussion Questions Discussion Guide: Fahrenheit 451 RA 2, Page 5

Additional Passages For Discussion Continued

5. "We need not to be let alone. We need to be really bothered once in a while."

   Points for discussion: What does it mean to be "let alone"? Why would Montag say we need NOT to be let alone? Why do we need to be really bothered once in a while? Generally, only things we care about bother us. Ask your students what bothers them and why it bothers them. Choose some things you think they would NOT care about and ask if they are bothered by those things. We shouldn't be bothered all the time; we need to pick and choose the things that we get upset about, or we would be upset all the time and not able to live. What kinds of things are important to care about? Why?

6. This time, Mildred ran. The yammering voices stopped yelling in the parlor.

   When Beatty tells Millie to shut off the parlor, she does it immediately. Why? What is it about Beatty that makes Millie spring to action when she would not do it for Montag? She should have cared enough for Montag to respect his wishes. Beatty is the authority figure whom she automatically (without thinking) respects and obeys.

7. "You ask Why to a lot of things and you wind up very unhappy indeed, if you keep at it. The poor girl's better off dead."

   Some points to discuss: Consider that Beatty is the one talking. Earlier he told Montag he had "seen it all," and he knew and understood the quote Mrs. Blake used. Could Beatty have come to the point Montag is at now? Is Beatty happy? Why would he think Clarisse is better off dead?

LESSON SEVEN
Fahrenheit 451

CCSS: L.9-10.1; L.9-10.2; L.9-10.4; L.9-10.4a; L.9-10.5;

Objectives:
- Students will review and discuss the vocabulary work for Reading Assignment 3
- Students will read Reading Assignment 3 orally in class
- Students will participate in an oral reading evaluation

Purposes:
The purposes of this lesson are:
- To make sure students have the correct understanding of the vocabulary words for RA 3
- To give students the opportunity to practice public speaking and oral reading
- To encourage students to speak up, speak clearly, and to read orally with the same expression as if they were just talking
- To evaluate students' oral reading so they can see where they need improvement and be given suggestions as to how to improve in these areas

Activity #1 (Optional)
Students were supposed to have done the vocabulary pages for Reading Assignment 2. Take a few minutes to review the answers to those pages with students so you're sure they're on the right track. Do this in whatever way suits your teaching style.

Activity #2
Have students read Reading Assignment 3 orally in class. You should determine the length of passages read based on your own students' needs and abilities.

As each student reads, help as necessary with word pronunciation and complete an oral reading evaluation form. When the student finishes, give appropriate praise. After all students have read, make constructive comments about difficulties that several students encountered with their reading--pronunciation, reading with expression, phrasing...whatever the issues are. Give some pointers as to ways these issues can be resolved.

Activity #3
Tell students to use the remainder of the class time to complete reading Reading Assignment 3 silently (or oral reading with a partner for practice, if you choose). While students are reading, finish writing up the oral reading evaluations. You may want to make a copy of each before giving them to students, or you may want to give them to students to review and then put the evaluations in any student work folders you might have for their term's work.

Students should complete reading Reading Assignment 3 prior to the next class meeting.

VOCABULARY WORK FOR ASSIGNMENT 3

PART I: Using Prior Knowledge And Contextual Clues
Use any clues you can find in the sentences from the text combined with your prior knowledge and write what you think the bold word means.

1. ...he talked in a **cadenced** voice...and when an hour had passed he said something to Montag and Montag sensed it was a rhymeless poem.

    With a rhythmic flow

2. The train radio vomited upon Montag, in **retaliation**, a great tonload of music made of tin, copper, silver, chromium and brass.

    Returning like for like

3. Books were only one type of **receptacle** where we stored a lot of things we were afraid we might forget.

    A container that holds matter

4. Proof of my terrible **cowardice**.

    Ignoble fear in the face of danger

5. On one wall a woman smiled and drank orange juice **simultaneously**. How does she do both at once, thought Montag...

    At the same time

6. For these were the hands that had acted on their own, no part of him, here was where the conscience first **manifested** itself to snatch books, dart off with Job and Ruth and Willie Shakespeare, and now, in the firehouse, these hands seemed gloved with blood.

    Showed; revealed

7. You towered with rage, yelled quotes at me, I calmly **parried** every thrust. Power, I said.

    Deflected; avoided

8. The folly of mistaking a metaphor for a proof, a torrent of **verbiage** for a spring of capital truths, and oneself as an oracle, is inborn in us, Mr. Valery once said.

    Wordiness

Vocabulary Work For Fahrenheit 451 Assignment 3, Page 2

PART II: Matching
Considering the usage in Part I, match the vocabulary words to their definitions.

H 1. cadenced   A. Ignoble fear in the face of danger

D 2. retaliation   B. A container that holds matter

B 3. receptacle   C. At the same time

A 4. cowardice   D. Returning like for like

C 5. simultaneously E. Wordiness

F 6. manifested   F. Showed; revealed

G 7. parried   G. Deflected; avoided

E 8. verbiage   H. With a rhythmic flow

Part III: Cloze Passage
Fill in the blanks with the appropriate vocabulary words from the list above.

The newscaster began his report with a CADENCED voice which MANIFESTED a VERBIAGE of unparalleled intensity. RETALIATION was his motive, for he was accusing another station of COWARDICE because of the underhanded way they were attacking his broadcasts. He had previously PARRIED their attacks, but now he was SIMULTANEOUSLY responding to them openly and hitting back with his own assertions about their station. At the end of his broadcast, he threw his notes into a trash RECEPTACLE to close with a dramatic flourish.

Vocabulary Work For Fahrenheit 451 Assignment 3, Page 3

PART IV: Words In Practice
Answer the questions and be able to give short explanations to justify your answers.

1. Does a cadenced march help keep soldiers in step together or make being in step difficult?

    helps keep them in step

2. If someone came up and slapped you in the face, is it likely you would want to retaliate?

    yes

3. What is one common household receptacle?

    trash can, laundry basket, electrical socket; any appropriate answer

4. Is cowardice on the battlefield usually considered to be heroic?

    no

5. Name two things that often happen simultaneously.

    announcers talking during a ball game; any appropriate answer

6. In what ways does the flu manifest itself?

    aches, fever, upset stomach

7. In what occupation is a lot of verbiage required?

    politician, lawyer, teacher; any appropriate answer

8. What is something that can be parried?

    a verbal insult; a punch thrown at you; any appropriate answer

VOCABULARY CROSSWORD KEY
READING ASSIGNMENT 3
Fahrenheit 451

```
C
O                           M
W                           A
A            R              N
RECEPTACLE   E    V         I
D            T    E         F
I       P A R R I E D
CADENCED     L    B         S
E            I    I         T
             A    A         E
             T    G         D
             I    E
             O
         SIMULTANEOUSLY
```

A container that holds matter (10)
Deflected; avoided (7)
Happening at the same time (14)
Ignoble fear in the face of danger (9)
Returning like for like, especially evil (11)
Showed; revealed (10)
With a rhythmic flow (8)
Wordiness (8)

ORAL READING EVALUATION
Fahrenheit 451

Name _____   Date _____

SKILL	Excellent	Good	Average	Fair	Poor
Fluency	5	4	3	2	1
Clarity	5	4	3	2	1
Audibility	5	4	3	2	1
Pronunciation	5	4	3	2	1
Expression	5	4	3	2	1
	5	4	3	2	1
	5	4	3	2	1
	5	4	3	2	1

Total Score ____ of ____   Grade _____

Comments & Suggestions:

LESSON EIGHT
Fahrenheit 451

CCSS: SL.9-10.1a-d; SL.9-10.4; RL.9-10.1; RL.9-10.2; RL.9-10.3; RL.9-10.4; L.9-10.4

Objectives:
- Students will participate in a group discussion of Reading Assignment 3
- Students will cite textual evidence to support their answers to discussion questions
- Students will analyze the characters and their relationships
- Students will consider the written details of the text and their effect on the story
- Students will complete the pre-reading vocabulary worksheet for Reading Assignment 4

Purposes:
The purposes of this lesson are:
- To review the main events and ideas in Reading Assignment 3
- To understand characters and their motivations
- To look for parallels to draw from the story into students' current lives
- To examine details for meaning and apply the meaning to the larger themes of the text
- To become familiar with selected vocabulary words, their definitions, and usage for the end purpose of assimilating the words into students' own vocabularies as well as providing for a better understanding of the text.

Activity #1 (Optional)
If you want to check to see that students have read the assignment, you can use the Multiple Choice questions for RA 3. Distribute copies (not in the student workbook), give students time to complete the quiz, and check the papers in your usual method.

Answer Key For Multiple Choice: Reading Assignment 3:
1. C   2. A   3. B   4. D   5. C   6. A   7. D   8. A   9. B   10. C

Activity #2
Work through the Characters, and Events and Points of Interest graphic organizers together as a class. Students should have taken some notes as they were reading. This review will help complete their notes for study purposes and serve as a review of the main events in the reading assignment.

Activity #3
Discuss the Discussion Questions for Reading Assignment 3. See Lesson Four for additional notes.

Activity #4
Prior to the next class meeting, students should do the vocabulary work and preview the study and discussion questions for Reading Assignment 4.

MULTIPLE CHOICE: READING ASSIGNMENT 3
Fahrenheit 451

1. Who is Faber?
    A. Faber is Montag's brother-in-law, and another sympathizer.
    B. Faber is second in command after Beatty.
    C. Faber is a retired English professor.
    D. Faber is the chief physician at Emergency Hospital.

2. Why does Montag first go to see Faber?
    A. He wants to duplicate a book before he gives it to Beatty.
    B. He thinks Faber can give him advice about how to help his wife.
    C. He wants to find out if Faber can translate books that are not in English.
    D. He wants to get information about others who have books, so he can turn them in to Beatty and further his career.

3. Faber thinks that three elements are missing from but necessary for the kind of life Montag wants. Which of the following is NOT one of those elements?
    A. Quality and texture of information
    B. The satisfaction of choosing one's own job
    C. Leisure time to think
    D. The right to carry out actions based on the other two elements

4. What is Montag's plan to begin changing the world?
    A. He plans to replace the kerosene with non-flammable liquid.
    B. He plans to collect all the books he can find and preserve them.
    C. He plans to hold meetings of small groups of people to begin talking about important things.
    D. He plans to plant books in firemen's houses then turn in alarms on the firemen.

5. What is Montag willing to do to convince Faber to help carry out the plan?
    A. He would pay Faber the money his wife wanted to use for the fourth parlor wall.
    B. He would quit his job and move in with Faber.
    C. He would destroy his book, page by page, until Faber would cooperate.
    D. He would do the first five operations himself so Faber would not be implicated.

6. How does Faber stay in contact with Montag when Montag leaves to go to the firehouse?
    A. Faber gives Montag a small radio transmitter and receiver that fits in his ear.
    B. Faber gives Montag a TV monitor that fits inside a watch mechanism.
    C. Faber gives Montag a thought-wave amplifier that fits behind his ear.
    D. Faber gives Montag a communications microchip.

Multiple Choice: Fahrenheit 451 Reading Assignment 3, Page 2

7. Why does Faber decide to go to St. Louis?
    A. He needs to put distance between himself and Montag.
    B. He wants to raise funds for their project.
    C. He is following up on a lead about a library there.
    D. He is going to meet with an unemployed printer.

8. Why does Montag burn the book of poetry in the wall incinerator in his home?
    A. Faber tells him to do it, to convince the ladies that he is joking.
    B. Montag knows it will make Mildred happy.
    C. Montag doesn't like the poems; he thinks they are jibberish.
    D. Montag wants to see the book burn; it gives him pleasure.

9. Where does Montag hide his books after the ladies leave?
    A. He hides them in the attic, above the vent.
    B. He hides them in the back yard.
    C. He hides them behind the ventillator grill.
    D. He hides them behind the parlor walls.

10. Whose house do the firemen visit on the night Montag returned to work?
    A. The firemen go to Clarisse's house.
    B. The firemen go to Faber's house.
    C. The firemen go to Montag's house.
    D. The firemen go to Beatty's house.

CHARACTERS SUGGESTED NOTES
Reading Assignment 3 Fahrenheit 451

As you read Assignment 3 use this graphic organizer to jot down information about characters.

MONTAG

-- Montag tries to figure out why he liked Clarisse and decides it's because she treated him as if he counted
-- realizes he needs help and remembers Faber, looks to him for help
-- digs deeper into the books looking for answers
-- flips out a little on the train on his way to Faber. Openly rants, holds book in public
-- commits to Faber's way of thinking, seeks to move forward in that direction
-- speaks with Millie's friends but gets angry at their lack of concern for real things, reads from a book to them against Faber's advice
-- wants to think on his own but can't yet
-- needs Faber to respond to Beatty

FABER

-- former English professor
-- calls himself a coward
-- also an inventor, devising radio
-- sees Montag's desire and is inspired to action
-- says 3 things are missing: quality of information, time to digest it, and the freedom to carry out actions based on the first two

MILDRED

-- tries to change the subject to more pleasant things
-- actually covers for Montag's having books and tries to make it seem ok for the women
-- comforts Clara Phelps by suggesting they turn on "the family"

BEATTY

-- quotes literature freely
-- says he's "been through it all"
-- seems to enjoy making Montag's pulse race and making Montag uncomfortable
-- knows the fire alarm is a "special case"
-- drives the truck himself

MRS. PHELPS

-- repeats that she isn't worried too many times
-- has no children and doesn't want any
-- encourages Montag to read poems
-- cried after hearing the poem

EVENTS & POINTS OF INTEREST SUGGESTED NOTES
Reading Assignment 3 Fahrenheit 451

As you read Assignment 3 make notes of the series of main events that take place. Put them in the order that they are given in the text.

- Montag reads from his books at home, with Mildred.
- The Hound comes sniffing at the door. Mildred is alarmed that the door-voice doesn't announce someone is there. Montag tells her to ignore the dog at the door.
- Montag tries to explain to Millie why they should read, but Mildred doesn't get it. The phone rings and she talks with Ann about the White Clown show.
- Montag remembers meeting a man in the park, a retired English professor named Faber. He decides to contact Faber.
- Montag takes the subway to Faber's neighborhood. He takes a book with him and carries it in plain sight. Loses patience with the annoying advertisement on the bus's PA system and yells for it to shut up, alarming the other passengers.
- Montag goes to Faber's house and asks for his help. Montag wants Faber to listen to what he has to say. Faber calls himself a coward and Montag brave. He tells Montag what Montag is looking for isn't books; it's what used to be in the books. Faber says three things are missing: quality of information, leisure time to digest it, and the right to act based on what one gets from the first two items.
- Montag tells Faber of his plan to get rid of the firemen by planting books in their homes and then turning in alarms on them. Faber likes the idea but thinks it wouldn't really change much and tells Montag to go home and go to bed. Montag begins tearing pages from the book he brought and won't stop until Faber agrees to help him.
- Faber shows Montag the ear-sized radio he made, gives it to Montag, and agrees to help Montag by listening to his conversations and giving him advice in his ear.
- Back at home, Montag tries to get Millie's friends to talk about important things. They try but don't seem capable.
- Mrs. Phelps insists (perhaps too much) that she does not worry and proclaims that she hates children. Mrs. Bowles sends her children to school and when they are home parks them in front of the parlor walls.
- Mildred suggests they talk politics to please Guy, but their discussion hinges on the looks of the candidates rather than the substance of the candidates' views.
- Montag brings out books. Millie tries to explain away why he has books. Mrs. Phelps encourages Guy Montag to read poetry but cries after hearing it. Everyone is upset. Montag throws the book in the incinerator. Millie suggests they turn on "the family." The ladies leave vowing not to return to this crazy fireman's house.
- Montag goes to work and turns over a book to Beatty. While playing poker, Beatty needles Montag by quoting literature. Montag is saved from the needling by the alarm bell.
- Montag is surprised that the house the alarm was called on is his own home.

Events And Points Of Interest Reading Assignment 3 Suggested Answers Continued

OTHER POINTS OF INTEREST TO IDENTIFY OR KNOW THE SIGNIFICANCE OF:

The White Clown is a show Millie and her friends watch on the parlor walls. Ask students to brainstorm ideas about the significance of the name of the show.

The Sieve and the Sand is the title of the second chapter, this reading assignment. It is taken from Montag's remembering trying to fill a sieve with sand and the frustration he felt at his failure to be able to do it. Discuss with your students how this parallels his struggle with his current situation.

Denham's Dental Detergent is the product for which there were constant ads on the train. Talk about the name of this product. It isn't "toothpaste"; it's "dental detergent." This is also an opportunity to discuss alliteration. Discuss why the advertisement is so upsetting to Montag when no one else on the train seems upset by it.

3 things that are missing are quality of information, leisure time to digest it, and the right to act based upon one's conclusions drawn from that. These are the things Faber says are missing in their society. Ask students how our society rates on these three items.

The green bullet is the radio device that fits inside Montag's ear so Faber can listen to Montag's conversations and can tell Montag how to respond when he needs help. Is it a kind of conscience? Is it like Big Brother listening in? Does it help Montag? Ask what your students think of this device. If they could have a green bullet radio, who would they want to be on Faber's end?

The Sea Of Faith is the name of the poem Montag read to Millie's friends, the poem that upset Mrs. Phelps and made her cry. Why would this poem make Mrs. Phelps cry? Why did Ray Bradbury choose this poem over the millions of others he could have referenced here?

STUDY & DISCUSSION QUESTIONS SUGGESTED ANSWERS
Reading Assignment 3 Fahrenheit 451

1. How do we know that the dog at the door is the mechanical hound?
    The phrases "an exhalation of electric steam" and "the smell of blue electricity blowing under the locked door" make it clear that the dog at the door is the mechanical hound.

    It is significant to note that Mildred acts as if it's just a regular dog, not necessarily distinguishing between something that is alive and something that is mechanical. To Mildred, whether something is alive or dead, real or fiction doesn't seem to make much difference. Another example of this is her considering the people on the parlor walls to be her "family."

2. Why is the event with the mechanical hound at the door significant?
    - It continues the notion that the hound is suspicious of Montag.
    - It shows Mildred's lack of differentiation between living things and mechanical devices.
    - It builds suspense within the story.

3. The details in this book are important. There are only a few sentences about the door-voice in the incident with the dog at the door, but they are important:
    "Someone--the door--why doesn't the door-voice tell us---"
    "I shut it off."
    What do we learn about Montag and Mildred from these two lines?
    - The use of the word "someone" followed by "the door" indicates Mildred's lack of distinction between living things and mechanical devices. She hasn't totally lost the distinction, though, as evidenced by her following-up with the more practical name of "door-voice."
    - This passage shows Mildred's dependence on devices. She is flustered when the door-voice doesn't alert her that someone or something is at the door.
    - It shows Montag's beginning to distance himself from the trappings of their society. Before he can break away, he has to shut out the things that keep him trapped in their way of life. Turning off the door-voice, locking the door, ignoring the hound... these are all things that show Montag's rejection of that lifestyle and/or need for uninterrupted time to stop and think.

4. Why does Montag insist on continuing to read the books?
    Montag feels like there is something important missing in the world, and he suspects that the answer might be in the books.

5. From Mildred's point of view, explain why the parlor walls are better than books.
    The parlor walls have people she can see and interact with. They are colorful, fun, and entertaining. Books have only printed words that she doesn't really understand. To Mildred, books are dead and the parlor walls are living.

Study & Discussion Questions Suggested Answers: Fahrenheit 451 RA 3, Page 2

6. Mildred asks Montag, "Why should I read? What *for*?" Summarize Montag's answer by finishing his sentence, "An hour a day, two hours, wth these books, and maybe . . ."

    Answers will vary, but most answers should have something to do with not repeating the same mistakes that have been made over and over again in history, learning how to live together without war, becoming more aware of each other both in our country and the world, and/or thinking and talking with each other to try to find true happiness rather than simply escaping into emptiness.

7. Compare and contrast Montag's first meeting with Faber in the park with his first meeting with Clarisse.

    While Clarisse and Faber were both surprised to see Montag, Clarisse had the curiosity and candor of youth. She was interested in him and in his life, and very vibrant. Faber on the other hand was initially fearful of Montag, but when he got over his fear he was more focused on his own inner life. He was described as being pale and grey. Both meetings were important for Montag because they both "talked the meaning of things" instead of talking about things themselves.

8. Montag asks Millie "Does the White Clown love you . . . does your 'family' love you?" What is the significance of Montag's questions?

    Millie consistently talks about the people on TV as if they are real, as if they are her actual family instead of mass-produced programming. Montag is asking her whether or not she experiences love from them, and if it is fulfilling the way real love is fulfilling, but she can't give him an answer. This is also an echo of Clarisse's statement: "What a shame you're not in love with anyone!"

9. What is the difference between talking "things" and talking "the meaning of things"?

    "Things" are superficial; they are at face value. "The meaning of things" requires thinking, questioning, forming opinions, evaluating, interpreting, and drawing conclusions--asking "How?" and "Why?" instead of just taking things at face value and accepting them. For example, the war planes fly over, and everyone knows that and occasionally remarks about it, but no one really knows why there is a war, who exactly is involved, how long it will last, or any other details. They simply accept that there is a war and the planes are a part of that.

10. "The train radio vomited upon Montag, in retaliation, a great tonload of music made of tin, copper, silver, chromium, and brass." What type of figure of speech is exemplified in this sentence? The music is in retaliation of what? Why is the music described as being made of metals?

    The sentence is an example of personification, which is interesting in view of the many references to things that are inanimate being alive and things that are alive being dead.

    The music is in retaliation of Montag's insistence on trying to memorize the Bible, but in a broader sense, the music tries to squelch Montag's dissention.

    Metals are cold and harsh; they're hard, and they echo sound and make it tinny. Harsh, cold music assaults Montag's longings for a more warm, loving, natural world.

Study & Discussion Questions Suggested Answers: Fahrenheit 451 RA 3, Page 3

10. Faber says that there are three things missing from the world. What are they?

    The first thing is quality, defined by Faber as "texture... life under the glass, streaming past in infinite profusion." The parlor families and the White Clown are too simple to have this quality. The second is leisure, time to sit and think and process. With the riot of sound from advertisements and fast cars everywhere, there is no room to process. The third is the opportunity to act on the things one has learned. In this world, people are not given choices. These opportunities are taken away through government and peer pressure.

11. Faber calls himself a coward for not speaking up against the bad changes in their society as they were happening, before it was too late. He later calls Montag "brave" after he learns that Montag stole the Bible. Do you think Faber is/was a coward and Montag is brave, or do you think their actions could be governed by something other than cowardice and/or bravery?

    Answers will vary. Some points for discussion are:
    - Define what it means to be a coward and what it means to be brave, then consider the characters' actions based on those definitions.
    - Consider motivation. Faber may have been the proverbial frog in the pot of cold water on the stove--he may not have realized what was happening until it was too late and he was cooked. Montag, on the other hand, has been living in the result of the changes and in his heart longs for something better.

12. Montag and Faber hatch a plan to plant books in Firemen's houses to help bring down the system, while also setting up clandestine reading rooms. Do you think this is a good plan? Evaluate their chances for success.

    Answers will vary.

13. Why are Millie and her friends made so nervous when Montag turns the TV walls off?

    They are nervous because Montag asks them to think about unpleasant topics, such as the war, without the distraction of the screens. Without the distraction they don't know how to handle their emotional content. Mrs. Phelps's answer to Montag sounds like a repetitive sound-bite from an advertisement. Then, she goes on and repeats that she's not worried so many times, one wonders if she's actually trying to convince herself that she isn't worried. Mildred jumps into the conversation and turns it to a more comfortable subject, a story shown on the parlor wall the evening before.

14. Describe Mrs. Bowles's parenting style and describe the type of children she is raising.

    Mrs. Bowles is a disengaged parent who doesn't really want anything to do with raising her children. She sends them away to school and only has them home three days a month, and for those three days, she "heaves them into the parlor and turns on the switch." Her children "would just as soon kick [her] as kiss [her]." She apparently kicks them back, treating them more like animals than people.

Study & Discussion Questions Suggested Answers: Fahrenheit 451 RA 3, Page 4

15. Earlier in the book, Beatty says "If you don't want a man unhappy politically, don't give him two sides of a question to worry him; give him one. Better yet, give him none." On what criteria do Millie and her friends judge the political candidates, and how does their political conversation between Millie and her friends relate to Beatty's statement?

   Millie and her friends judge the candidates based on how they look, not what they stand for. They describe the two choices for president: one a fat, balding man who picks his nose named Hubert Hoag and a tall, handsome man who speaks warmly named Winston Noble. Those in power know that the masses of people are superficial and judge on superficial evidence, so everything about the two candidates is designed to make it seem like people have a choice, but in reality no one would vote for Hoag. It is a ploy to keep the people who have power in control of that power.

16. Why does Mrs. Phelps start crying in response to the poem?

   Answers will vary. Students should be able to connect the description of the world in the poem to the condition of Montag's world and understand that on some level Mrs. Phelps has experienced the truth of the poem, though she seems unable to understand the reason for her emotional response. No one in the room seems to know how to cope with Mrs. Phelps's emotional response, to discuss the issue or comfort her. They turn to distractions and attempt to abandon the poem and discussion. Mrs. Bowles vows never to return to "this fireman's crazy house again." Re-read the poem with your students, and discuss it.

17. Chapter Two is entitled "The Sieve and the Sand." To what does this refer?

   It refers to Montag's desperate attempt to memorize part of the Bible while on the train. The feeling of futility reminds him of a time in his childhood when he tried to fill a sieve with sand at the beach. In a broader sense, it could also be referring to Montag's attempts to fill Mildred and her friends with knowledge and awareness, and their sieve-like lack of acceptance or retention of the ideas he is trying to convey.

Study & Discussion Questions Discussion Guide: Fahrenheit 451 RA 3, Page 5

ADDITIONAL PASSAGES FOR DISCUSSION

1. Faber tells Montag "It's not the books you need, it's some of the things that once were in books. The same things could be in the 'parlor families' today." What do you think he means by this?

    Faber means that the qualities we look for in a good book are not inherently linked to that format. There are other ways to gain knowledge, connection, and meaning in life.

2. "We are living in a time when flowers are trying to live on flowers, instead of growing on good rain and black loam."

    Discuss the idea of flowers living on flowers. That which is pretty, fun, and entertaining is the blossom, not the food of life. A steady diet of only the blossom will leave the plant malnourished. Likewise, a steady diet of fun and entertainment without substance leaves our lives malnourished.

3. "We cannot tell the precise moment when friendship is formed. As in filling a vessel drop by drop, there is at last a drop which makes it run over; so in a series of kindnesses there is at least one which makes the heart run over."

    Discuss the idea of what makes a good friend. What do your students look for in their friends? Without being specific in their answers get them to either agree or disagree that they knew the exact moment when their best friends became their best friends. Are their friends like Clarisse? Do they make them feel like they "count" the way Clarisse made Montag feel like he "counted"?

4. Mildred kicked the book. "Books aren't people. You read and I look all around, but there isn't *anybody*!...my 'family' is people. They tell me things; *I* laugh, *they* laugh! and the colors!"

    Try to get your students to see the irony that Millie's "family" isn't any more "people" than books are; they are not real. But because Millie can *see* them and interact with them, they seem real to her. What she doesn't know is that people who read "see" the characters and events taking place in their mind's eye as vividly as on a screen, as vividly as Millie sees her "family." The pleasure from a book comes from imagining it how you think it looks and being able to think about the words and ideas without someone having drawn it all out for you with their own interpretation.

5. "Who's more important, me or that Bible?" She was beginning to shriek now, sitting there like a wax doll melting in its own heat."

    This is a fabulous image. Alert students to look for the wax doll image in other places throughout the book. Note a wax doll is fake but smooth and perfect, like the people on television commercials. A melting wax doll is the perfect image for a distressed Mildred.

Study & Discussion Questions Discussion Guide: Fahrenheit 451 RA 3, Page 6

Additional Passages For Discussion Continued

6. "My wife's dying. A friend of mine's already dead. Someone who may have been a friend was burnt less than twenty-four hours ago. You're the only one I knew might help me. To see. To see . . ."

    Points For Discussion: Is Montag's wife dying? If so, of what? If not, why would Montag say that? What does Montag want to see?

    Mildred would have been dead if she hadn't had her stomach pumped out, so maybe Montag is accurate in saying that his wife is dying. She might be successful next time. Also, she certainly looks like death, all pale and sometimes speaking in a faint voice. See what your students think and guide the discussion, inviting different ideas.

    As to what Montag wants to see...mostly he wants to understand what's wrong with his world, and he thinks understanding what is in the books will help him accomplish that.

7. "Nobody listens anymore. I can't talk to the walls because they're yelling at *me*. I can't talk to my wife; she listens to the *walls*. I just want someone to hear what I have to say. And maybe if I talk long enough, it'll make sense. And I want you to teach me to understand what I read."

    Montag is so alone. He has no one to talk with about his new thoughts and feelings. He is looking to Faber to be his sounding board, to share information with, to help him understand. It's sad, really. Clarisse is gone. Mildred is not interested. Beatty is a part of the establishment that hunts down people with these kinds of thoughts.

8. "And don't look to be saved in any *one* thing, person, machine, or library. Do your own bit of saving, and if you drown, at least die knowing you were headed for shore."

    Faber is telling Montag that we each are responsible for our own lives; no one can live our lives for us, and we should not believe that the answers to our lives' questions are available from one source, nor that any one source outside of ourselves could be blamed for our failures. Our choices are our own, to be made thoughtfully with knowledge from many sources, but nevertheless, our own. If Montag should die following the path he believes to be the right one, he has the satisfaction of knowing he was doing what he thought was the right thing.

9. "Remember, the firemen are rarely necessary. The public itself stopped reading of its own accord. . . . People are having *fun*."

    Faber makes an excellent point. The masses of people really don't *want* to read; they don't *care* about what's going on in the world; they don't *care* about anything outside of what immediately affects them. As long as they have food, shelter, and entertainment, they're happy. Few people want more than that. Montag is a minority trying to speak up for a small percentage of the population.

Study & Discussion Questions Discussion Guide: Fahrenheit 451 RA 3, Page 7

Additional Passages For Discussion Continued

10. I remember the newspapers dying like huge moths. No one wanted them back. No one missed them. And then the Government, seeing how advantageous it was to have people reading only about passionate lips and the fist in the stomach, circled the situation with your fire-eaters."

    Ask students, "Why would a non-reading, non-thinking public be advantageous to the government?"

11. "I don't want to change sides and just be *told* what to do. There's no reason to change if I do that."

    Montag is right; there is no point in fighting for the freedom to read, think, and express and act on your thoughts if you relinquish the freedom you are fighting for to another oppressor.

12. "He is no wise man who will quit a certainty for an uncertainty."

    Is this true? Perhaps it depends on what the certainty IS as to whether or not risking the uncertainty is worth it. Discuss this idea with your students.

13. "But remember the Captain belongs to the most dangerous enemy to truth and freedom, the solid unmoving cattle of the majority."

    Discuss why the "solid unmoving cattle of the majority" are the most dangerous enemy to truth and freedom.

14. The men ran like cripples in their clumsy boots, as quietly as spiders.

    Discuss this imagery with your students. It's contradictory...men running like cripples in clumsy boots ought to be noisy and rather out-of-control, unlike a spider that is stealthy with each move planned and executed with precision.

LESSON NINE
Fahrenheit 451

CCSS: L.9-10.1; L.9-10.2; L.9-10.4; L.9-10.4a; L.9-10.5;
W.9-10.2; W.9-10.2a; W.9-10.2c; W.9-10.2e; W.9-10.2f; W.9-10.4; W.9-10.5;

Objectives:
- Students will review and discuss the vocabulary work for Reading Assignment 4
- Students will imagine what they think the world will be like 50 years from now and write a descriptive essay detailing what they imagine

Purposes:
The purposes of this lesson are:
- To make sure students have the correct understanding of the vocabulary words for RA 2
- To practice creative thinking while considering how things might actually progress and change over the next 50 years
- To gain an appreciation for Ray Bradbury's insights and conclusions as he wrote in 1951

Activity #1
Students were supposed to have done the vocabulary pages for Reading Assignment 4. Take a few minutes to review the answers to those pages with students so you're sure they're on the right track. Do this in whatever way suits your teaching style.

Activity #2
Distribute Writing Assignment 2 (located in the Student Workbook in the Writing Assignments section as well as on page 212 for your convenience). Discuss the directions in detail and advise students as to when the assignment will be collected for grading.

Students should use the remainder of this class time to work on the writing assignment.

VOCABULARY WORK FOR ASSIGNMENT 4

PART I: Using Prior Knowledge And Contextual Clues

Use any clues you can find in the sentences from the text combined with your prior knowledge and write what you think the bold word means.

1. The other firemen waited behind him, in the darkness, their faces illumined faintly by the **smoldering** foundation.

    Burning with little smoke and no flame

2. The other was like a chunk of burnt pinelog he was carrying along as penance for some **obscure** sin.

    Not clear; partially hidden

3. Two dozen of them flurried, wavering, **indecisive**, three miles off.

    Not able to make a decision

4. And there on the small screen was the burnt house, and the crowd and something with a sheet over it and out of the sky, fluttering, came the helicopter like a **grotesque** flower.

    Bizarre; distorted

5. ...Montag might...see himself dramatized, described, made over, standing there, **limned** in the bright small television screen from outside....

    Described; portrayed; delineated

6. He saw a great **juggernaut** of stars form in the sky and threaten to roll over and crush him.

    Overwhelmingly advancing sight crushing all in its path

7. He smelled the heavy musk like perfume mingled with blood and the gummed exhalation of the animal's breath, all **cardamon** and moss and ragweed odor in this huge night where the trees ran at him....

    An Indian spice

8. The most important single thing we had to pound into ourselves is that we were not important; we mustn't be **pedants**; we were not to feel superior to anyone else in the world.

    Those who flaunt their knowledge

9. There was a silly damn bird called a Phoenix back before Christ; every few hundred years he built a **pyre** and burned himself up.

    A pile of combustible materials for burning a corpse

Vocabulary Work For Fahrenheit 451 Assignment 4, Page 2

PART II: Matching
Considering the usage in Part I, match the vocabulary words to their definitions.

E 1. smoldering   A. Described; portrayed; delineated

H 2. obscure   B. Not able to make a decision

B 3. indecisive   C. A pile of combustible materials for burning a corpse

D 4. grotesque   D. Bizarre; distorted

A 5. limned   E. Burning with little smoke and no flame

F 6. juggernaut   F. Overwhelmingly advancing sight crushing all in its path

I 7. cardamon   G. Those who flaunt their knowledge

G 8. pedants   H. Not clear; partially hidden; remote

C 9. pyre   I. An Indian spice

Part III: Cloze Passage
Fill in the blanks with the appropriate vocabulary words from the list above.

The PEDANTS predicted that a meteor would fall. An object initially appeared OBSCURE in the sky, but suddenly the full JUGGERNAUT approached no longer leaving the skeptics INDECISIVE about the forecasted event. The rather GROTESQUE presence of this phenomenon in the night sky was now before them. When it hit, the meteor created a SMOLDERING crater that gave off smells of sulphur and a faint hint of CARDAMON, as it had landed in a field where this spice was grown. Depending on the conditions LIMNED in his insurance policy, the farmer might get reimbursed for the loss of his crops, but probably not for the cow that dropped dead at the shock of the event. The farmer would have to make a PYRE and dispose of the poor animal.

Vocabulary Work For Fahrenheit 451 Assignment 4, Page 3

PART IV: Words In Practice
Answer the questions and be able to give short explanations to justify your answers.

1. Would a smoldering fire keep you very warm on a cold winter's night?

    not very

2. Name an obscure person in the field of sports, music, or movies.

    any relatively unknown person

3. In what occupation would it be bad to be indecisive?

    surgeon, traffic cop, any appropriate answer

4. At what holiday might you wear something grotesque?

    Halloween

5. What kind of a document might have conditions limned in its pages?

    insurance policy; any appropriate answer

6. Is a juggernaut something to embrace or run from?

    run from

7. Would cardamon be more likely to be used by a chef or a mechanic?

    chef

8. What characteristics would someone who is a pedant have?

    smart, egocentric, probably not well-liked; any appropriate answer

9. What foreign people from long ago are known for funeral pyres?

    Vikings; any appropriate answer

VOCABULARY CROSSWORD KEY
READING ASSIGNMENT 4
Fahrenheit 451

```
                    J
                    U
    L I M N E D     G
      N             G
P E D A N T S       E
Y   E       S       R
R   C A R D A M O N
E   I       O   A
    S       L   U
    I       D   T
    V       E
    E     G R O T E S Q U E
            I       C
            N       U
            G       R
                    E
```

A pile of combustible materials for burning a corpse (4)
Bizarre; distorted (9)
Burning with little smoke and no flame (10)
Described (6)
Italian herb (8)
Not able to make a decision (10)
Not readily noticed or seen; not commonly known (7)
Overwhelming, advancing sight crushing all in its path (10)
Those who flaunt their knowledge (7)

WRITING ASSIGNMENT 2
Fahrenheit 451

PROMPT

Ray Bradbury wrote Fahrenheit back in 1951, yet his work is still very relevant today. It is amazing that he was able to foresee the progression of so many things so accurately. When he wrote this book, television had just been invented. There were no such things as "ear buds" or "ear phones." The world of micro-technology and computers had not yet been discovered.

No one really knows how things will be in the future, but at one time or another, we all think about it. What is your vision of the future? What do you think our world will be like 50 years from now?

Your assignment is to describe our world as you believe it will be 50 years from now.

PREWRITING

- Choose five major topics for your composition--five areas of our lives you will describe. Some areas to consider are government, ecology, business, lifestyle, transportation, jobs/workplaces, family, economy, food, shelter, clothing, music, architecture, agriculture, and entertainment, but don't feel limited by these; you may consider other areas as well.
- Make five columns on a piece of paper and title each with one of the five topics you have chosen. Under each topic, in the appropriate columns, jot down notes about how you think each will be in 50 years.

DRAFTING

- Write a paragraph in which you introduce the idea that you believe life will be different in 50 years, especially in the areas you have chosen to write about (your five topics).
- In the body of your composition, write one paragraph for each of your topics. Use a topic sentence to state exactly how you believe that topic will be different in 50 years, and then fill in your paragraph with specific examples from your column of notes. Do this for each of your five topics, one paragraph for each topic.
- Write a paragraph in which you summarize your ideas and conclude your composition.

When you finish the rough draft of your paper, ask a student who sits near you to read it. After reading your rough draft, he/she should tell you what he/she liked best about your work, which parts were difficult to understand, and ways in which your work could be improved. Reread your paper considering your critic's comments, and make the corrections you think are necessary.

PROOFREADING

Do a final proofreading of your paper, double-checking your grammar, spelling, organization, and the clarity of your ideas. Make a final, good copy to submit for grading.

LESSON TEN
Fahrenheit 451

CCSS: L.9-10.1; L.9-10.2; L.9-10.4; L.9-10.4a; L.9-10.5;
W.9-10.2; W.9-10.2a; W.9-10.2c; W.9-10.2e; W.9-10.2f; W.9-10.4; W.9-10.5;

Objectives:
- Students will complete Reading Assignment 4
- Students will participate in writing conferences to receive evaluation of and help with their writing skills

Purposes:
The purposes of this lesson are:
- To finish reading Fahrenheit 451
- To conference with students one-on-one regarding their writing skills

Activity #1
During this class time, students will read the remainder of Fahrenheit 451. You need to decide how you want them to do this, whether you want them to read silently, orally in pairs, or orally in small groups. Direct students accordingly.

Activity #2
While students are reading, hold writing conferences with individual students. You can use Writing Assignment 1 or Writing Assignment 2 as the basis for your conference. Offer praise for positive points about the students' work, and suggest ways in which the writing could be made better. Talk with students to find out if they like to write, what kinds of writing they like to do, or if they don't like to write, find out why not. Just try to get an idea of how each student feels about writing in general and about the writing assignment you are evaluating, in particular.

A Writing Evaluation Form is included in this guide for your convenience.

WRITING EVALUATION
Fahrenheit 451

Name _____ Date _____

Assignment _____

SKILL	Excellent	Good	Average	Fair	Poor
Grammar	5	4	3	2	1
Spelling	5	4	3	2	1
Punctuation	5	4	3	2	1
Organization	5	4	3	2	1
Content	5	4	3	2	1
Support &/or Development	5	4	3	2	1
Legibility	5	4	3	2	1
	5	4	3	2	1

Strengths:

Weaknesses:

Comments:

LESSON ELEVEN
Fahrenheit 451

CCSS: SL.9-10.1a-d; SL.9-10.4; RL.9-10.1; RL.9-10.2; RL.9-10.3; RL.9-10.4; L.9-10.4

Objectives:
- Students will participate in a group discussion of Reading Assignment 4
- Students will cite textual evidence to support their answers to discussion questions
- Students will analyze the characters and their relationships
- Students will consider the written details of the text and their effect on the story
- Students will complete the pre-reading vocabulary worksheet for Reading Assignment 4

Purposes:
The purposes of this lesson are:
- To review the main events and ideas in Reading Assignment 4
- To understand characters and their motivations
- To look for parallels to draw from the story into students' current lives
- To examine details for meaning and apply the meaning to the larger themes of the text
- To become familiar with selected vocabulary words, their definitions, and usage for the end purpose of assimilating the words into students' own vocabularies as well as providing for a better understanding of the text.

Activity #1 (Optional)
If you want to check to see that students have read the assignment, you can use the Multiple Choice questions for RA 4. Distribute copies (not in the student workbook), give students time to complete the quiz, and check the papers in your usual method.

Answer Key For Multiple Choice: Reading Assignment 4:
1. D   2. A   3. D   4. B   5. A   6. C   7. D   8. B   9. A   10. D   11. D   12. A   13. C   14. D

Activity #2
Work through the Characters, and Events and Points of Interest graphic organizers together as a class. Students should have taken some notes as they were reading. This review will help complete their notes for study purposes and serve as a review of the main events in the reading assignment.

Activity #3
Discuss the Discussion Questions for Reading Assignment 4. See Lesson Four for additional notes.

MULTIPLE CHOICE: READING ASSIGNMENT 4
Fahrenheit 451

1. Who is the final informant on Montag's home?
    A. Faber
    B. Mrs. Phelps
    C. Beatty
    D. Mildred

2. Why does Montag kill Captain Beatty?
    A. Montag kills Beatty to protect Faber.
    B. Montag kills Beatty for revenge.
    C. Montag kills Beatty to protect Mildred.
    D. Montag kills Beatty by accident; his finger slips on the flame thrower trigger.

3. Why doesn't Montag run away before he kills Beatty?
    A. He is mesmerized by the fire at his house.
    B. He wants to make sure Mildred is safe.
    C. Faber tells him to stay where he is.
    D. He knows the mechanical Hound is in the neighborhood and will kill him.

4. Where does Montag go after killing Beatty?
    A. He goes to the firehouse.
    B. He goes to Faber's house.
    C. He goes to St. Louis to meet Faber.
    D. He goes to find Mrs. Phelps.

5. Why does Montag go to the river?
    A. The river is away from the city; it is his best chance for survival.
    B. Faber tells him to collect books that are stashed there, then to meet him in St. Louis.
    C. The river will lead him to the train tracks, where he can jump a train to safety.
    D. Montag is hungry and thirsty; he plans to find food and water to drink there.

6. Why does Montag take whiskey, a suitcase, and some of Faber's dirty clothes with him?
    A. He will use them to disguise himself as a drunken bum, to get out of the city.
    B. He takes the whiskey as an antiseptic, the clothes to wear, and the suitcase to collect any books he may find out in the country.
    C. He needs some strong-smelling things to throw the Hound off of his scent.
    D. Faber gives them to Montag and indicates he will let him know later what they are for.

7. What unusual sight does Montag see near the railroad tracks?
    A. Montag sees the remains of a mechanical Hound.
    B. Montag sees flowers growing.
    C. Montag sees milk and fruit left there.
    D. Montag sees men warming themselves by a fire.

8. During the manhunt for Montag, why do the authorities identify an innocent man as Montag and kill him?
    A. They don't know what Montag looks like; they make a mistake.
    B. They want to look successful to their viewers and put a neat ending on the event.
    C. The tracking computer malfunctions, idenifying the wrong man.
    D. Faber gives Montag's clothes to an innocent man so the authorities will follow him instead of Montag.

9. Who are the men Montag meets away from the city?
    A. They are former teachers and philosophers, outcasts from society.
    B. They are all former firemen, just like Montag.
    C. They are the men who taught Beatty all about literature.
    D. They are farmers who are unaware of the conditions in the city.

10. How is literature being preserved?
    A. There is an old mine being used to house books the men collect.
    B. Each man carries one book to safeguard.
    C. The men hide books under the railroad tracks.
    D. Each man memorizes a chapter or a book.

11. What book does Montag preserve?
    A. He saves *War And Peace*.
    B. He saves *The Constitution Of The United States*.
    C. He saves *Macbeth*.
    D. He saves *The Book Of Ecclesiastes*.

12. What happens to the city?
    A. It and its residents are obliterated by bombs in the war.
    B. It suffers extreme damage, but the residents are able to rebuild.
    C. It miraculously escapes damage.
    D. It is, ironically, destroyed by fire.

13. What is the mission of Montag and the others after the war ends?
    A. They want to teach everyone how to read.
    B. They want to find any remaining family members.
    C. They want to learn from previous mistakes and always remember.
    D. They want to convert any survivors to their way of thinking.

14. What are the leaves of the tree of life for?
    A. They are food for the starving people.
    B. They are clothing for the survivors.
    C. They are poultices for the radiation burns.
    D. They are for the healing of the nations.

CHARACTERS SUGGESTED NOTES
Reading Assignment 4 Fahrenheit 451

As you read Assignment 4 use this graphic organizer to jot down information about characters.

MONTAG

-- did what Beatty told him to do & burned his own home
-- "hands" still acting on their own, as a separate entity...killing Beatty
-- thinks Beatty wanted to die
-- berates himself as a fool but plunges forward instead of turning himself in
-- seems to take some satisfaction in calling in the alarm on fireman Black's house
-- commits himself to running away, goes to the river (baptism to a new life)
-- meets Granger & seems to fit in with Granger & friends
-- looks forward, not back

BEATTY

-- seems confident that he'll get rid of Montag
-- pushes Montag by being condescending
-- figures out about the green bullet
-- threatens to find Faber
-- is killed by Montag...set on fire
-- Montag thinks Beatty wanted to die
-- berates Montag for reciting poetry and reading literature but does significantly more of that himself, than Montag did

FABER

-- commits to action by going to St. Louis
-- helps Montag escape
-- by going to St. Louis, he escapes the annihilation of the city (though we don't know if St. Louis was also annihilated)

MILDRED

-- turns in the alarm on her own house
-- speaks of the house in 3rd person
-- is pale...no lipstick, floured face
-- doesn't even acknowledge Montag
-- zooms away in the beetle

GRANGER

-- practical, book-lover & well-read
-- tells story of Phoenix
-- is bothered by city events, but has a calm resolve to do what he feels he needs to do
-- seems to accept his lot in life while doing what he can to preserve and sustain

EVENTS & POINTS OF INTEREST SUGGESTED NOTES
Reading Assignment 4 Fahrenheit 451

As you read Assignment 4 make notes of the series of main events that take place. Put them in the order that they are given in the text.

- Beatty makes Montag burn his own house with a flamethrower, not kerosene & match.
- Beatty discovers the green bullet & threatens to track down the person on the other end (Faber), so Montag sets Beatty on fire and Beatty dies.
- The Mechanical Hound attacks Montag. Montag sets the Hound on fire but gets a short dose from the needle before the Hound is destroyed.
- Montag grabs a few remaining books and leaves the scene, escaping as well as he can.
- He is almost run over by a car full of teenagers, out for fun.
- Montag hides books at fireman Black's home and calls in an alarm.
- Montag arrives at Faber's house, chats a bit, & gives him some money. Faber advises Montag to head for the river and to follow the railroad tracks into the country, where he may find hobo camps. Faber says he will be leaving for St. Louis early in the morning, that Montag should later try to contact him there. Montag takes Faber's dirty clothes and whiskey to throw the Hound off of his scent.
- He makes it to the river, floats downstream, and later finds the railroad tracks and follows them until he finds a hobo camp.
- At the hobo camp, Montag meets Granger and his friends. On TV, he watches the authorities pursuing him until they arrest the wrong person (to bring the case to a close).
- Granger explains that he and his friends--and people all over the country--have memorized books or parts of books, waiting for a time when they can be written down again. Montag becomes the Book of Ecclesiastes.
- The city is bombed, obliterated by the planes' bombs.
- Granger talks about the Phoenix.
- The men head towards the city.

OTHER POINTS OF INTEREST TO IDENTIFY OR KNOW THE SIGNIFICANCE OF:
The river is ultimately Montag's means of escape from the Hound & his past. Montag has a symbolic baptism into a new life in the river.

The railroad tracks lead Montag to a new life with Granger and the other literate hobos.

The Book of Ecclesiastes is the book of the Bible that Montag "becomes." It is considered to be the "teaching" book of the Bible, one book that is exceptionally full of wisdom and practical living advice.

Phoenix The story of the phoenix is the story of mankind. Mankind destroys itself (the city & bombs) and rises from the ashes of the destruction to be new and better again. It is also Montag's story, as he rises from the ashes of his home and starts a new life.

STUDY & DISCUSSION QUESTIONS SUGGESTED ANSWERS
Reading Assignment 4 Fahrenheit 451

1. Beatty confesses that he sent the Hound to Montag's home. Why did he send it?
   Beatty was trying to warn him away from the books and to scare him back into line.

2. Compare the Mildred we saw at the beginning of the book with the Mildred who flees the house and zooms off in a beetle.
   When we first met Mildred, she was pale and oblivious to Montag. When she flees the house, she is again pale and oblivious to Montag. She speaks of "the poor family" in the third person, as if it is someone else's home being destroyed.

3. What is the significance of the vacuum that occurs when Montag destroys the TV walls?
   Older television sets were made with cathode ray tubes which contained a vacuum, or space in which there was no air or pressure. When broken, the tubes would release the vacuum, which most of the time just caused a lot of sparks and lights, but sometimes could seriously hurt a person if they were close by and the toxic portions got into their lungs, something Montag holds his breath to avoid. The vacuum he releases by burning the TV walls however is symbolic of the vacuum caused by the TV, as well as the lack of meaningful content on the screen.

3. What motivates Montag to pull the trigger on the flame-thrower and set Beatty on fire?
   Beatty says he'll track down the person on the other end of Montag's green bullet radio device. Montag knows this means Faber will be killed.

4. Montag believes Beatty wanted to die. Explain why you agree or disagree with him.
   Answers will vary.

5. Montag wonders if the teenagers who almost ran him over just for fun were the ones who ran over Clarisse. Is there any evidence to support this thought? Based on evidence in the book, would you say Clarisse's death was likely a random or a premeditated act?
   Based on the fact that Clarisse's whole family deserted their house and the way Beatty talked about her, Clarisse's death was more likely a premeditated act since she was a known free-thinker. We're never told whether or not Beatty suspected she was affecting Montag and actually had her eliminated or not. Either way, her death does not seem to be accidental.

6. Is what Montag does to Mrs. Black's house a just thing to do? Is it moral? Is it right? Explain why or why not.
   Answers will vary.

7. Explain the symbolism of the things that Montag does in the river.
   Montag is baptized into a new life. He sheds his old life, his old self as he sheds his own clothes. He puts on the new clothes of Faber's old life, a life of books, of thinking, of living. The river holds Montag "comfortably" and he leisurely floats down the river, finally having a time to consider all that has happened.

Study & Discussion Questions Suggested Answers: Fahrenheit 451 RA 4, Page 2

8. How is the fire in the countryside different from the fire Montag has experienced?

    The fire lit by the men in the countryside is a warming fire, not a destructive one. It brings people, including Montag, together rather than tearing them apart. Montag realizes "He had never thought in his life that it [fire] could give as well as take."

9. Montag listens to the silence and wonders how Millie would take it. What do you think Millie would do if she were with Montag? Do you think she could adapt?

    Answers will vary. Some points to consider:
    - Millie overdosed on the sleeping pills. Was she as unhappy as Montag, just unable to face it, seeing no alternative?
    - Millie didn't understand why Montag longed for books; she couldn't see their value.
    - When Montag confronted the group of women with conversation and books, Mildred kept turning the conversation towards things from the parlor walls.
    - Millie burned the books and turned in Montag.
    - When the parlor walls were turned off, Millie was uncomfortable, looking towards them.

10. Why does the search team find someone else to kill in place of Montag?

    The government needs to maintain the order they have developed by allowing society to remain distracted and complacent. In order to provide a satisfying story that will keep people feeling good and not thinking too hard, they needed to find a scapegoat.

11. The men in the countryside have a plan for saving books. What is it, and do you think it is a good plan?

    The men plan to memorize all the books they can in order to copy them down again one day. Answers will vary for the second half of the question.

12. Explain Granger's metaphor of the Phoenix.

    The phoenix is a mythical bird that burns itself every thousand years, and is reborn again from the ashes. Granger compares humanity to that bird, saying that humans have a tendency to make the same mistakes every few generations, and are then forced to rebuild everything from those ashes. Granger also states that a few more people learn from those mistakes each time it happens, and hopes that in time there will be enough of these people that the cycle will not have to begin again.

13. Explain why Granger misses his grandfather but Montag won't miss Millie.

    Granger's grandfather interacted with him; he did things and was a part of Granger's life. Millie was never a part of Montag's life in the same way Granger's grandfather was a part of his life. Montag and Millie lived in the same house, but they never did any meaningful activities together and rarely even spoke of anything beyond the surface of the daily routine. She only interacted with the parlor walls.

14. Why did Ray Bradbury make Montag the Book of Ecclesiastes rather than some other book?

    Some consider the Book of Ecclesiastes to be the "teaching" book of the Bible, the one with the most wisdom for the daily life of mankind.

Study & Discussion Questions Discussion Guide: Fahrenheit 451 RA 4, Page 3

ADDITIONAL PASSAGES FOR DISCUSSION

1. "By the time the consequences catch up with you, it's too late, isn't it, Montag?"
    Beatty is lecturing Montag, condemning him for not heeding warnings that the consequences of his actions would one day become real, for thinking nothing would happen to *him*. The irony is that the consequences of Beatty's nettling Montag caught up with *him*; he was set on fire and killed before he could defend himself.

2. "Now, Montag, you're a burden. And fire will lift you off of my shoulders, clean, quick, sure; nothing to rot later. Antibiotic, aesthetic, practical."
    Again, ironically, Beatty is the one that is destroyed. He became a burden to Montag, and fire lifted Beatty off of Montag's shoulders--clean, quick, and sure.

3. Beatty . . . twisted in on himself like a charred wax doll and lay silent.
    The wax doll image returns. Previously used to describe Mildred, here it describes the dead Beatty.

4. [Montag] stood and he had only one leg. The other was like a chunk of burnt pine log he was carrying along as a penance for some obscure sin.
    Points For Discussion: Discuss what "sin" is and what "penance" is, then have your students try to figure out what Bradbury means by this sentence. What could Montag's "sin" have been? Is his leg really burned? What is wrong with his leg? Why would this imagery have been used?
    His leg is not burned but is feeling the effects of the drugs from the needle of the Mechanical Hound. His "sin" could be going against society, going against the accepted lifestyle of the masses of people. Oppositely, it could be his penance for NOT taking action against that lifestyle sooner. Or perhaps it was a penance for the sin of ruining so many innocent people's lives while he was a fireman. There are many possible answers.

5. . . . simply a number of children out for a long night of roaring five or six hundred miles in a few moonlit hours, their faces icy with wind, and coming home or not coming at dawn, alive or not alive, that made the adventure.
    Points For Discussion: The "children" (presumably teenagers) are "cruising" or "joy riding," just out for "fun." What do they consider "fun"? What does it say about their society, that they come home at dawn "alive or not alive" but either way have had an adventure?

6. They would have killed me, thought Montag. . . . For no reason at all in the world they would have killed me.
    The teens cruising in the car are the society's next generation. The present generation doesn't mind killing people who go against it's policies. Perhaps Bradbury is suggesting that the next step in the degeneration of society is to not value any life at all--either one's own or anyone else's.
    Points For Discussion: Ask your students if they have heard of this kind of thing in the news--random killings. What does that say about our society? How can we curb this disturbing activity?

Study & Discussion Questions Discussion Guide: Fahrenheit 451 RA 4, Page 4

Additional Passages For Discussion Continued

7. Mrs. Black, are you asleep in there? . . . The house did not reply.

   Houses have voices. After all, Mildred expected the door voice to tell her when someone was on the outside of her home, waiting to be let in. This is a reversal of that. Montag is outside. Is Mrs. Black inside? This is an extension of the living house metaphor that has been used throughout the book as well as the continuation of the animate/inanimate confusion. Mrs Black... asleep. Inanimate? House speaking. Animate? Certainly at least an example of personification.

8. He felt as if he had left a stage behind and many actors. He felt as if he had left the great seance and all the murmuring ghosts. He was moving from an unreality that was frightening into a reality that was unreal because it was new.

   Points For Discussion: Why would Montag feel like he had left a stage and actors? Note that the "murmuring ghosts" is also an example of foreshadowing, since everyone in the city will later die in the bombing. Point out the juxtaposition of reality and unreality in this quote. See how many different examples of reality and unreality they can see in it. How can a reality be "unreal because it [is] new"?

   In light of this quote, consider the wax doll imagery that has been used. Also consider the parlor walls. What is the stage? Who are the actors? Is the "family" actors? Or are people like Beatty actually the actors?

9. . . . the river was mild and leisurely, going away from the people who ate shadows for breakfast and steam for lunch and vapors for supper.

   Discuss the imagery in this quote. What do shadows, steam, and vapors all have in common? Can they be eaten? If not, then what is this quote actually saying? And why would Bradbury choose to say it this way rather than straight out in plain words?

   Shadows, steam, and vapors are all impossible to hold; they are nothing concrete. Of course people can't eat them. These are images saying that the people intellectually and emotionally consumed nothing substantial. Like the dialogue from the parlor walls...the "family" didn't ever really say *anything*. They spoke empty, meaningless words. The whole society is built on nothing.

10. This was all he wanted now. Some sign that the immense world would accept him and give him the long time he needed to think all the things that must be thought.

    Points For Discussion: Isn't wanting the immense world to accept us something we all want? Why would Montag want that, in particular? What does Montag want to think about? Have your class brainstorm a list of things Montag would think about. Answers may include his marriage, Clarisse, why Beatty knew so much literature, what Faber is doing in St. Louis (if St. Louis exists), how society will rebuild itself...any reasonable answer related to the book would be acceptable; there are many, many things Montag would think about.

Study & Discussion Questions Discussion Guide: Fahrenheit 451 RA 4, Page 5

Additional Passages For Discussion, Continued

11. And he was surprised to learn how certain he suddenly was of a single fact he could not prove. Once, long ago, Clarisse had walked here, where he was walking now."
    Point For Discussion: Why would Montag think Clarisse had walked there? Is this meant to be taken literally, or is it a figurative suggestion? Perhaps Montag finally understood Clarisse's appreciation for nature.

12. . . . there was a foolish and yet delicious sense of knowing himself as an animal come from the forest, drawn by the fire.
    Discuss the primeval imagery used here. It fits in with Montag's rebirth after his baptism in the river.

13. But you can't *make* people listen. They have to come round in their own time, wondering what happened and why the world blew up under them.
    Points For Discussion: Is it true that you can't make people listen? Does it mean "listen" literally, or does it mean you can't make people change their minds to your point of view? Did Mildred and her friends "listen" to Montag? How can you tell when you *should* listen to what someone else says? How can you tell when you should follow someone else's advice? To whom should we listen?

14. ". . . shake the tree and knock the great sloth down on his ass."
    Granger's grandfather was speaking about security, that security is like a sloth. He believed that to live life to its fullest, one needs to throw security out the window and go do things, see things, and experience all that one can.
    Points For Discussion: Is this good advice? Is it wise to always throw caution to the wind and just "go for it" all the time? What indicators are there to let you know when you should or shouldn't throw caution to the wind?

15. Silently, Granger arose, felt of his arms and legs, swearing, swearing incessantly under his breath, tears dripping from his face.
    Why are tears dripping from Granger's face? How is this detail more effective than just saying, "Granger was sad because the city was destroyed"? Why is he swearing? Do swearing and crying go together? Why or why not? What is Granger feeling when he arises?

16. In the trees, the birds that had flown away quickly now came back and settled down.
    This is a small detail, but it speaks volumes. Mankind has dealt himself a blow, but nature resumes the routine it has observed for eons.

LESSONS TWELVE - UNIT END
Fahrenheit 451

ASSIGNMENTS AND ACTIVITIES

Now that the reading of the book is completed, it is up to you how much more you want to do with the book. The next section of this teaching guide has a variety of mini-lessons, lessons, projects, activities, and writing assignments from which you may choose to fill out and complete the study of Fahrenheit 451.

The first lessons are based on the elements of fiction and cover the whole book. Following those are additional lessons, writing assignments, and activities related to each reading assignment.

The Student Workbook section has all the student materials necessary for completing all of these lessons and activities.

NOTE! Be sure to look through the Student Workbook. There are some extra pages in there that are not duplicated in the Teacher's Guide. There are some graphic organizers, reader response sheets and a few other things.

LESSON: HISTORICAL CONTEXT
Fahrenheit 451

CCSS: W.9-10.7; W.9-10.8; W.9-10.9; SL.9-10.1

Objectives:
- Students will review US and world events from 1941-1951
- Students will consider, evaluate, and discuss the effect of US and world events on Bradbury's writing of Fahrenheit 451
- Students will correlate specific elements of Fahrenheit 451 to their historical context

Purposes:
The purposes of this lesson are:
- To show the historical context of the novel Fahrenheit 451
- To get students to correlate events from the past with current events and policies and to project what these things may mean for the future

Prior To Class: Set up your classroom in such a way that allows all students to see your computer screen.

Activity #1
Have students write down 5 things they know or think happened in the 1940's. Collect the lists and (without identifying the writers) briefly run through student responses orally, writing the most important ones on your board. Allow for short, light discussions.

Activity #2
Search "News 1940s" on the Internet. There are many sites that give the main events of each year and/or decade. When you find a good site, review its contents in detail with students. You might even go into 1950-1952, since Fahrenheit 451 was published in 1953.

Activity #3
Ask students to think for a few minutes about the events you have discussed and to think about them in context of the book Fahrenheit 451. Guide your students through a discussion exploring the effects of the events of 1940-1950 on Bradbury and his writing of Fahrenheit 451.

The following Historical Context worksheet is in the Student Workbook. You may give it to students prior to Activity #2, to fill in as you do the Internet research together as a class, or you may want to have students take notes on it during your class discussion, while you use the Suggested Answer key to the worksheet as your discussion guide.

HISTORICAL CONTEXT SUGGESTED ANSWERS
Fahrenheit 451

In 1951 Ray Bradbury wrote a short story ("The Fireman") on which Fahrenheit 451 (published in 1953) was based. What was going on in Bradbury's world and in his mind to prompt him to create Montag's world? Take a few minutes to jot down some things that were going on between 1941-1953. Then, see which of these things you can make correlations to in Fahrenheit 451.

World Events:
1941: Pearl Harbor, Siege of Leningrad 1942: Anne Frank Goes Into Hiding, Battle of Midway, Manhattan Project begins 1944: D-Day 1945: FDR dies, Germans surrender, UN founded, US drops atomic bombs on Japan & Japan surrenders 1946: Nuremberg trials, Peron becomes President of Argentina 1947: Marshall Plan, Taft-Hartley Act 1948: Gandhi Assassinated, Apartheid begins, State of Israel is founded 1949: China becomes Communist, NATO established, USSR gets atomic bomb 1950: Korean War begins, McCarthy begins Communist hunt 1951: Rosenbergs sentenced to death

Entertainment:
1941: *Citizen Kane* film 1942: *Casablanca, White Christmas* 1944: first network censorship 1945: Steinbeck's *Cannery Row,* Wright's *Black Boy* 1947: Jackie Robinson joins the Dodgers, Babe Ruth dies 1949: Orwell's *Nineteen Eighty-Four,* 45 rpm records, abstract expression 1950: first Peanuts cartoon

Science & Technology:
1941: Jeep invented 1942: napalm & radar invented 1944: DNA discovered, ballpoint pens 1945: first computer, microwave oven, penicillin invented 1946: carbon-14 dating method is developed 1947: sound barrier broken, Polaroid cameras invented 1948: big bang theory, Planned Parenthood founded, World Health Organization founded, Orville Wright dies 1949: high-compression V8 car engines 1950: first organ transplant (kidney) 1951: 1st color tv, first solo flight across the North Pole, oral contraceptive developed, first nuclear power plant in US

Social:
1946: bikinis, Dr. Spock's baby & child care book 1948: Truman ends racial segregation in military, Hollywood Ten jailed for refusing to say if they were Communists or not 1950: first credit card

Historical Context: Fahrenheit 451 Suggested Answers Page 2

Below are a few examples of how the many changes in lifestyle, advances and developments in science and technology, and world events may have influenced *Fahrenheit 451*. You may want to include much more, depending on how in-depth you want to dig into historical context.

EVENT	EFFECT IN FAHRENHEIT 451
WWII, Korean War, atomic bombs developed & used	References to the War, planes flying over, the final annihilation of the city
Development & expanded use of television, invention of color TV	Parlor walls, insipid programming
V-8 engines, sports cars, improving roads	Fast driving, kids cruising
Dr. Spock's baby book, Planned Parenthood, oral contraceptives	Mildred's friends' attitudes towards children
Censorship	Burning of the books, media censorship
McCarthyism	Persecution of those who think other than the State

LESSON: POINT OF VIEW
Fahrenheit 451

CCSS: None of the CCSS relate specifically to point of view, but it is included in this guide as an important element of fiction.

Objectives:
- Students will review the types of point of view.
- Students will decide which point of view fits Fahrenheit 451 and explain why.
- Students will state why it is important for this novel to be from Montag's point of view.

Purposes:
The purposes of this lesson are:
- To review point of view as an element of fiction
- To apply point of view to Fahrenheit 451
- To evaluate the use of point of view in the novel

Suggested Lesson Plan

Review Point of View as an element of fiction with your students. Discuss the various types of point of view. A very basic list is included on the following page. If you want to expand upon that, there is room for students to add more on their Student Workbook page.

Give students time individually or in groups to respond to the questions on the following page, which is also in their Student Workbooks, then discuss the questions and answers in detail.

POINT OF VIEW SUGGESTED ANSWERS
Fahrenheit 451

Point Of View

Point of View is the lens through which the story is told.
There are several different kinds of Point of View:
- **First Person:** Told by a character in the story using "I"
- **Third Person Limited:** Told by a character in the story without "I"; we only know what the character knows
- **Third Person Omniscient:** Told by the author (someone outside the book); all-knowing

Based on these descriptions, which do you think fits Fahrenheit 451? Why?
The Third Person Limited point of view is used in Fahrenheit 451. The story is told from Montag's point of view without his directly being the narrator; we learn everything from a third person who seems like a narrator, but it's all from Montag's point of view. No information that Montag doesn't know is given.

Why is it important that the story is told from Montag's point of view?

Montag is Everyman; the average person, trying to make it through life as well as he can. We can relate to him as he discovers a lifestyle he had not previously known existed; we feel for him when Mildred doesn't respond to him; we root for him as he tries to break away from being a fireman of destruction and plunges forward into a new and thoughtful life.

More than that, though, he makes it to the end of the book (unlike Beatty and Mildred, for example) so that we know there are folks like him and Granger who will start civilization anew from the ashes. This is key in the broadest message of the book.

LESSON: SETTING & CONFLICT
Fahrenheit 451

CCSS: None of the CCSS actually address setting and conflict, but a brief study of them is included since they are important elements of fiction.

Objectives:
- Students will respond to the question, "Why doesn't the exact year of the setting matter?".
- Students will review main types of conflicts and will give examples of them from the text.

Purposes:
The purposes of this lesson are:
- To touch upon two important elements of fiction: setting and conflict
- To make students aware of the setting of the novel
- To review types of conflicts and apply them to Fahrenheit 451

Suggested Lesson Plan
Take a few minutes to review the main elements of fiction with your students:
- point of view
- setting
- conflict
- character
- plot
- symbolism
- theme
- style, tone, language

Use the page which follows as a guide to discussing setting and character in Fahrenheit 451. It can be done orally, together as a class--or you could have students do it individually or in small groups (or some combination thereof). If it is not done together as a whole-class activity, take time to discuss it after students have developed responses.

SETTING & CONFLICT SUGGESTED ANSWERS
Fahrenheit 451

Setting

Though it is never stated, we assume the setting is in the United States, at some time in the future. Enough time has passed for two nuclear wars to have happened since the year 2022. Perhaps Bradbury set it 100 years into the future from 1950; it's never made completely clear, but it doesn't really matter what the exact year is. Why not?
- First of all, Mr. Bradbury wouldn't be able to know exactly how far in the future it would take to progress this far.
- Secondly, the book is a warning of how things could become at some point in the future if people stay on the same path they were on when he wrote it.
- Also, the book is a broader statement on humanity and the cycle of civilizations, so assigning a particular year would limit the scope of the work.

Conflict

The basic types of conflict are:
- person vs. person
- person vs. self
- person vs. society
- person vs. nature

Main conflicts usually occur with the main character being the "person" against something. There can also be conflicts with other characters against the same elements. Think about Fahrenheit 451 and complete the exercise below with examples from Fahrenheit 451.

Examples of Person vs. Person
Montag vs. Beatty *
Montag vs. Mildred
Montag vs. Mildred's friends

Examples of Person vs. Self
Montag vs. himself *, wondering if he is a fool to step outside of the norm
Faber vs. himself, wishing he had the courage to take action

Examples of Person vs. Society
Montag vs. society *
Clarisse & her family vs. society
Granger & friends vs society

Examples of Person vs. Nature
Humanity vs the natural world *
Montag in the natural world when he leaves the city, though he actually is being more helped by nature than going against it.

* is the main conflict of this type   This is not an exhaustive list.

LESSON: CHARACTER DEVELOPMENT
Fahrenheit 451

CCSS: RL.9-10.1; RL.9-10.3

Objectives:
- Students will review the terms "protagonist" and "antagonist" and determine into which of these two categories characters from Fahrenheit 451 belong.
- Students will consider the purpose and importance of each major and minor character in Fahrenheit 451.
- Students will determine which character(s) in Fahrenheit are dynamic and which are static.
- Students will trace the development of the dynamic character Montag throughout the book.

Purposes:
The purposes of this lesson are:
- To review the elements of characterization and character development
- To show students how to evaluate a person's character by examining words, actions, and appearance
- To examine the cause-effect relationship between events that happen and ways those events can cause thought and personality changes
- To learn to look for subtle changes in speech or behavior that indicate changes going on within a person

Notes: This lesson may take more than one class period. It basically can be broken into three parts:
- Review of characterization and character development as an element of fiction
- Study of each of the characters in the novel Fahrenheit 451
- Study of Montag's development throughout the book

The student workbook has graphic organizers with questions to guide students through each of these parts. How you use these worksheets is up to you.
- Have students work in small groups or in pairs to complete them then discuss them as a class. This might especially be effective with Part 2, the study of characters other than Montag.
- Have students complete them individually then discuss them as a class
- Work through them together as a class having students take notes on the pages as the discussion unfolds
- Use your interactive whiteboard and let different students write up the "answers" and/or lead the discussions
- You may use all or only some of the worksheets
- You might use a different strategy for each of the three parts to add variety to covering the information

Suggested Answers to the worksheets are on the following pages. You may wish to elaborate or go into more depth in your class discussions, depending on the level of your students.

CHARACTER DEVELOPMENT SUGGESTED ANSWERS
Fahrenheit 451

PART I: Character As An Element Of Fiction

1. Define "protagonist" Main character

2. Define "antagonist" Main opposition to the main character

3. The protagonist in Fahrenheit 451 is Guy Montag

4. The antagonist(s) in Fahrenheit 451 is/are Beatty, representing the establishment

5. Define "dynamic character" Character who changes over the course of the story

6. Define "static character" Character who does not change over the course of the story

7. What is a "stereotyped character"? Character whose traits are based on typical or common elements of a particular type of person; usually static; usually a minor character filling a need for a character of that particular type

8. Which character in Fahrenheit 451 is dynamic? Montag

9. Which characters in Fahrenheit 451 are static? all the others but Montag

10. Are any characters in Fahrenheit 451 stereotypes? If so, which ones?
    You could make a case that Faber is a stereotype. The other minor characters each serve a function in the novel and are developed to the extent needed, but they aren't true stereotypes.

Below are the names of characters in Fahrenheit 451. On the blank to the left of each name, identify the person as having a major or minor role in the story. On the blank to the right of the name, identify the character

major	Capt. Beatty	Montag's boss; represents the establishment
major*	Clarisse McClellan	Introduces Montag to the possibility of an alternate lifestyle
minor	Granger	Literary hobo who accepts Montag into a new way of life
major	Guy Montag	Fireman who searches for happiness and a better way of life
major	Mildred	Montag's "wax doll" wife
minor	Mrs. Black	Wife of Montag's co-worker, whose house Montag calls an alarm on
minor	No. Elm Woman	Sets her own house and herself on fire rather than give up her books
minor	Mrs. Bowles	Mildred's friend who has children but wants nothing to do with them
minor	Mrs. Phelps	Mildred's friend who claims not to be concerned with anything but cries at the poem.
major*	Professor Faber	Helps Montag from his old way of life to his new one
minor	Stoneman and Black	Firemen Montag works with

*One could argue that Clarisse and Faber are minor characters with limited roles, but because their roles are so important, we've chosen to call them major characters.

CHARACTER DEVELOPMENT SUGGESTED ANSWERS
Fahrenheit 451

PART 2: Character Studies - Beatty, Clarisse, Mildred, Faber, Mrs. Phelps

Beatty

1. List some of Beatty's physical characteristics.

Beatty looked like all the other firemen...sunburned face, charcoal hair, soot-colored brows, ash-smeared cheeks.

2. What is one habit Beatty has that is symbolically important?

Beatty smokes a pipe.

3. Find & list 5 events in Fahrenheit 451 in which what Beatty does or says is important.
There are many examples. Here are a few:
- When Montag says he wouldn't want the Hound after him, Beatty asks if Montag has something to hide. After seeing Montag's reaction, he laughs softly.
- Beatty knows all about the quote Mrs. Blake uses when she refuses to leave her home.
- Beatty gave Montag a history of firemen and then explained how things came to be the way they are.
- Beatty says, "Let's not quibble over individuals with memoriams. Forget them. Burn all, burn everything. Fire is bright and fire is clean."
- Beatty knows what happened to Clarisse.
- He gives Montag opportunities to be a good fireman--doesn't go after him immediately and gives Montag plenty of warnings about what the consequences of his actions will be.
- Beatty says, "By the time the consequences catch up with you, it's too late, isn't it, Montag?"
- Beatty calls Montag a "burden" and says "fire will lift you off my shoulders, clean, quick, sure; nothing to rot later...."
- Beatty discovers the green bullet and threatens to track down Faber.

4. Is Beatty *for* or *against* Montag? Support your answer with evidence from the book.
Answers will vary, as a case could be made either way. As long as the answer is appropriately supported, it is acceptable.

5. Montag thinks Beatty wanted to die. Do you agree or disagree with him? Use evidence from the book to support your answer.
Some students will agree and some will disagree. The point is to get them to look at the text and the facts to come to their own conclusions.

CHARACTER DEVELOPMENT SUGGESTED ANSWERS
Fahrenheit 451

PART 2: Character Studies - Beatty, Clarisse, Mildred, Faber, Mrs. Phelps

Clarisse

1. List some of Clarisse's physical characteristics.
Clarisse's face is "slender and milk-white. She has dark eyes that are "shining and alive," and she wore a white dress when Montag first met her.

2. Give a few examples of the natural elements associated with Clarisse.
Natural elements are associated with Clarisse: moonlight, leaves, snow, whispering wind.

3. What is the single most important question Clarisse asks Montag?
Clarisse asks Montag if he is happy.
    Why is that question important? What effect does it have on Montag?
He thinks on that question and comes up with the realization that he is not happy. This spurs on his desire for happiness and a feeling of fulfillment.

4. What is the one thing about Clarisse that most attracts Montag to her? Tell *why* it attracts Montag to her.
Montag feels like Clarisse genuinely cares what he has to say. She listens to him and thinks about what he says before she responds. She generates a human connection with him, something even his wife does not do.

5. Explain why Clarisse's death is important in Fahrenheit 451.
Clarisse's death is important for a number of different reasons:
- It makes Montag have to move on towards a new life on his own.
- It makes the introduction of Faber necessary and believable.
- When Montag understands how and why Clarisse dies, it helps him understand the injustice of his society.
- Clarisse's death eliminates the possibility of any further development in the relationship between herself and Montag. Culmination of the attraction is not what the book is about.

CHARACTER DEVELOPMENT SUGGESTED ANSWERS
Fahrenheit 451

PART 2: Character Studies - Beatty, Clarisse, Mildred, Faber, Mrs. Phelps

Mildred

1. List some of Mildred's physical characteristics.

Mildred is pale, sometimes described as a "wax doll."

2. Choose one word or phrase you believe best sums-up Mildred's personality. Support your choice with examples from the text.

Word choices will vary. They may include words like *shallow, unhappy, distant, pale*, or others. Any appropriate word is acceptable as long as it is sufficiently supported. The point is to make students think about Mildred enough to be able to define her in an appropriate word or phrase.

3. What are 3 things Mildred routinely does?

Mildred listens to the radio on her "Seashells," watches television on the parlor walls, and takes sleeping pills.

What do these three things have in common, and what does that say about Millie?

All three of these activities are means of escaping reality. Millie either doesn't like her lifestyle, or it makes her unhappy. Perhaps she just can't emotionally handle real life, or maybe she just doesn't know what reality is or how to interact with it. It's possible her love of radio, tv, and pills is some combination of some or all of these things.

4. Why does Mildred call in the alarm on her own house?

It's hard to say for sure why Millie calls in the alarm because it is never directly stated, but some possible reasons are:
- Self-preservation; she sees where things are headed and realizes the consequences that will happen if she does not make the call.
- Like the Mechanical Hound, she is so programmed to follow the script, the rules, that she inevitably has to turn in the alarm.
- Perhaps her friends have warned her that they have called in alarms. Rather than being seen as a part of the problem, she chooses to be on record as on the right side of the law.
- Turning in the alarm is another means of escaping from reality; she can't handle the reality that Montag is forcing on her.

CHARACTER DEVELOPMENT SUGGESTED ANSWERS
Fahrenheit 451

PART 2: Character Studies - Beatty, Clarisse, Mildred, Faber, Mrs. Phelps

Faber
1. List some of Faber's physical characteristics.

Faber is old enough to be "retired." He had on a black suit when Montag first met him in the park. He responded with a "pale voice." At their second meeting (first at Faber's apartment), Faber looks old and fragile and afraid, but less so after he saw Montag's book.

2. Faber is a relatively minor character in Fahrenheit 451, but he is important. What function does Faber's character have in the story?

Faber is the bridge between Montag's old life and his new life. His character helps and enables Montag to cross over from a hopeless world into a world of hope, from ignorance into knowledge, from a culture of death into new life.

3. Give a verbal snapshot of Faber before Montag solicits his help and afterwards.

Before: Faber characterizes himself as being a coward. He sits at home, afraid to act on his desires to try to change the way things are.

After: After Faber agrees to help Montag, he becomes more "alive." He becomes a part of Montag's battles from a distance via the green bullet and then becomes fully immersed in Montag's fight when the Hound is hot on Montag's trail. Finally he graduates to taking action on his own as he goes to see about getting copies of the books printed.

4. Did Faber live at the end of the story? What evidence is in the text? Does it matter if Faber lives or dies at the end of the story?

We are led to believe that Faber lives. He supposedly left the city early in the morning before the bombings began, and even if other cities were hit, it is unlikely Faber would have yet arrived at another city.

Whether Faber lives or dies is thematically not especially important. We know that there are others, like Montag and Granger, who will carry on the work of reformation.

CHARACTER DEVELOPMENT SUGGESTED ANSWERS
Fahrenheit 451

PART 2: Character Studies - Beatty, Clarisse, Mildred, Faber, Mrs. Phelps

Mrs. Phelps
1. List 5 of the most important things Mrs. Phelps says or does.
- Mrs. Phelps protests too much that she doesn't worry about the war.
- Mrs. Phelps says, "Anyway, Pete and I always said, no tears, nothing like that. It's our third marriage each and we're independent."
- Mrs. Phelps says, "...No one in his right mind, the Good Lord knows, would have children!"
- Mrs. Phelps encourages Montag to read his "little poem," and she cries afterwards.
- Mrs. Phelps turns in an alarm on Montag.

2. Which of the 5 things you listed above gives us the most insight into Mrs. Phelps's character? Why?
A case could be made for any of these, but her crying after hearing the poem is probably the most revealing. She is in control of all the other things she says and does, but her crying shows her real emotion and true feelings.

3. Compare and contrast Mrs. Phelps and Mildred.
Similarities: Both are wax-doll-like in that they focus on things that are shallow. They watch the same kinds of things on the parlor walls, and they seem to adhere to the same social rules.

Differences: The biggest difference is that under her veneer Mrs. Phelps has some depth of emotion, some sense of reality (like Montag does), which Mildred does not have. Mildred does not cry after the reading of the poem. She is flustered and tries a flurry of things to make Mrs. Phelps feel better, but there is no substantial "underneath" to Millie. She is empty of real feelings to feel sympathy or empathy. She recognizes there is a problem but has no tools with which to cope with the situation. Mrs. Phelps is touched by the poem. She doesn't really have tools to deal with her emotions, but her emotions are still present; she is more human, more alive than Millie.

4. What is Mrs. Phelps's use as a character in the story?
In a way, she acts as a foil to both Millie and Montag. She isn't as "far gone" as Millie is, in the sense of being empty of emotion...but neither does she have as much of a taste for reality as Montag has.

Each character in the book actually shows a different facet of, response to, or progression of the type of society in which they live.

CHARACTER DEVELOPMENT SUGGESTED ANSWERS
Fahrenheit 451

PART 3: Montag's Development Through The Book

1. Montag goes through a number of events that transform him from the obedient Fireman Montag into the Book Of Ecclesiastes. Give a brief explanation of how or why each listed event changed him.

EVENT	EFFECT OF THE EVENT ON MONTAG
Montag meets Clarisse	Clarisse awakens Montag's emotions and intellectual curiosity. She shows him an alternative to his current lifestyle, an alternative Montag finds interesting.
Mildred's stomach is pumped	Montag is upset that Mildred overdosed on sleeping pills and over the casual way the men treated the "clean up." It all seems unreal and nasty to him, and he begins to wonder why things are the way they are.
Montag realizes he is not happy	Once Montag comes to the realization that he is NOT happy, he tries to figure out *why* he isn't and then tries to find what *will* make him happy.
No. Elm Woman lights the fire	Before the woman's actions, Montag could ignore the effects of his work on real people. After this, he does not want to continue being a fireman.
Clarisse dies	When Clarisse dies, Montag isn't transformed yet and has to find someone else like Clarisse to give him more information and answer his questions. He remembers Faber.
Montag realizes he does not love Millie	Montag realizes his life with Millie has been empty; he does not love her, and she cannot help him find happiness. He knows their relationship is over.
Faber agrees to help	This sends Montag forward into action to learn more and to try to effect some change on society.
Montag burns down his own house	After totally losing Millie and burning down his own home, Montag has nothing left to lose. He can go forward uninhibited.
Beatty verbally assaults Montag and threatens to get Faber	With nothing to lose and worried for Faber's safety, Montag kills Beatty. After this, there can be no return to the old life for Montag.
Montag meets Granger	Montag is accepted into the lifestyle that Clarisse, Faber, and Granger represent; the lifestyle that promises to give Montag some true happiness and may enable him to begin changing (rebuilding?) society.

CHARACTER DEVELOPMENT SUGGESTED ANSWERS
Fahrenheit 451

PART 3: Montag's Development Through The Book, page 2

2. In a work of fiction, the author can simply tell you about the character. That's called **Direct Characterization**.

In fiction, as in real life, we can also learn about the character
- through the character's physical appearance
- through the character's own words, thoughts, and actions
- through the comments of other characters

This is called **Indirect Characterization.**

Look through the text and find examples of each of these kinds of indirect characterization as they apply to Montag. Include the words from the text and, if not evident, what we learn about Montag from the example given.

Physical Appearance Montag looks like all the other firemen: black hair, sooty face, 5 o'clock shadow beard

Character's Own Words There are too many to list here. Any of Montag's words showing something about his character would be acceptable.

Character's Own Thoughts There are too many to list here. Any passages from the text stating Montag's thoughts which show something about his character would be acceptable.

Character's Own Actions There are too many to list here. Any example students find from which we can see something about Montag's character would be acceptable.

Comments Of Other Characters
- Clarisse says, "You laugh when I haven't been funny and you answer right off. You never stop to think what I've asked you."
- The morning after Mildred overdoses on sleeping pills, she tells Montag he doesn't look so great either.
- Beatty calls Montag a "burden."
- There are many other examples.

CHARACTER DEVELOPMENT SUGGESTED ANSWERS
Fahrenheit 451

PART 3: Montag's Development Through The Book, page 3

3. A character who changes has to be motivated by something. What is Montag's motivation to change? What does he want more than anything else, enough to lose his home, his wife, and his job? Support your answer with textual evidence.

One could make a case that Montag wants happiness or that he is seeking knowledge of a past and more natural world. In a larger sense, Montag ultimately wants humanity...real emotions, thoughtfulness, empathy, sympathy, personal interaction, creativity--things used to inherently belong to people before society stripped people of these things and made them empty.

4. Clarisse dies. Do you think Montag's development would have been different if Clarisse hadn't died? Explain.

Answers will vary. Any answer should be well-supported and thought-through. It is likely Montag would have eventually taken a similar path to what he took, searching for that which would make him satisfied inside. Whether or not he would have achieved this before dying is debatable. The point is to get students to consider the strengths and weaknesses of Montag's character and to do mini-forecasts of how things might have turned out if Clarisse had lived. This is a thinking exercise more than a question with a right-or-wrong answer.

5. Mildred is incapable of sharing Montag's journey. Do you think Montag's development would have been different if Millie had been able to share Montag's passion for finding a new life? Explain.

Again, this is debatable and answers will vary. The point of this question is to get students to think through different scenarios to project logical outcomes based on their knowledge of the characters.

LESSON: SYMBOLISM
Fahrenheit 451

CCSS: RL.9-10.1; RL.9-10.4; RL.9-10.10;
RI.9-10.2; RI.9-10.3; RI.9-10.8
W.9-10.2a-f; W.9-10.4; W.9-10.9; W.9-10.10
SL.9-10.1; L.9-10.5

Objectives:
- Students will study and interpret symbolic images within Fahrenheit 451
- Students will locate and analyze passages with symbolic images
- Students will read and evaluate informational texts about symbolic images in Fahrenheit 451
- Students will respond to questions about the informational texts
- Students will participate in discussions about symbolism in Fahrenheit 451
- Students will create and write an analysis of the symbolic use of rain in Fahrenheit 451

Purposes:
The purposes of this lesson are:
- To broaden students' understanding and knowledge of symbolic imagery
- To deepen students' understanding of Fahrenheit 451
- To show part of the craft of writing fiction
- To evaluate informational texts
- To learn the process of evaluating symbolic imagery
- To practice writing an analysis

Notes: This lesson will take more than one class period. It basically can be broken into three parts:
- Study of the imagery of the chapter titles
- Study of the symbols and recurrent images within the text
- Analysis and evaluation of the symbolic use of rain in the text

The materials provided can be used in any way you choose:
- All students independently complete all materials with class discussions to enhance and reinforce the materials studied
- Groups of students each complete a different part of the lesson and then lead class discussions to share the materials studied
- Some parts can be done in groups and some independently

The informational articles can be used as independent work for students or groups of students, class discussion guides, oral reading samples, or in a variety of other ways.

The questions following the informational articles could be used as quizzes, discussion guides, independent work, or any way you would like to use them.

The informational article evaluation page could lead to an additional writing assignment...to rewrite the article implementing the changes students feel would make it better.

LESSON: SYMBOLISM page 2
Fahrenheit 451

The materials provided for this lesson are:

Part 1
- Article about symbolism in the chapter titles
- Questions about the chapter titles article & suggested answer key
- Evaluation form to evaluate the chapter titles article (can also be used for the Part 2 article)

Part 2
- Article about symbols and images in the text
- Questions about the article & suggested answer key

Part 3
- Assignment: Analyzing and Evaluating the Symbolic Use of Rain in Fahrenheit 451
- Graphic organizer worksheet for student pre-writing notes
- Student page on which to write the analysis

Suggested Plan

Part 1
Read the article about the chapter titles orally together in class and discuss the appropriate elements of each chapter as you go through the article. Follow up with the questions as a short review. Have students do the Informational Reading Evaluation independently. Discuss their evaluations. Follow up with a re-write of the article as a writing assignment.

Part 2
Divide your class into 9 groups, one for each of the symbols/images listed. Have each group read and discuss the symbol/image they have been assigned. Come back together as a class and have each group lead a discussion about its symbol/image. Guide the discussions as necessary. Have all students complete the follow-up questions as a self-test. Discuss the answers.

Part 3
Allow students to work in pairs or small groups to find the passages referencing rain and to discuss what rain might mean or symbolize in those passages. Students should then work independently to complete their own written analysis. Collect them for grading.

Teacher Notes:
- All of this work and study of symbols and images should set up a good lesson about themes in the novel.
- The articles & other materials (except answer keys) are also printed in the Student Workbook.
- If you have to develop differentiated lesson plans, consider using Part 2 for your "low" group, Part 1 for your "middle" group and Part 3 for your college-bound group.
- You could also have your "low" group do just 1 part, your middle group do 2 parts, and your college-bound group do all 3 parts.

SYMBOLISM & IMAGERY
Fahrenheit 451

PART 1: The Chapter Titles
The passages below are about symbolism and the relevance of each chapter's title to the contents of the chapter and the book. Read these passages and answer the questions that follow.

The Hearth And The Salamander

A "hearth" is the brick or stone part of a fireplace that extends out into the room. Often the hearth is raised up from floor level, but it doesn't have to be. Sometimes "hearth" is used to refer to the fireplace as a whole.

In the days before other home heating methods and gas or electric stoves were available, big fireplaces with huge hearths were located in the kitchen or in the kitchen/living/dining room space. Family life centered around these hearths. Food would be cooked in kettles or pans that were heated by the fire. Dinner would be served at a table near the hearth, and after dinner family members would sit near the hearth to keep warm while reading, doing needlework, or conducting other activities. Because the hearth was so central to family life, it often is a symbol of "home."

Salamanders are amphibians. Like many frogs, they live in or near water or in other cool, damp places. In appearance, they resemble a lizard in form with skin more like a frog's in texture. Salamanders can be poisonous, so many are brightly colored to warn predators of their toxicity.

The important thing about salamanders, as far as their symbolic importance in Fahrenheit 451, is their association with fire. In ancient times, people thought salamanders were born from fire! Actually, they lived in rotten logs and when the logs were burned, the salamanders came out to escape the flames. For centuries people thought that salamander skin was fireproof and that salamanders could even put out fires.

In Fahrenheit 451 the fire trucks are called salamanders. Why? It's probably because of the ancient legends about salamanders coming from fire and being able to put out fires.

(continued on next page)

Symbols In Fahrenheit 451: Chapter Names, Page 2

But how do "hearth" and "salamander" go together to be an appropriate name for this chapter? Yes, the fire trucks are called salamanders but they carry firemen who start fires in homes; they don't put out fires. Consider that the salamander might represent something other than the firetrucks. To figure out what that might be, look at what the chapter is about.

Montag is the central character in this chapter, and he's a fireman. Therefore there's a good chance that he is somehow connected with this salamander symbolism. Salamanders were thought to be born from fire. Montag in his current occupation starts fires; fire is a big part of his life. Salamanders were thought to come out of the fire. Montag meets Clarisse and sees Mrs. Blake set fire to herself and her home--events which start to bring him away from (out of) his life of starting fires and into a state where he doesn't want to start fires anymore. In fact, he wants to stop the fires from being set. Hmmm. Salamanders were thought to put out fires. Are you seeing the connections? "Salamander" in the title refers to Montag. The new Montag comes from a life of fire and goes into a life of stopping fires, wanting the book and home burnings to stop.

So what does "hearth" have to do with any of this? Traditionally, as previously explained, "hearth" is a symbol of "home." Notice it isn't a symbol of "house." "Home" encompasses family, safety, warmth, and love; it is associated with tradition and roots, wholeness and togetherness.

In this chapter, Montag burns homes along with the books. Montag's own home is not "homey" at all; in fact, it is cold, almost sterile in nature. There's no warmth, no hearth, no good smells, no love, no togetherness, no sharing. Our salamander Montag sees the contrast between his own house and Clarisse's home, his own lifestyle and Clarisse's lifestyle--and realizes how empty his life is. He begins to want the emptiness of his life to be filled up.

So, The Hearth And The Salamander is a very appropriate name for this chapter. Montag, the salamander, is born from a life of fire. He is brought out of this life of fire through meeting Clarisse and realizing how empty his life is. He sees his own house is not a home and he begins looking for something that will satisfy his yearnings. He thinks books hold the answer. Burning books, burning homes, burning people becomes directly opposed to what Montag most wants; in fact, he wants the burning of books, homes, and people to stop. He becomes a catalyst, a force for the goal of stopping the fires.

(continued on next page)

The Sand And The Sieve

A sieve is a device, usually shaped like a shallow bowl or a tall cup, with holes punched in the bottom. The purpose of a sieve is to let smaller particles through the holes while retaining the larger parts, to separate the larger particles from the smaller ones.

The title of this chapter comes from Montag's remembering that as a child at the beach, a cousin offered him a dime if he would fill a sieve up with sand. The sand, of course, went right through the holes in the sieve. He tried and tried to fill it up, but he just couldn't do it. He sat there and cried.

What basically happens in chapter two? Montag remembers Faber, finds his address, and takes a book to him. While on the train, Montag realizes he'll have to give the book to Beatty very soon, so he tries to memorize it on the train ride to Faber's house. But he can't. The PA system on the bus is busy blaring an advertisement for Denham's Dentifrice, Denham's Dandy Dental Detergent. It's impossible to concentrate, to think, to remember with the ad blaring. He gets really frustrated and finally bursts out yelling for the thing to shut up. He tries to retain the words, but they slip through his mind like sand through a sieve.

That's one connection. But is it enough to name a whole chapter for it? What else goes on in the chapter? At this point in the novel, Montag has some knowledge: he knows he is unhappy; he has discovered some things that seem like a better way of life; he believes books hold the information he needs to find happiness and fulfillment. This is a great discovery, and he wants to share it with someone. He tries to share it with Millie and then with Millie and her friends, but they don't "get it." No matter how hard he tries to make them enlightened in the way he has become enlightened, they just don't "get it." He tries and tries to fill them up with these wonderful, new ideas but Millie and her friends are incapable of understanding or retaining the ideas he is trying to share with them, just like the sieve was incapable of holding the sand he tried to put in it.

Symbols In Fahrenheit 451: Chapter Names, Page 4

Burning Bright

The title of this chapter is a reference to a poem called "The Tyger" by William Blake:

> Tyger Tyger, burning bright,
> In the forests of the night;
> What immortal hand or eye,
> Could frame thy fearful symmetry?
>
> In what distant deeps or skies.
> Burnt the fire of thine eyes?
> On what wings dare he aspire?
> What the hand, dare seize the fire?
>
> And what shoulder, & what art,
> Could twist the sinews of thy heart?
> And when thy heart began to beat,
> What dread hand? & what dread feet?
>
> What the hammer? what the chain,
> In what furnace was thy brain?
> What the anvil? what dread grasp,
> Dare its deadly terrors clasp!
>
> When the stars threw down their spears
> And water'd heaven with their tears:
> Did he smile his work to see?
> Did he who made the Lamb make thee?
>
> Tyger Tyger burning bright,
> In the forests of the night:
> What immortal hand or eye,
> Dare frame thy fearful symmetry?

The idea is, "Who made the tiger, so beautiful on the outside, yet with such a fierce heart? And, was the maker pleased with his creation?" The connection to Fahrenheit 451 is "Who made mankind, so beautiful on the outside but so prone to all the things that lead to self destruction and war? And is the maker pleased with his creation?" Notice, too, that tigers' coats are orange and black and white--important colors in Fahrenheit 451: fire, evil, purity.

The chapter title is also appropriate literally: Montag's house burns brightly, Beatty burns brightly, the Mechanical Hound burns brightly, and the city burns brightly as it is annihilated.

SYMBOLISM: CHAPTER TITLES SUGGESTED ANSWERS
Fahrenheit 451

PART 1: The Chapter Titles - Questions For Review

1. The hearth is usually a symbol of home.

2. People used to think that salamanders were born from fire and were fireproof.

3. The title Burning Brightly is a reference to a poem named "The Tyger" by William Blake

4. Four things burn brightly in chapter three:
   Montag's house
   Beatty
   The Mechanical Hound
   The City

5. The salamander is a good symbol for Montag because Montag is a fireman, with his new life coming out of the fire. Legends say people used to believe that salamanders were born from fire. As Montag begins his new life, he wants to stop the book and house burnings, to stop the fires, which relates to the legends about salamanders being able to put out fires.

6. Mildred and her friends are like a sieve because they can't understand or retain the new ideas Montag wants to share with them.

7. While on the train, Montag yelled, "Shut up!" because he wanted to memorize his book, but he couldn't because the train PA system was so loud talking about Denham's Dentifrice.

8. Montag's house is not a home because there is no love, no human warmth, no sharing, no togetherness.

ARTICLE EVALUATION
Fahrenheit 451

Reading & Evaluating Informational Texts

1. What is the purpose of the article? How well did it achieve this purpose?

2. What is the central idea of the article?

3. Are the points that are made logical; is the reasoning sound? Give an example or two.

4. Are the points well developed? Explain why you think so or not.

5. Do you think this article is well-done as-written, or do you think it should be revised to be better? What would make it better?

SYMBOLISM & IMAGERY
Fahrenheit 451

PART 2: Symbols & Imagery Within The Text
There are many symbols within the text of Fahrenheit 451. Read about some of them below and then complete the exercise that follows.

Fahrenheit 451
Paper burns around 451 degrees Fahrenheit. This number isn't exact because the actual number depends on the chemical composition of the paper, moisture content, and so on. However, for the purposes of this novel, 451 is symbolic of the temperature at which book paper burns.

Snake Imagery
Here are some passages where the snake imagery is found:
- "One of them [the machines] slid down into your stomach like a black cobra down an echoing well...."
- "...a silly empty man near a silly empty woman, while the hungry snake made her still more empty."
- "There's a Phoenix car just drove up and a man in a black shirt with an orange snake stitched on his arm coming up the front walk."
- "I saw the damnedest snake in the world the other night. It was dead but it was alive. It could see but it couldn't see."
- "A voice drifted after him, 'Denham's Denham's Denham's,' the train hissed like a snake. The train vanished in its hole."

Traditionally, snakes are the bad guys--evil incarnate. This started with the story of Adam and Eve in the Garden of Eden in the Bible, when the Devil, disguised as a snake, tempted Eve to eat the forbidden fruit from the Tree of Knowledge.

In the passages above, the stomach-pumping machine is like a snake, Beatty has the symbol of a snake on his arm, and the train hisses like a snake. The need for stomach-pumping (and having it done in such a cold, uncaring manner like a janitorial mop-up), and the train's PA system's pounding noise and advertising at the occupants so they could think of nothing else are bad things in and for people, signs of an unhealthy society.

In the other three references noted, the snake represents whomever is creating the rules and pushing for this kind of lifestyle. Beatty is Captain of the firemen, definitely an enforcer of the rules. The hungry snake that "made her still more empty" is the society that has so emptied its citizens. And the snake that was dead but was alive--the stomach-pumping apparatus that looked inside Mildred to suck out all the junk--also could represent the seemingly intangible yet ever-present forces that created Montag's society. Rules and laws are not living things, yet they can suck the life out of the living by stripping people of the ability to think for themselves, by eroding freedom and choices, and by taking all the fun, creativity, and "meat" out of daily life.

Book Burning

Books are the traditional method of recording knowledge. Therefore, books represent knowledge and are the record of all the things people have thought, done, and imagined for all of recorded time. When there is no written record of something, it is easy to forget (as well as to modify) the facts. "Oh, that never *really* happened. Someone just made it up." "Firemen never put out fires; that's an old tale." In this sense, the burning of the books is symbolic of the new regime getting rid of the past so it can indoctrinate the people into believing what it wants them to believe.

Books hold ideas. Ideas spark imagination and creativity. They inspire people to think, to suppose, to wonder, and to want to find truth in life. If a regime wants to control people, to make people fall in line and do what they are told, books are the enemy and must be destroyed. Creativity, thinking, and questioning go against being controlled. Burning books can therefore also represent the destruction of creativity and thought as well as the emergence of the dominance of a regime attempting to control a population.

You might also note that in Fahrenheit 451, the firemen not only burn the books, they also burn the houses and relocate the residents to asylums or elsewhere. It isn't just about removing the books; it's about totally eliminating any opposition, anyone who might disagree or want things to be different.

Phoenix

Granger tells the story of the Phoenix, the bird that every few hundred years built a pyre and burned himself up and then rose again from the ashes to start anew. The image of the Phoenix is visible on Montag's chest when he meets Clarisse as well as on the Captain's hat and car. It is often a part of the symbology for firemen because of the Phoenix's destruction by fire.

When Granger tells about the Phoenix, he says it "must have been first cousin to Man....it looks like we're doing the same thing." This not only speaks to Mankind's past, it foreshadows the bombing of the city and the renewal that will occur afterwards.

Parlor Walls

In the past, homes often had rooms called parlors. These rooms were like a formal living room where family and guests would gather, often after dinner. Men would discuss politics, business, or other intellectual matters. A wife might do needlework or read; children were either not present or would sit and read or quietly play a game. At some point in the evening, a child or the wife might play the piano or provide some other kind of entertainment such as reciting, singing, or acting. Parlors were before television. If no guests were present, spouses might discuss family matters, neighborhood news, church or social club events, or the like.

Fahrenheit 451 Symbols & Imagery Within The Text, Page 3

In contrast, the Parlor Walls in Fahrenheit 451 are television on steroids; opposite in almost every way to the old-fashioned parlor. The walls are loud, colorful, and bright. Mildred is passive except for a few scripted lines she may have as "interaction." She takes in and is entertained by the sights and sounds on the big screens, but she never has to do or think anything. So it's ironic that Bradbury named them the "parlor" walls. One could make a case that Mildred meets her "family" and interacts with them in her Parlor Walls, but the "family" isn't real, and the shows don't have any substance.

This kind of mindless entertainment for hours on end is one part of the erosion of Mildred to emptiness. During the time of the Roman Empire, the politicians devised (and carried out) a plan to give the people cheap food and lots of entertainment so they would be happy and distracted from the political issues of the day, making their rise to power easier and practically uncontested. No one cared. "Give them bread and circuses" is the often-used phrase coined by Roman satirist and poet Juvenal. In the same way, Mildred and her friends don't really care about politics or much of anything except their shows. They don't even know or care why their country is at war.

The Parlor Walls, therefore, become symbolic of the ignorance and shallowness developed and encouraged by those in power to keep the masses of people happy and unconcerned with what the politicians are doing. It is also part of the metaphoric "hungry snake" that "made her [Mildred] still more empty."

Finally, Parlor Walls are also a means of escape for Mildred and her friends. Being entertained with happy and shallow programming, they can avoid facing the reality of their lives.

Seashells
Think of the "Seashells" as modern day ear buds. When Mildred isn't absorbed by the Parlor Walls, she is plugged in to her Seashells, being entertained by music or the radio. Before going to bed, she takes sleeping pills and plugs in her Seashells to drown out any thoughts of the day that will keep her awake. Like the Parlor Walls, they are a means of escape that promote lack of thought, and they are symbolic of the ignorance and shallowness encouraged by those in power.

The Green Bullet
So what about the Green Bullet, then? It's like a Seashell, isn't it? In form, yes, it is. It is a small, green, and bullet-shaped radio that fits into Montag's ear, as a Seashell would. But in substance it is quite different. Let's look at the name. What is green? Natural, living things like plants are green. But then there's that word "bullet," which usually is associated with killing, bringing death. What does the Green Bullet do? It provides a communications link between Faber and Montag, so Montag can have some help in responding to Beatty and others. Faber is a part of those with a green, "living" lifestyle--full of life, full of thoughts, real emotions, ideas, and creativity. Faber and Montag want to deliver a verbal bullet, a response that stops Beatty. In a larger sense, the Green Bullet becomes symbolic of finding a way to stop the erosion of humanity.

Fahrenheit 451 Symbols & Imagery Within The Text, Page 4

Mirrors
Look for a minute at the places where mirrors are used in the text:

- "He [Montag] knew that when he returned to the firehouse, he might wink at himself, a minstrel man, burnt-corked, in the mirror."
- "How like a mirror, too, her [Clarisse's] face. Impossible; for how many people did you know that refracted your own light back to you?"
- "These men [the firemen] were all mirror images of himself!"
- "There was a crash like the falling parts of a dream fashioned out of warped glass, mirrors, and crystal prisms." (as Mildred left the house in the beetle)
- "The look of you is enough. You haven't seen yourself in a mirror lately." (Granger to Montag)
- "...because in the millionth part of time left, she [Millie] saw her own face reflected there, in a mirror instead of a crystal ball, and it was such a wildly empty face, all by itself in the room, touching nothing, starved and eating of itself...."
- "Come on now, we're going to go build a mirror factory first and put out nothing but mirrors for the next year and take a long look in them."

That which is seen in a mirror is not real; it is a reflection of that which is real. Also, we cannot see ourselves without a mirror. We cannot see what we really look like without examining our own reflections. Go back and re-read the quotes above considering these ideas.

This whole book is filled with things that are real but not real, living but not living, seeming to be real but...not. The Mechanical Hound is mechanical, but it seems alive to Montag. The door-voice is not real, but it is personified. The "family" is not real, but Mildred treats them as if they are. The war is very real, but seems like it is not (until it's too late). History is real but is made into a fairy tale, a made-up story. These are just a few examples. Mirrors, reflections, distortions, and ironies abound in a close reading of Fahrenheit 451.

Think about this again: We cannot see what we really look like without examining our own reflections. This is physically true, but it also applies to our character. Without looking at our own actions, reflecting on the things we do, thinking about the effects of what we do and the meaning of what we do, we cannot know ourselves as individuals or as a society.

The Mechanical Hound
The Hound, like Beatty is a symbol of the establishment. In addition, the Hound represents the blurring of the non-living and living in Montag's world.

SYMBOLISM & IMAGERY
Fahrenheit 451

Symbols & Imagery Within The Text - Questions For Review

1. List 9 things that are important images or symbols in Fahrenheit 451:
Fahrenheit 451, snake imagery, book burning, Phoenix, Parlor Walls, Seashells, Green Bullet, mirrors, the Mechanical Hound

2. Name three things or people that represent the establishment, those in control:
Beatty, the Mechanical Hound, Parlor Walls

3. Name three things that are a means of "escape" from the reality of life:
Parlor Walls, Seashells, sleeping pills, beetle

4. Years after people read Fahrenheit 451, the thing they remember is that it is about book burning. What does the book burning actually symbolize?
The burning of the books can represent the destruction of history, creativity, and thought as well as the emergence of the dominance of a regime attempting to control a population.

5. Why are the Parlor Walls important in Fahrenheit 451?
The Parlor Walls are symbolic of the ignorance and shallowness developed and encouraged by those in power to keep the masses of people happy and unconcerned with what the politicians are doing. It is also part of the metaphoric "hungry snake" that "made her [Mildred] still more empty."

6. Explain how the story of the Phoenix relates to the city.
The Phoenix periodically burns itself to death, and a new Phoenix is born from the ashes. This story foreshadows the bombing of the city and the renewal that will occur afterwards.

SYMBOLISM & IMAGERY
Fahrenheit 451

PART 3: Analyzing And Evaluating The Symbolic Use Of Rain - Assignment

Your assignment is to analyze and evaluate the symbolic use of rain in Fahrenheit 451.

- Find the passages where rain is mentioned and write them down (with page numbers). (Hint: If you have access to a digital form of the book, you can search "rain" to find passages then look them up in your book.)
- Skim before and after the passages to see what is happening in that part of the story.
- Look at the possible symbolic meaning rain might have in each passage & make notes about it.
- Review your notes about each passage and see what is in common.
- Draw conclusions based on your passage analysis.
- Write an analysis of the symbolic use of rain in Fahrenheit 451

A few observations about rain:
    Rain can be cleansing or renewing.
    Rainy/stormy weather can foreshadow bad things happening.
    Rain helps things grow.
    Rain is water, which is life-giving.

[An alternate assignment could be to do the same for "hands."]

Teacher Note: Students' workbooks have a page that is a graphic organizer and a page for writing the analysis. They are included here in your packet so you don't have to go searching for a copy to see what they are.

SYMBOLISM & IMAGERY
Fahrenheit 451

PART 3: Analyzing And Evaluating The Symbolic Use Of Rain: Notes

Page	Passage	Notes

SYMBOLISM & IMAGERY
Fahrenheit 451

PART 3: Analyzing And Evaluating The Symbolic Use Of Rain: Written Analysis

LESSON: THEME
Fahrenheit 451

CCSS: RL.9-10.1; RL.9-10.2
SL.9-10.1; SL.9-10.1c
W.9-10.2; W.9-10.10

Objectives:
- Students will study the text of Fahrenheit 451 to determine the main theme of the novel.
- Students will consider the historical context of the novel to help determine the reasons this theme was thought to be important enough to write a book emphasizing it.
- Students will make a list of what Mr. Bradbury's advice would be to them.
- Students will evaluate the list of advice, decide if it is good advice or not, and create a task list of things they should start doing and things they should stop doing or do less to implement the advice given.

Purposes:
The purposes of this lesson are:
- To determine the main theme of the book Fahrenheit 451
- To understand why the theme of Fahrenheit 451 are important
- To evaluate and apply what they have learned from reading this book

Teacher's Notes:
This lesson may take more than one class period. It is composed of three main parts:
- Study of the text to get the "big picture" of the novel
- Looking at the "big picture" to determine the theme
- Understanding the theme in context and applying practical application of the theme

The following 6 pages are in the Student Workbook. Suggested answers are provided for you where appropriate. Page 6 is here in your teacher edition so you know what it is; student answers will vary.

Teacher's Pet Publications plans to create multimedia presentations of the materials covered in this teacher guide. Check at http:www.tpet.com under materials for Fahrenheit 451 to see what, if any are currently available.

Suggested Use Of Materials:
One way to approach this lesson is to use the pages provided as a discussion guide. You could present the materials to the students in a lecture format with students taking notes or filling out the Discussion Notes graphic organizer (Theme page 4)as you speak. Students would have your entire presentation available in their Student Workbooks for further review and study purposes.

As you get to the pages where student responses are required, Theme pages 5-7, end the lecture portion and have students either independently or in groups fill in appropriate responses. You could also do this as a whole-class activity, though page 6 is probably best done individually.

THEME
Fahrenheit 451

There are many ways to approach studying the themes of Fahrenheit 451, but any approach has to start with the text, for it is through the text that the themes are developed.

You have already read the text from beginning to end. You may have looked at specific passages to consider the symbols within the story or to study character development. Let's pull out some things now that will help us understand the larger themes of the work.

Our study will be based on:
- Montag's Realizations
- Words & Actions Of Mildred And Her Friends
- Beatty's Commentaries
- Clarisse, Faber, & Granger's Contributions
- The Ending

Montag's Realizations
We all get pretty used to our own daily routines and our own way of life. We accept that what we do is how life *is*. That's how Montag is...until Clarisse slips into his world that evening on his way home from work. Her world is very different from his. It seems interesting to him. And she asks a simple question--almost as an afterthought before parting: "Are you happy?".

Montag goes home to find his wife in bed with her Seashells plugged into her ears. Motionless. Pale. Dull. None of which is unusual. In fact, he doesn't realize she has overdosed on sleeping pills until he kicks the empty bottle. The men come to pump out her stomach and fix her up, but their casual attitude toward this "clean up job" is annoying and upsetting to Montag. It doesn't take Montag long in the beginning of the novel to realize that he is *not* happy.

Then there's Clarisse. What is it about her that intrigues him? He likes talking with her. Unlike his wife, she is responsive and thoughtful, a breath of fresh air in his stale life. Again, it doesn't take Montag long to realize that he wants *that* kind of a life...one of conversation and thought and genuine interaction rather than thoughtless, automatic responses.

On top of all that, Montag witnesses a woman who is willing to die rather than live her life without her books. That's pretty powerful. Even more powerful is Montag's witnessing her light the match that starts the fire--and realizing that what he does for a living has real consequences for real people.

Montag realizes he is unhappy, realizes what kind of a lifestyle he wants, realizes that books have something that is important enough to die for, and realizes what he has been doing as a fireman is not such a great thing.

There's one more important realization. He can't share his new life quest with Millie. She's just not capable of understanding what he has discovered.

Fahrenheit 451: Theme, page 2

Words And Actions Of Millie And Her Friends

"Why?" we must ask, "Why is Mildred incapable of understanding and sharing Montag's quest for a new life?" The answer is pretty simple, really: she's just too shallow of a person. Montag reads to her, but the words have no meaning, they're just words. "It doesn't mean anything! The Captain was right!" she says. Then she is relieved to pick up the ringing telephone, to talk with her friend about the White Clown show.

Millie spends all of her time watching mindless shows on the Parlor Walls, listening to the radio through her Seashells, and talking with her friends about nothing in particular, the way her Parlor Wall "family" talks but says nothing of substance.

Children are a bother. No one in their right mind would want them. So ship them off to school to be taken care of by others. When they're home, plunk them in front of the Parlor Walls. There's a war, but no one knows why; it doesn't really matter. It happens somewhere else. Husbands go off to war and are expected back with no consequences. Elections are won on looks alone. Nothing that is troublesome or unpleasant is allowed in. Millie and her friends haven't a care in the world. In fact, Mildred says, "I am happy...and proud of it!"

How do Millie and her friends cope when things come into life that aren't so pleasant? They run away; escape to the Parlor Walls, the Seashells, the pills. They have no coping skills whatsoever. They are totally unprepared to meet real life. It overwhelms them. After the firetruck arrives at Montag's house, Mildred comes out...ignores Montag, like he is a stranger...talks to herself about the house as if it is someone else's...gets into the beetle and rides away.

Beatty's Commentaries

How did people become like Mildred...incapable of coping with reality? Ah, let's look back at Captain Beatty's commentaries and consider his words. Ironically, here is a condensed version of what Beatty says, with a whole bunch of stuff left out:

> "Whirl man's mind around about so fast under the pumping hands of publishers, exploiters, broadcasters that the centrifuge flings off all unnecessary, time-wasting thought! ... School is shortened, discipline relaxed, philosophies, histories, languages dropped....Life is immediate, the job counts, pleasure lies all about after work. ... Empty the theaters save for clowns and furnish the rooms with glass walls and pretty colors running up and down the walls.... More sports for everyone, group spirit, fun, and you don't have to think, eh? ... More pictures. The mind drinks less and less. Impatience. Highways full of crowds going somewhere, somewhere, somewhere, nowhere. ... Don't step on the toes of the dog-lovers, the cat-lovers, doctors, lawyers, merchants, ... There was no dictum, no declaration, no censorship, to start with, no! Technology, mass exploitation, and minority pressure carried the trick.... Today, thanks to them, you can stay happy all the time...."

> "We must all be alike. Not everyone born free and equal, as the Constitution says, but everyone made equal. Each man the image of every other; then all are happy, for there are no mountains to make them cower, to judge themselves against. ... A book is a loaded gun in the house next door. ... Who knows who might be the target of the well-read man?"

"... Ask yourself, What do we want in this country, above all? People want to be happy....Well, aren't they? Don't we keep them moving, don't we give them fun? That's all we live for, isn't it? For pleasure, for titillation? ..."

"Colored people don't like *Little Black Sambo*. Burn it. White people don't feel good about *Uncle Tom's Cabin*. Burn it. Someone's written a book on tobacco and cancer of the lungs? The cigarette people are weeping? Burn the book. ... Funerals are unhappy and pagan? Eliminate them, too. ... Burn all, burn everything. Fire is bright and fire is clean."

"...So bring on your clubs and parties, your acrobats and magicians, your daredevils, jet cars, motorcycle helicopters, your sex and heroin, more of everything to do with automatic reflex."

And there you have it. That's basically how Beatty says the Mildreds and their friends came to be.

Clarisse, Faber, & Granger's Contributions
But the figurative door is left open, you see, because of Clarisse, Faber, Granger, and folks like them. Not *everyone* fell into the automatic reflex, always-happy trap. There are still people who like to have conversations and stand around, kicking leaves and thinking (Clarisse). There are still people who know that what has happened isn't a good thing, though they don't have the courage or the wherewithal to take action to change things on their own (Faber). There are still people who know, appreciate, and try to save that which has been burned, that which has been lost (Granger). And there are still people like Montag who say, "Hey! I want something more than this shallow, pretend-happy life."

The End
And in the end of the book, what happens? The shallow life Mankind acquiesced to over time brought itself down--and the outcasts, the thinkers, the do-ers, the people who could cope with reality, stepped in to start civilization anew.

Fahrenheit 451: Theme, page 4

Theme Notes
Use this page to jot down notes about theme in Fahrenheit 451.

1. Montag makes these important realizations:
   - He realizes he is not happy.
   - He realizes what kind of a lifestyle he wants.
   - He realizes books have something that is important enough to be willing to die for.
   - He realizes what he has been doing as a fireman is not such a great thing.
   - He realizes that he can't share his new life's quest with Millie.

2. Mildred is incapable of being a part of Montag's quest for a new lifestyle because
   She is too shallow to understand it or to want to participate.

3. Mildred and her friends can't cope with unpleasant realities. When they are faced with such things, their response is to run away by turning to the Parlor Walls, Seashells, or pills.

4. Beatty gives a long speech stating how he thinks their society came to be as it is. Towards the end he says: "...So bring on your clubs and parties, your acrobats and magicians, your daredevils, jet cars, motorcycle helicopters, your sex and heroin, more of everything to do with automatic reflex."

5. Not *everyone* fell into the automatic reflex, always-happy trap. There are still people who like to have conversations and stand around, kicking leaves and thinking (Clarisse).

   There are still people who know that what has happened isn't a good thing, though they don't have the courage or the wherewithal to take action to change things on their own (Faber).

   There are still people who know, appreciate, and try to save that which has been burned, that which has been lost (Granger).

   And there are still people like Montag who say, "Hey! I want something more than this shallow, pretend-happy life."

6. At the end of the book, the shallow life Mankind acquiesced to over time brought itself down-- and the outcasts, the thinkers, the do-ers, the people who could cope with reality, stepped in to start civilization anew.

Fahrenheit 451: Theme, page 5

From Text To Theme
We have looked at the text in a "big picture" way. Now, how do we get from this to that elusive thing called "theme"?

First we need to know what "theme" is.
Theme is the central idea of the book. It is the comment the book makes about life.
- Theme addresses the nature of humanity
- Theme addresses the nature of society
- Theme addresses the nature of humankind's relationship to the world and/or
- Theme addresses the nature of our ethical responsibilities

What is the nature of humanity as set forth in Fahrenheit 451?
Most people just want to be happy.

What is the nature of society as set forth in Fahrenheit 451?
As society becomes more technologically advanced and gets segmented into an infinite number of minority groups who don't allow for anything offensive to anyone, society degenerates to a washed-out sameness in which people become more mechanical with auto-responses and machines become personified.

What is the nature of humankind's relationship to the world in Fahrenheit 451?
The natural world remains what it is created to be while humans repeat a cycle of building civilizations which inevitably collapse and give birth to the next civilization.

What is the nature of our ethical responsibilities as set forth in Fahrenheit 451?
The more people give up their responsibilities of facing life in the real world--of reflecting on and monitoring their behavior toward the goal of maintaining a good society--the more the society will degenerate and ultimately collapse.

All of that being said, and considering the "big picture" of the text that we have just examined, write one phrase or sentence that best states the main theme of Fahrenheit 451.
Becoming a people who want nothing more than to be entertained, who give up the responsibilities of thoughtful reflection and maintenance of ethical behavior, is a sure path to self-destruction.

Are there other themes that are not the main theme? Did you have to choose among several things to determine the main theme? What other themes are in Fahrenheit 451?
- Being happy requires more than having fun or being entertained.
- When we relinquish our rights in exchange for "bread and circuses" and fail to monitor those who make the laws that control us, enslavery or annihilation are inevitable because those with power want to stay in power at all costs, which includes making war with each other. Either way, we become the victims because through apathy or cowardice we allow it.

Fahrenheit 451: Theme, page 6

Theme In Context
You've read the book and by studying it and getting to the theme, you know what it is really about, not just the story line. The next question to ask is, "Why?". Why would Ray Bradbury back in 1950 put pen to paper to write this book? And what did he intend for his readers to get from it? In a sense, the "theme" is what we get from the book, but until we turn that into his advice for us, his efforts are in vain, worthless.

Why Did He Write It?
Think about Ray Bradbury's lifetime. (He was born in 1920 and died in 2012.) His childhood took place in the Roaring Twenties, followed by the Great Depression, WWII, the rise of Communism, and the Korean War. In his lifetime, technological advances were astounding. Any thoughtful person would look at the world and wonder where all this would lead, as did Ray Bradbury.

Bradbury's book is a cautionary story, warning people of the possible consequences of the direction he saw the country going.

What Would Ray Bradbury's Advice Be To Us, His Readers?
Think about Fahrenheit 451 and all that is in it. Think about the characters, the themes, the ideas presented and discussed. Make a list of items of advice Ray Bradbury would give to you.

Do These Things: Here are a few suggested answers; other valid answers are possible:
- Read and learn as much as you can.
- Understand as much as you can about history.
- Take time to reflect on what you read, what you say, and what you do.
- Help others to understand the importance of participating in life and society in a thoughtful, meaningful way rather than becoming passive and living only for "bread and circuses."
- Mind your civic responsibilities; be informed and voice your opinions.
- Be a part of and appreciate the natural world.
- Do what you can in your own circle of family, friends, and neighborhood to promote good habits and ethical behavior.
- Find people you believe are thoughtful, ethical, and live the lifestyle you want to live, and join them.
- Be responsible for yourself and your own actions.

Don't Do These Things: Here are a few suggested answers; other valid answers are possible:
- Don't let technology run your life.
- Don't give automated responses; think before your speak.
- Don't stay plugged-in to mindless media.
- Don't run away from reality; develop coping skills.
- Don't look for happiness in a bottle or in the media.

Fahrenheit 451: Theme, page 7

Now you have a decision to make: you need to decide if this is good advice or not. It might all be good advice, some might be good and some not so good, or it all could be bad advice. What do you think? Is Bradbury's advice good or not? Answer completely below, explaining your answer fully.

_____
_____
_____
_____
_____
_____
_____
_____
_____
_____
_____
_____

It is wise to take good advice, and we usually benefit from that in the long run. If you believe any of Mr. Bradbury's advice is good, think for a few minutes how that might apply to you. Make a list of things you should probably stop doing and things you should probably start doing to act upon the advice given.

Start Doing These Things: Stop Doing/Do Less Of These Things:

_____   _____
_____   _____
_____   _____
_____   _____
_____   _____

Anytime someone gives you advice, you have to evaluate it. Decide if it is good advice or not, and then act accordingly. Consider the source, think about the consequences of following the advice, and evaluate what that might mean for you.

DISCUSSION ACTIVITY: CENSORSHIP THEME
Fahrenheit 451

CCSS: SL.9-10.1; SL.9-10.1c; SL.9-10.1d

Objectives:
- Students will participate in a class discussion about censorship.

Purposes:
The purposes of this lesson are:
- To make students aware of what censorship is and the many ways in which it is manifested.
- To explore and discuss the many facets of censorship

Teacher's Notes:
Censorship is an important theme in Fahrenheit 451. Montag's government controls the media and schools and only allows books, programming, and information that furthers its policies. This government censorship of everything from history to news is not the only form of censorship examined by the novel, though. The people had a hand in censorship, too, through what they chose to watch and read. They chose to have fun instead of becoming educated, so newspaper and magazine circulations dropped while inane programming on television increased.

In many of your communities, there are debates raging about what books should be put into the library, which books should be taught in the classrooms, and/or what books should be banned from both places. One purpose of this lesson is to make students aware of these debates. If such a thing is happening in your school district, bring in the books that are under question and explain both sides of the debate in detail to your students. In fact, you may want to arrange a debate between the arguing parties right in your classroom so students can see first-hand the arguments being made.

In addition, students should be made aware that almost everything they see/read/hear is biased. It is very rare to find anything truly objective in print these days. Even the news we hear is biased: someone decides which stories to put over the air waves, and which ones will be shelved. Someone decides which stories will be printed in the newspaper and which ones will be trashed. Advertising bombards us all constantly; it is most definitely biased. The point is to make students aware that the media is controlled by people, and it is often used to directly or indirectly express the opinions of those people or to sway others to a particular viewpoint.

Fahrenheit 451: Discussion Activity Censorship Theme, page 2

Activity

Use these questions to guide a class discussion about censorship:
- Are there good books and bad books? What's the difference?
- What is the First Amendment?
- Who decides what news will be published or broadcast? What effect does that have on what we see and hear?
- Are there certain things that should not be published? If so, what? If not, why not?
- Who has a right to privacy? Who has a right to know private things? What is private?
- What is a journalist's responsibility to the public? What is a journalist's responsibility to the person being interviewed? Are there or should there be limitations placed on journalists?
- Who has the right to decide what is good for you or me? Who gave them that power?
- If you control the media, what do you control?
- One of Bradbury's warnings is about censorship based on "offending minorities," with "minorities" meaning *any* subgroup within the culture. "Don't step on the toes of the dog-lovers, the cat-lovers, doctors, lawyers, merchants, chiefs, ..." What is the result if nothing that could be in any way construed as offensive to anyone were not allowed to be published or said? What is the danger of that?
- What would our world be like without books, magazines, newspapers, and the freedom of the press?
- How does censorship take away or limit freedom?
- Is *any* kind of censorship good?
- In what ways does the Internet combat censorship? Do you think the Internet will eventually be regulated and censored?
- What can you do to help combat censorship?

ACTIVITY: EXPLORATION OF ADDITIONAL THEMES
Fahrenheit 451

CCSS: RL.9-10.1; RL.9-10.2; RL.9-10.4; RL.9-10.9; RL.9-10.10;
W.9-10.2a-f; W.9-10.4; W.9-10.5; W.9-10.7; W.9-10.9; W.9-10.9a
SL.9-10.1b-d; SL.9-10.4; L.9-10.1; L.9-10.3; L.9-10.5

Objectives:
- Students will participate in a small group to analyze an assigned theme or motif in Fahrenheit 451.
- Students will scan the text for references to the assigned theme.
- Students will analyze and discuss the references to their theme to draw some conclusions regarding the cumulative meaning of those references.
- Students will orally share information and conclusions regarding the themes and motifs in the novel.

Purposes:
The purposes of this lesson are:
- To have students work together to explore additional themes and motifs in the novel and to present their conclusions to their classmates in both oral and written form.

Teacher's Notes:
The idea of total governmental control over an apathetic people and the censorship that goes along with that are not the only two themes in Fahrenheit 451. Some of the others include:
- knowledge versus ignorance
- the natural order & elements of the world versus a man-made world
- the blurring of the lines between animate and inanimate objects
- religion, religious imagery, and scriptural references
- conscious versus subconscious, often shown by hands acting on their own

This is not an exhaustive list, but it does hit many of the highlights of themes and motifs in the novel.

Activity
1. Divide your class into groups, one group for each theme or motif you want to explore. Students will scan the text to find references to their topics and note the places where those references occur. *The student assignment and notes pages are reprinted on the following pages for your convenience. They are in the Student Workbook as well.*
2. Students should review and discuss the references they have found and come up with some observations, thoughts, and ideas as to what these references cumulatively mean. They should jot down a few sentences to summarize their conclusions and be prepared to share their information with classmates.

Follow-up:
- Each group should create a written summary of its findings and conclusions, and each of these summaries could be combined into a booklet, published and distributed to all class members for study purposes.
- Students should read articles written by others about the themes and motifs in the novel and compare their own conclusions with the conclusions of others.

EXPLORATION OF ADDITIONAL THEMES
Fahrenheit 451

The idea of total governmental control over an apathetic people and the censorship that goes along with that are not the only two themes in Fahrenheit 451. Some of the others include:

- knowledge versus ignorance
- the natural order & elements of the world versus a man-made world
- the blurring of the lines between animate and inanimate objects
- religion, religious imagery, and scriptural references
- conscious versus subconscious, often shown by hands acting on their own

This is not an exhaustive list, but it does hit many of the highlights of themes and motifs in the novel.

Your assignment is to fully explore one of these themes in Fahrenheit 451.

You will scan the text for references to this theme and note the references on the chart on the following page. Your group should assign each person in the group one of the reading assignment sections to scan for references to your theme.

When you finish noting references, you should come back together as a group to discuss each of the references you have found and try to draw some conclusions about the cumulative meaning of the references. Write these down in a few sentences at the bottom of the Notes page.

When all groups have completed these tasks, the class will come back together as a whole to share information and discuss each theme/motif that has been explored. Be prepared to share your information with the whole class.

After your textual research is over, you should find and read at least two articles written by others about your assigned theme or motif in the novel.

Finally, each group member should write a summary about your theme or motif, clearly stating what your theme or motif is and explaining its use in the novel, using specific examples from the text to support your statements and including (and citing) any appropriate information from the additional articles you read.

THEME/MOTIF NOTES
Fahrenheit 451

Theme/Motif _____

PAGE	REFERENCE

Use an additional sheet of notebook paper if needed for more references.

Notes About Cumulative Meaning Of The References:

_____
_____
_____
_____
_____
_____
_____
_____

LESSON: USE OF LANGUAGE
Fahrenheit 451

CCSS: RL.9-10.1; RL.9-10.4; W.9-10.10; SL.9-10.4
L.9-10.3; L.9-10.4a; L.9-10.5; L.9-10.5a

Objectives:
- Students will study passages from Fahrenheit 451 to see how Bradbury crafted the text
- Students will study some types of figurative language found in Fahrenheit 451
- Students will find and identify figurative language in Fahrenheit 451

Purposes:
The purposes of this lesson are:
- To show students that writing is a craft in which language is used as the author's tools to create his work
- To show students *how* language is used to convey the author's message
- To give students an appreciation for Ray Bradbury's exceptional talent as a writer
- To reinforce material covered in previous lessons
- To review a few kinds of figurative language as a refresher/reinforcer of that subject

Teacher's Notes:
This lesson is in two parts:
- study of passages from Fahrenheit 451 to show Bradbury's use of language
- study of figurative language in Fahrenheit 451

The first few pages that follow give a commentary about use of language in the first few paragraphs of the novel Fahrenheit 451. You can use these pages as lecture notes, a class discussion guide, group or independent study, or in any other way you choose.

After the example commentary pages, there is an exercise for students to complete in which they analyze the provided paragraph in the same way that the commentary was done on the previous pages. Again, this could be done as an individual or group assignment--or as a whole-class activity. A key with suggested answers is provided for you, though you may want to add more to it.

The next page is a brief review of some kinds of figurative language, with examples from Fahrenheit 451. It is probably best used as a discussion guide.

Finally, there is an exercise in which students find more examples of figurative language in the text of Fahrenheit 451. You might consider breaking the class into groups and having each group take a section of the book in which to find examples. This will provide a wide variety of examples to discuss as a follow-up activity. A copy of the figurative language exercise is provided for you, though no answer suggestions are given...students will find a wide variety of examples in the text.

All of the Use Of Language pages are in the Student Workbook.

USE OF LANGUAGE
Fahrenheit 451

Writing is often referred to as a "craft." You may hear authors say they've spent years working on their craft. Well, a "craft" is an occupation that requires special skills or particular attention to details. A woodworker, for example, may craft a fine piece of furniture, taking great time and effort to make every joint, every angle, every carved detail perfect. The same is true with writing: authors take a great deal of time and effort to make every word, every sentence, every chapter fit the purposes of their book perfectly. Ray Bradbury was a master at this.

We can't look at every passage in the whole book; there just isn't enough time. But we can look at a few passages that show Mr. Bradbury's mastery very well, then you can go on to look at other passages on your own to truly appreciate his finely crafted work. At some point you should go back and reread the novel from start to end after completing this study. You will see so many things you missed the first time around.

Let's take a look at the beginning of the book.

Passage	Commentary
It was a pleasure to burn.	What? A *pleasure* to burn? How odd! It grabs our attention, lets us know something unusual is going on, & lets us know this person *likes* burning things. It introduces a main element of the book: burning.
It was a special pleasure to see things eaten, to see things blackened and *changed*.	Why "eaten" instead of "burned"? "Eaten" is much more graphic; it personifies the fire, right away giving lifelike qualities to an inanimate thing, introducing the theme of "living but not living, inanimate but perceived as alive" paradox in the book. "Changed" is in italics; this whole book is about change of one kind or another.
With the brass nozzle in his fists, with this great python spitting its venomous kerosene upon the world, the blood pounded in his head, and his hands were the hands of some amazing conductor playing all the symphonies of blazing and burning to bring down the tatters and charcoal ruins of history.	Calling the hose a python brings it to life & begins the snake imagery often used in the book. "Blood pounding in his head" graphically tells us he's excited, working hard, energized. The element of "hands" often used throughout the book is introduced. Who would think to liken using a fire hose to conducting a symphony? What are tatters? They are torn pieces; bits of shredded clothing. What does "to bring down the tatters and charcoal ruins of history" mean? It brings a mental image of old charred buildings falling down but we know it's more than that. How do you "bring down" or destroy history?! Yet, that is also an important element in the book. Remember how Montag was told firemen never put out fires; that was just an old tale? That is shredding history, turning history into charcoal ruins. And here it is at the very start of the book!

Fahrenheit 451: Use Of Language, page 2

Passage	Commentary
With his symbolic helmet numbered 451 on his stolid head, and his eyes all orange flame with the thought of what came next, he flicked the igniter and the house jumped up in a gorging fire that burned the evening sky red and yellow and black.	Bradbury *tells* us 451 is symbolic; he leaves no doubt. Montag's head is "stolid": not easily stirred or moved mentally; unemotional. One word introduces the unemotional, lethargic, passive nature of people in this society. When you look at someone's eyes, you can tell a lot about them. Montag's are all orange flame. Orange is a bright color, a warning color, as in a yellow/orange light of a traffic light or "road work ahead" signs--fire. Danger. The house "jumped up." That's personification (giving inanimate objects human qualities). Again, very graphic. It's a "gorging" fire; "gorging," as in gorging on a meal--feasting; overeating (which brings back the eating image from the previous paragraph). The fire "burned the evening sky red and yellow and black"--the sky (nature) is being burned (destroyed), another subtheme in the book...humankind's unnatural existence in the city. Red and yellow and black--colors of danger and evil.
He strode in a swarm of fireflies. He wanted above all, like the old joke, to shove a marshmallow on a stick in the furnace, while the flapping pigeon-winged books died on the porch and lawn of the house. While the books went up in sparkling whirls and blew away on a wind turned dark with burning.	"Fireflies" gives a living quality to the bits of glowing embers in the air, which are not alive. The idea of shoving a marshmallow on a stick in the furnace refers to toasting a marshmallow on a stick over a fire, but the idea has degenerated through the years. People no longer have campfires, so they relate to doing it via the furnace, which is something they *do* have. And, it's an old joke now, not something that people really used to do. History has been changed, and it makes no sense, so it's a joke. Again, there's more personification with the flapping pigeon-winged books dying on the porch and lawn, as if they had life and they were being killed. Why pigeon-winged instead of some other bird? Carrier pigeons carry messages, as books do. The book sparks blow away on a "wind turned dark,"...wind (nature) turned dark (perverted) with burning.
Montag grinned the fierce grin of all men singed and driven back by flame.	Why does Montag "grin," and why is it a "fierce" grin? A "grin" is a broad smile, usually to show pleasure. "Fierce," in this case, is as in a *fierce* competition: furiously eager or intense. He's loving what he does and is right in there giving it his all. Notice, too, that he is the same as "all men singed..." and later in the book he realizes he looks like all the other firemen.

Fahrenheit 451: Use Of Language, page 3

Passage	Commentary
He knew that when he returned to the firehouse, he might wink at himself, a minstrel man, burnt-corked, in the mirror. Later, going to sleep, he would feel the fiery smile still gripped by his face muscles, in the dark. It never went away, that smile, it never ever went away, as long as he remembered.	Winking at oneself is usually an indication of happy self-congratulations. The minstrel-man image is one of being someone other than who you appear to be, doubly appropriate because minstrel-men often performed in "black face," with their white faces artificially blackened--and the firemen have sooty, blackened faces. The mirror introduces the idea of self-examination, mirrors, reflections, and crystals that appear throughout the book. His smile never went away. He, like others in his society, are perpetually happy, and he can't remember not having that smile. Remember, though, that he laughs when he doesn't know how to respond to Clarisse--and that is an auto-response laugh, not because she says anything funny. Perhaps this perpetual smile is an auto-response, too...just always there. And, finally, it says, "as long as he remembered," not "as long as he could remember." We usually say we've been doing something as long as we can remember. One reading of this last line could beg the question, "As long as he remembered *what*?".

And yet, when we read these passages for the first time, it just seems like a regular beginning of a story. Little do we suspect that Mr. Bradbury has given us such a thorough introduction to the book and has packed all of this symbolism and imagery into a few short paragraphs. *That* is use of language, professionally crafted.

Ray Bradbury doesn't just tell a story. He manipulates us, his readers, by careful use of language to tap into our emotions and to bring images to mind. This is what brings the story to life; we see things in our mind. We can *see* Montag holding a python hose and those poor little books flapping as they die on the porch.

Fahrenheit 451: Use Of Language, page 4

Now it's your turn. Read the passage in the left column then create a commentary about the use of language in the passage, as was done above.

Passage	Commentary
The autumn leaves blew over the moonlit pavement in such a way as to make the girl who was moving there seem fixed to a sliding walk, letting the motion of the wind and the leaves carry her forward. Her head was half-bent to watch her shoes stir the circling leaves. Her face was slender and milk-white, and in it was a kind of gentle hunger that touched over everything with tireless curiosity. It was a look, almost, of pale surprise; the dark eyes were so fixed to the world that no move escaped them. Her dress was white and it whispered. He almost thought he heard the motion of her hands as she walked, and the infinitely small sound now, the white stir of her face turning when she discovered she was a moment away from a man who stood in the middle of the pavement waiting.	Student responses will vary, but here are some suggestions: Clarisse is identified with natural things: autumn *leaves, moonlit* pavement, & wind. Milk-white face, a natural white. White dress, innocence, purity. White stir of her face turning--a stir doesn't have color; interesting use of "white" Dark eyes...deep, thoughtful. Hand imagery again A moment away--usually a distance measurement; this uses time. Montag is in the *middle* of the pavement; about to be in the middle of old lifestyle vs new one

Fahrenheit 451: Use Of Language, page 5

Figurative Language

In the passages above, some inanimate objects were given qualities of living things--the python (hose) spitting its venomous kerosene upon the world, for example. This is an example of figurative language called *personification*. There are many kinds of figurative language an author can use to craft his work. Here are a few:

Personification: Giving inanimate objects qualities of living things

Hyperbole: Exaggerating or making an overstatement

Metaphor: Comparing two unlike things without using *as* or *like*

Simile: Comparing two unlike things using *as* or *like*

Understatement: Opposite of hyperbole; emphasizing something by significantly lessening its degree

Here are some examples from Fahrenheit 451:

Personification:
- ...the flapping pigeon-winged books died on the porch...
- A fountain of books sprang down upon Montag...

Hyperbole:
- He felt his chest chopped down and split apart.
- I don't know anything anymore...

Metaphor:
- ...her eyes were two miraculous bits of violet amber...
- People were more often...torches, blazing away until they whiffed out. (This is sort-of a trick one. In the book it says "he searched for a simile" but what he actually used was a metaphor. If he had said "People were more often...*like* torches..." it would have been a simile.)
- The woman on the bed was no more than a hard stratum of marble...

Simile:
- How like a mirror, too, her face.
- ...she was like the eager watcher of a marionette show...
- Her face was like a snow-covered island upon which rain might fall...
- [The Mechanical Hound] was like a great bee come home from some field where the honey is full of poison wildness...

Understatement:
- The breath coming out the nostrils was so faint it stirred only the furthest fringes of life, a small leaf, a black feather, a single fiber of hair.
- A fountain of books sprang down upon Montag as he climbed shuddering up the sheer stairwell. How inconvenient!

Fahrenheit 451: Use Of Language, page 6

Figurative Language Exercise

How many examples of figurative language can you find in Fahrenheit 451? Jot them down and identify the type of figurative language for each (as well as the page number in the text) in the chart below.

Type = personification, hyperbole, metaphor, simile, or understatement

Type	Page	Example

ADDITIONAL LESSONS, ACTIVITIES, & ASSIGNMENTS FOR EACH READING ASSIGNMENT

Fahrenheit 451

ASSIGNMENTS AND ACTIVITIES
TO STUDY DIFFERENT ASPECTS
OF EACH READING ASSIGNMENT

NOTES
Fahrenheit 451

COMIC STRIP CHARACTERS
ACTIVITY FOR READING ASSIGNMENT 1
Fahrenheit 451

CCSS: RL.9-10.7; SL.9-10.1; SL.9-10.1c; SL.9-10.1d;

Objectives:
- Students will make graphic representations of specified characters and scenes from Reading Assignment 1
- Students will compare and contrast the graphic representations they have created

Purposes:
The purposes of this lesson are:
- To review the text of key scenes related to characters in the first reading assignment
- To encourage students to envision the characters and to translate those mental images into paper or computer images
- To give students the opportunity to work in a creative medium that is fun and motivating

Teacher's Notes:
This assignment can be done as an in-class or out-of-class project, can be done as individual work or as a group project, and can be done in any media that is acceptable to you--paint, watercolors, markers, as jpg images or Powerpoint slides from the computer...whatever suits you and your students.

<u>Bring in stacks of comic books, graphic novels, or comic strips from the newspaper</u> for students to use to get ideas as to layout, perspective, etc.

Discuss the assignment in detail with students. Be sure to tell students any additional requirements you might have and tell them by when the assignment must be completed.

After the graphic images have been completed, have a show-and-tell discussion about the various representations, comparing and contrasting the elements of like character representations. (Compare/contrast images of Montag, then compare and contrast images of Beatty and The Hound, then compare/contrast images of Clarisse.)

Here are some points on which to guide the comparison/contrast discussion:
- What facial expressions are used? Why?
- Does everyone see the characters in the same way?
- What other details are included? Why?
- How effective is the use of color?
- What elements of the images have symbolic importance?

The assignment page which follows is in the Student Workbook.

COMIC STRIP CHARACTERS
Fahrenheit 451

The first reading assignment has some great material for making a comic-strip-style representation of the characters.

At the opening of the story, there's <u>Montag</u>, a larger-than-life fireman holding that python hose spewing venomous kerosene.

Later, a few pages from the end of the reading assignment section, <u>Beatty and the Mechanical Hound</u> provide excellent material for a cartoon artist to run with.

And then, there's <u>Clarisse</u>...dear, sweet Clarisse with all the images of nature associated with her. You can find 3 different scenes involving Clarisse in this section of the book, from which you can draw on for ideas.

Your assignment is to draw 3 comic strip cells, one for each of the three references above.
- You can make them any size you want, but no smaller than 3 x 3, so details can be included and seen.
- They should be done in color.
- Have fun exaggerating their qualities, as a comic strip artist would!

Here's how to go about doing it:
1. Go back to the text and re-read the parts relating to each character before you begin to draw, to get ideas and mental pictures to work from.
2. Jot down notes about what will be included in your images, notes for each of the three drawings. Consider things like: characters' facial expressions, body stance, other things in the image (like background images, things the character would be holding, etc.), colors that will be used, and size of the images, etc.
3. Look at some comic strip images to see how different artists draw within the individual cells and how they show faces and other elements--angles, perspectives, etc. Choose some cell layouts that you think might work well for your images, and use them as models as you do your own work.
4. Decide on the media you will use (markers, computer, paints) and gather your materials.
5. Make rough-draft sketches showing the layouts of each image.
6. Proceed with creating your masterpieces!

LESSON: CLARISSE'S POEM (SONG)
ACTIVITY FOR READING ASSIGNMENT 1
Fahrenheit 451

CCSS: W.9-10.3d; W.9-10.4; W.9-10.5; W.9-10.10

Objectives:
- Students will review portions of the text relating to Clarisse
- Students will characterize Clarisse through poetry or song lyrics

Purposes:
The purposes of this lesson are:
- To review the texts of key scenes related to Clarisse in the novel
- To analyze Clarisse's character and translate the essence of her character into words in the form of poetry

Teacher's Notes:
This assignment can be done as an in-class or out-of-class project, can be done as individual work or as a group project, and can be done in any media that is acceptable to you--a poem, rap music, or song lyrics.

Discuss the assignment in detail with your students. Tell students any additional requirements you might have and when this assignment will be due.

You might consider telling students that the best work (as judged by you) will be put on display, included in your school's literary publication or newspaper, or be awarded some other appropriate prize you have devised.

The assignment page which follows is in the Student Workbook.

CLARISSE'S POEM (SONG)
Fahrenheit 451

Isn't it a nice time of night to walk? I like to smell things and look at things, and sometimes stay up all night, walking, and watch the sun rise.
--- Clarisse

She isn't physically present in any scenes after the first reading assignment section, yet her presence is felt throughout the novel. Have you ever met someone like that...someone whose personality sticks with you in a positive way long after he or she has left the room...someone like Clarisse?

Your assignment is to write a poem (or lyrics) entitled Clarisse's Poem (or Song), in which you convey the essence of Clarisse's character based on her scenes in the novel.

There is no specific length requirement, but it is highly unlikely you could do this assignment justice in just a few lines.

Here's how to go about doing it:
1. Skim through the text of Reading Assignment 1 to locate and reread the passages in which Clarisse participates.
2. Make notes about the things she does, what she says, how she is described. You can use words or phrases directly from the text.
3. Analyze what you have read and the notes you have made to construct in your own mind the key things that made Clarisse the person she was. What is the essence of her character?
4. Circle, jot down, or note what words or phrases would best convey "Clarisse."
5. Choose a form for your work: If you do a poem, what kind of a poem will you do? Free form? A poem with a strict rhyming pattern? A series of Haiku poems? If you do song lyrics, will they be in the form of rap? To the tune of a particular song you know or like or think would be appropriate for Clarisse?
6. Begin a rough draft of organizing words and phrases into your form. Don't be afraid to add your own words, not just words from the text. This is *your* work; you're not stuck with only Mr. Bradbury's words. Be descriptive. Make your readers *feel* who Clarisse was.
7. Rework, reword, rearrange, edit. Craft your poem (or song) about Clarisse carefully, to be the best you can make it.
8. Then, write a final draft. Decorate your final draft with appropriate illustrations if you are so inclined.

BACK IN THE DAY
ACTIVITY FOR READING ASSIGNMENT 1
Fahrenheit 451

CCSS: W.9-10.3; W.9-10.3a; W.9-10.3d; W.9-10.3e; W.9-10.4; W.9-10.10
SL.9-10.1a; SL.9-10.1c; L.9-10.1; L.9-10.2

Objectives:
- Students will read background information about how this assignment relates to Fahrenheit 451
- Students will prepare interview questions
- Students will conduct an interview of a grandparent-aged person (or older)
- Students will write a narrative about the interview

Purposes:
The purposes of this lesson are:
- To connect Fahrenheit 451 to real life
- To impress upon students the importance of talking with people of an older generation about their life experiences, to know what has really happened in the past
- To engage students in conversation with someone of a different generation
- To expose students to information they may not have known before
- To make students think about the interview in a concrete way by having them relate their interview experience in a narrative
- To practice the conventions of writing

Teacher's Notes:
Discuss the assignment in detail with your students. Tell students any additional requirements you might have and when this assignment will be due.

Be sensitive to the fact that some students may not have a grandparent still living. The assignment interview can be done with any grandparent-aged (or older) person.

A good follow-up would be to hold a class discussion after all the interviews are done, to let students share interesting aspects of their interviews.

The assignment pages which follow are in the Student Workbook.

BACK IN THE DAY
Fahrenheit 451

Have you ever found an old coin, maybe dated 30 or 40 years ago, and wondered where all that coin had traveled in all those years...who else had it, what they bought with it? It's fun to imagine where it has been. The sad part is that you can never really *know*; it's not like the thing can tell its life's story.

Old *people*, on the other hand, can. They can tell you where they've been, what they've seen first-hand, what they remember about how things used to be, back in the day...like Clarisse's grandfather.

In terms of the message in Fahrenheit 451, people didn't *know* what had been done in the past; they just assumed that whatever they were being told was the truth. That often is a good assumption...but not always. If you don't know that firemen used to put out fires, and you see that they only start fires now...then it would be easy to assume that they never put out fires, if no one ever told you that they did. Did you know that all gas stations used to be full service and you never had to pump your own gas? The attendant did it--and he washed your windshield and checked your oil, too! ...Or did you just assume that everyone always pumped his or her own gas? A thing like that doesn't make a lot of difference, but some other things *do*.

If we don't talk to our grandfathers and grandmothers, our great-aunts and great-uncles, the old fella who lives down the street, or that old woman in the nursing home, we lose the passing-on of first-hand information. 30 or 40 years from now when your grandchild asks you how something was back in the 1900's, you may not have experienced it, but you can say, "My mother, my grandmother, or that old fella down the street once told me..." And *their* first-hand experience is passed on through several generations. You (thankfully) might never know what it was like to not be able to drink from the same water fountain as another person...but someone else can express to you the humiliation, the anger, the frustration he or she felt. And you know it was real. And because you know it was real, your grandchild will know it was real, too, when you tell her about it.

So *talk* with an old person...frequently. Listen to the stories of his life experiences, ask her about how things were different back in the day. What was it like when he came home from Vietnam? What did it mean to her to see the first man walk on the moon? What things did his grandfather tell *him* about why he came to America? Ask questions, listen, and remember. Then, some day in the future, if the history books say Americans never went to the moon; that's just an old story, you will recognize the lie, you will *know* what really happened.

Your assignment is to talk (and listen) to an old person. If you don't have old relatives, visit the American Legion or a nursing home, explain your assignment, and ask for some time to talk with someone there.

Fahrenheit 451: Back In The Day Activity, page 2

Some things to keep in mind:
- *Speak clearly and be patient.*
- *Be prepared with a list of questions.* If you really listen to what is said and if you think about it rather than just letting it go in one ear and out the other, you will probably also naturally have questions within the conversation.
- *Take notes so you can refer to them later.* If you have a recording device, ask the person you talk with if you may record the conversation rather than taking notes during it. Then go back later to make notes from the recording.
- *Be polite.* You may bump into a topic that the person is uncomfortable talking about. Just go on to something else. Your goal is not to upset anyone. Also, "please" and "thank you" are still appreciated by most people.

Here are some sample questions to get you started:
- What things from your childhood do you remember most vividly?
- What world events have had the most effect on you in your lifetime?
- What was your favorite thing to do when you were my age?
- Did you know your grandparents or great-aunts and uncles, and if so, what do you remember about them? What did they do for a living?
- What's the most important thing you have learned in your lifetime?

Add more of your own questions to this list. The point of the questions is to find out what really happened and what things were really like "back in the day," at a time before you can remember.

After you complete your interview, write a narrative telling about your experience with the interview. Here are some guidelines for this writing assignment:

Write an *introductory paragraph* in which you state the name and age of your interviewee and your relationship to that person. You could also mention how you felt about doing the interview. Were you nervous? Were you looking forward to it? Were you dreading it?

The body of your narrative should tell about the interview itself.
- You could organize the body of the narrative by making a paragraph for each of the questions you asked for which the interviewee had lengthy or interesting answers. Based on the first question above, the topic sentence for the paragraph might be something like this: "The thing [interviewee name] remembers most vividly about [his/her] childhood is...." And then your paragraph would include some of the details from the interviewee's reply.
- Another way to organize the body of the narrative would be by your reactions to the information you received in reply to your questions. For example, "I was surprised to find out that..." or "The most touching moment, for me, in the interview was..." or "It made me sad to find out that..." Think about how you felt about different parts of the interview conversation to come up with your own topic sentences. Then, fill out your paragraphs with details about what was said that made you feel that way, and why.

Write a concluding paragraph stating what you will remember most about this interviewing experience, and why.

MINI-LESSON: WRITING TECHNIQUE
ACTIVITY FOR READING ASSIGNMENT 1
Fahrenheit 451

CCSS: RL.9-10.1; RL.9-10.4; SL.9-10.1; SL.9-10.1c; SL.9-10.2

Objectives:
- Students will review a passage from the text that exemplifies the stream of consciousness writing technique
- Students will discuss the meaning of the passage and how this writing technique achieves the desired effects

Purposes:
The purposes of this lesson are:
- To explore the stream of consciousness writing technique
- To show how Mr. Bradbury uses this technique in Fahrenheit 451
- To evaluate the effectiveness of using this technique

Teacher's Notes:
Read to students the passage beginning, "One drop of rain. Clarisse. Another drop. Mildred. A third. The uncle...." Students should follow along in their books. (60th Anniversary edition, page 15)

After reading the passage, explain that to understand the passage, you need to look at the events that lead up to it. Briefly review those events with your students
- Montag went to work as a fireman.
- Montag met Clarisse on his way home.
- When he got home, he discovered Mildred had overdosed.
- The men came and pumped out Mildred.
- Montag overheard conversation at Clarisse's house.

Discuss briefly what effect each of these events had on Montag, and have students conjecture what the cumulative effect may have been.

Read the "conversation" Montag overheard at Clarisse's house, then reread the "One drop of rain" passage and explain to them that it is written using the "stream of consciousness" writing technique.

Discuss the passage with students. Sample discussion questions:
- What does the passage mean?
- What are the effects of writing the passage this way?
- What is conveyed in this passage that would be difficult or impossible to convey in another way?
- What would it be like if the whole book were written like this? (So...this is a technique that is most often used sparingly.)

Optional follow-up: Have students try writing using the stream of consciousness technique as a quick-write in class.

ARE YOU HAPPY?
DISCUSSION ACTIVITY FOR READING ASSIGNMENT 1
Fahrenheit 451

CCSS: SL.9-10.1; SL.9-10.1c; SL.9-10.1d; SL.9-10.4

Objective:
- Students will participate in a group discussion about happiness, things that make us unhappy, and ways to cope with things that make us unhappy

Purposes:
The purposes of this lesson are:
- To explore what it means to be "happy"
- To show students ways of evaluating their own happiness
- To show students ways of coping with and changing unhappiness

Teacher's Notes:
Clarisse asks Montag a simple question: Are you happy?. It doesn't take Montag long to realize that he is not happy.

This lesson is an exploration of what it means to be happy and how to achieve happiness. Originally, this was planned as a writing assignment, but that left students alone to discover how happy or unhappy they are, without any support and without giving them any coping devices. This lesson, therefore, is not just about discovering what makes us happy or unhappy; it is about what to do when we realize we are unhappy--what can we do to cope with unhappiness?

Below is a discussion guide. Use whatever parts of it you think are appropriate for your students. The writer of this guide is not a psychologist or counselor; these are just some common-sense suggestions. For more professional advice and suggestions, you might consider speaking with a professional in this area or even having a professional on hand in the room during the discussion.

A follow-up writing assignment after the discussion would be appropriate. Some topics for a follow-up assignment are:
- What did you learn from the class discussion about happiness?
- What is one thing that makes you unhappy, and what can you do to improve or cope with that?
- Rate your happiness on a scale of 1 to 10 and briefly explain your numerical choice.

Lesson: Are You Happy? page 2

Introductory Activity
Ask students what makes them happy. Brainstorm a list and write students' responses on your board. Then, ask what makes them unhappy. Again, brainstorm a list and jot down student responses.

Transition:
Clarisse asks Montag this simple question: Are you happy?. Prior to this, Montag had just sort-of assumed he was happy. He did his daily routine every day. However, it doesn't take Montag long to realize that he is *not* happy--and to search for something he believes will make him feel more satisfied...happier.

Sample Discussion Questions:
- Do you ever stop and think about whether you're happy or not?
- Is that a good thing to do now and then? Why or why not?

- What does it mean to be "happy"? Are there different kinds of happiness?
- You've said that these things make you happy: [Review the list on the board of things that students said make them happy.] Do all of these things give one the same kind of happiness?
- What, then, are the most important kinds of happiness?

- Are there, then, also different degrees of unhappiness?
- Which of the things that make you unhappy [refer to the list students brainstormed earlier] are more important than the others? Which are less important?

Look at the items on the "unhappy" list. Discuss ways of coping with these things.

Small Things (Like having to do household chores)
- Try to be thankful for the related items like
    having a bed that needs to be made...some people have no bed
    having to do dishes...some people have had no meal
    taking out the trash...to have had the things that were used

Medium Things (Like disagreements with parents, not being allowed to do something you want to do, or feeling "wronged" by a friend)
- Try talking things out calmly & respectfully
- Attempt a compromise
- Try to keep things in perspective; how important is the problem in a cosmic sense will it make a real difference to you 20 years from now? Is it really worth being miserable over

Big Things (Like being abused or bullied, being hooked on drugs)
- Seek professional help. Talk to a teacher or counselor to find the appropriate steps to take. [Provide students with appropriate contact information.]

Follow-up: Discuss with students how to evaluate their own happiness and keep things in perspective. Remind students that a positive attitude and being thankful for all the positive things helps to make the negative things less important.

WHAT'S IN YOUR WINDOW?
WRITING ASSIGNMENT FOR READING ASSIGNMENT 1
Fahrenheit 451

CCSS: W.9-10.4; W.9-10.5; W.9-10.10;

Objective:
- Students will describe what Montag would see if he were standing outside the window of their homes one typical evening

Purposes:
The purposes of this lesson are:
- To tie the novel to students' lives
- To have students evaluate, from an objective perspective, what goes on in their homes on a typical evening.
- To practice envisioning something and turning those thoughts into words on paper so someone else can see what was envisioned

Teacher's Notes:
Discuss the assignment in detail with your students, including the due date you have set and any other requirements you might want to add to those stated.

A follow-up discussion (after the descriptions are written) would be appropriate. You could discuss how sometimes we fall into a rut without really thinking about it...and ways to avoid doing that.

Alternately, a follow-up writing assignment could be having students write what they *wish* Montag would see if he were looking in their windows.

The assignment sheet for this writing assignment is also in the Student Workbook.

WHAT'S IN YOUR WINDOW?
Fahrenheit 451

He stood outside the talking house in the shadows, thinking he might even tap on their door and whisper, "Let me come in. I won't say anything. I just want to listen. What is it you're saying?" --Guy Montag

Guy stood outside of Clarisse's home that evening, listening to the conversation. He wanted to hear more. If Montag were to stand outside your home, looking in your window, what would he see and hear on any typical evening?

Your assignment is to describe from Montag's point of view what he sees and hears while standing outside of your home one evening, looking in your window.

You may write this in any format you choose:
- as a descriptive essay
- as a play scene
- as a poem or song lyrics
- as a comic strip

Here's how to begin:
1. Choose the setting. In what room are things most likely to be going on at your house in the evening?
2. Make some notes describing the room--essential as well as unusual characteristics.
3. Make some notes about who will be in the room.
4. Make notes about what kind of conversation or activity that will typically be going on.
5. Go back and sketch in any dialogue that might be happening
6. Decide on the format for your description.
7. Begin writing a draft.

Think about and be prepared to state what Montag's reaction to what he sees and/or hears might be (and why you think he would feel that way).
- Would he want to come in just to listen?
- Would he be bored?
- Would he want to stay at the window watching?

PLAY THE MAN, MASTER RIDLEY
WRITING ASSIGNMENT FOR READING ASSIGNMENT 2
Fahrenheit 451

CCSS: W.9-10.4; W.9-10.5; W.9-10.10; L.9-10.1

Objective:
- Students will compose a letter from the North Elm woman to her daughter (or son), explaining why she chose to end her life in this way and giving her daughter (or son) her parting words.

Purposes:
The purposes of this lesson are:
- To put students in the mindset of the North Elm woman, to get them to think about these things: why someone would be willing to die rather than live without her books, what effects this action would have on family members, and what advice or parting words would be appropriate in this situation
- To write considering point of view, audience, and purpose

Teacher's Notes:
Discuss the assignment in detail with your students, including the due date you have set and any other requirements you might want to add to those stated.

The assignment sheet for this writing assignment is also in the Student Workbook.

PLAY THE MAN, MASTER RIDLEY
Fahrenheit 451

The woman on North Elm decided she would rather die than live without her books. Perhaps she also had heard that people with books were sometimes sent to the insane asylum. At some point, though, she made up her mind to deliberately stay in her burning home with her burning books. No doubt she had thought about this before the alarm was ever called in. When you break the law, you usually think about the consequences and what you would do if you got caught.

We're going to diverge from the actual story of Fahrenheit 451 for a little bit. Suppose the North Elm woman knew ahead of time that the alarm was going to be called in, and she had already decided to go down with her books. After making this decision, she wrote a letter to her daughter, which she mailed when she found out the alarm had been called in. What would she have said to her daughter in that letter?

Your assignment is to write a letter from the North Elm woman to her daughter (or son, your choice) explaining why she refused to leave her home, and giving her daughter (or son) her parting words.

- Be thorough in your explanations
- Use a friendly letter format

Here's a way to go about doing this assignment:
1. Pretend you are the North Elm woman.
2. Think about why you would do what she did, knowing what you know about her world. Jot down any reasons you can think of as to why she would choose to do this.
3. Think about what you would say to your child, knowing you would soon be gone. What words of advice, what final words would you say? Jot down any ideas you have.
4. Look over your notes. Choose the best reasons and advice. Organize them in a logical way. Do any thoughts go together or naturally flow from one to another? Identify those kinds of things in your notes.
5. Write a rough draft of your letter. A few words of introduction, stating your intentions, would be appropriate. Follow that with your reasons. Follow that with any advice or final words you have.
6. Re-read, revise, have someone else read your letter and make suggestions. Edit and revise as necessary until you are happy with the final draft.

BOOKS, BOOKS, BOOKS
ACTIVITY FOR READING ASSIGNMENT 2
Fahrenheit 451

CCSS: RL.9-10.10,

Objectives:
- Students will brainstorm as many different kinds of reading material as possible.
- Students will go to the library, find 10 different kinds of reading material, briefly investigate each one, and complete a graphic organizer with the information found.
- Students will choose one item from their graphic organizer lists to read and read it.
- Students will give a brief oral report to the class about the materials they read.

Purposes:
The purposes of this lesson are:
- To get students thinking about reading and the many different kinds of things that are available to read.
- By investigating many different kinds of reading material, reluctant readers may find a kind of reading they enjoy, and active readers may consider something other than what they usually read.
- Reporting to the class is a quick way to evaluate whether or not the reading has been done, it exposes all students to many reading materials (which might sound interesting or be recommended for further reading), and it gives the reporter the opportunity to practice public speaking skills.

Introduction To Share With Students
Piles of books and shovel-fulls of magazines bombarded Montag as he faced the attic at North Elm. The woman must have practically had a whole library up there! Just think of how many different kinds of things there are to read! Take a minute to brainstorm as many different kinds of reading materials and genres of literature as you can!

[Your students may need a brief review of what a "genre" is. Tend to that if necessary. Then write down on your board all the different answers students give. When they start to run out of ideas, guide them with some suggestions to get them to add more.]

Activity
Take your students to your library or media center. Send them on a hunt to find at least 10 different kinds of books or magazines. They should fill out the graphic organizer on the following page, noting the kind of reading material it is, its title, what it seems to be about (based on the cover information), and whether or not it seems interesting. Give students ample time to complete the assignment.

Follow-up: Have students check out and read one of the items on their lists that seemed interesting to them. Tell them by when their reading has to be completed, then use part of a class period for students to report back to the class about their reading. A brief oral report would suffice; just enough for you to know the book has been read. Make a note as to which item each student chooses from his or her list so you will know at report time if that title has been read or not.

BOOKS, BOOKS, BOOKS
Fahrenheit 451

Find 10 different kinds of reading materials in your library or media center. Tell what kind each is, list the tiles, read the covers to see what they are about and fill in the About column, and then tell if each looks interesting to you or not. A few boxes are bigger in case you need more room for some titles

Kind	Title	About	Interesting To You?

DOVER BEACH
DISCUSSION ACTIVITY FOR READING ASSIGNMENT 3
Fahrenheit 451

CCSS: RL.9-10.1; RL.9-10.4; RL.9-10.9; RL.9-10.10; W.9-10.9a
SL.9-10.1; SL.9-10.1c; SL.9-10.1d; L.9-10.3; L.9-10.5; L.9-10.5a

Objectives:
- Students will read the poem "Dover Beach" in its entirety.
- Students will discuss the literal and figurative meaning of the poem.
- Students will discuss the relationship of the poem to Fahrenheit 451.

Purposes:
The purposes of this lesson are:
- To study in more depth the relationship between "Dover Beach" and Fahrenheit 451
- To practice interpreting figurative language and poetry
- To show how using source material strengthens and enriches a work

Activity
Read the poem "Dover Beach" in its entirety (included after these directions) with your class. Discuss the literal and figurative meaning of the poem, line by line.

Then, conduct a discussion of how the poem relates to Fahrenheit 451. Below are some discussion questions to get you started.

- How does the "turbid ebb and flow of human misery" correlate to the Phoenix in Fahrenheit 451?
  - The "turbid ebb and flow of human misery" indicates that times of prosperity and more dismal times are cyclical for humankind. In Fahrenheit 451, the Phoenix bird who burns itself up and rises anew from the ashes represents this same kind of cyclical nature in human society.

- What is the "sea of faith" that has abandoned the world in "Dover Beach"? Has the "sea of faith" also abandoned Montag's world? Explain.
  - The "sea of faith" could be many things but is most often thought to be "faith" in a religious sense. When people are no longer rooted in a belief in something larger than themselves, civilization tends to deteriorate. Yes, most people in Montag's world are only interested in themselves and their own pleasure.

- Left without faith, all the two people in the poem have left is each other to count on in the world. In what ways is this similar to Montag and Mildred? Can Montag and Mildred count on each other?
  - Like the speaker in the poem, Montag wants to count on Mildred, to go forward together in this quest for a new life. Unfortunately for Montag, he can't count on Mildred. She isn't interested.

Dover Beach Discussion Activity, page 2

- How does the last line of the poem, "Where ignorant armies clash by night" relate to Fahrenheit 451?
  - The planes frequently fly over, reminding Montag of the War. In Fahrenheit 451 War is portrayed as senseless, as it is in the poem.

- What effect does adding this little poem to Fahrenheit 451 have on the work as a whole?
  - It enriches the depth of the book.
  - We get a sample of the works being destroyed.
  - We see that many elements of Fahrenheit 451 are timeless...have been considered by others previously. That in itself also underscores the cyclical nature of the human condition.
  - Including it shows Montag is strong enough in his feelings about the books to read it and take a chance on getting turned in. It shows us more about Mrs. Phelps, as she reacts to it by crying. It shows us more about the other characters, as they react to Mrs. Phelps.

Note: The "Dover Beach" discussion activity page which follows is also included in the Student Workbook.

Follow-up: Have students do a quick-write activity in which they summarize your class discussion by answering this question:

What does the poem "Dover Beach" have to do with Fahrenheit 451?

This will make them think back through your discussion and recall the information presented--to help solidify it in their minds, and it will give you a way to assess what students got out of the discussion. Plus it is a good opportunity to get students to practice summarizing and writing.

DOVER BEACH
Fahrenheit 451

Dover Beach
BY MATTHEW ARNOLD

Notes:

The sea is calm tonight.
The tide is full, the moon lies fair
Upon the straits; on the French coast the light
Gleams and is gone; the cliffs of England stand,
Glimmering and vast, out in the tranquil bay.
Come to the window, sweet is the night-air!
Only, from the long line of spray
Where the sea meets the moon-blanched land,
Listen! you hear the grating roar
Of pebbles which the waves draw back, and fling,
At their return, up the high strand,
Begin, and cease, and then again begin,
With tremulous cadence slow, and bring
The eternal note of sadness in.

Sophocles long ago
Heard it on the Ægean, and it brought
Into his mind the turbid ebb and flow
Of human misery; we
Find also in the sound a thought,
Hearing it by this distant northern sea.

The Sea of Faith
Was once, too, at the full, and round earth's shore
Lay like the folds of a bright girdle furled.
But now I only hear
Its melancholy, long, withdrawing roar,
Retreating, to the breath
Of the night-wind, down the vast edges drear
And naked shingles of the world.

Ah, love, let us be true
To one another! for the world, which seems
To lie before us like a land of dreams,
So various, so beautiful, so new,
Hath really neither joy, nor love, nor light,
Nor certitude, nor peace, nor help for pain;
And we are here as on a darkling plain
Swept with confused alarms of struggle and flight,
Where ignorant armies clash by night.

tranquil = peaceful; calm

tremulous = trembling
cadence = rhythmic pace

Aegean = the Aegean Sea, part of the Mediterranean Sea
turbid = muddy; cloudy; not clear

The sound of the sea waves reminded Sophocles of the coming and going of good and bad times for humankind.

----

girdle = something that encircles or confines
furled = rolled tightly in upon itself

At one time, humankind had faith, but people no longer do.

----

certitude = certainty

Without faith, there is no certainty or peace in the world. All we have left is each other, so let's be true to one another in a confused world full of war.

TV FAVORITES
ACTIVITY FOR READING ASSIGNMENT 3
Fahrenheit 451

CCSS: SL.9-10.1; SL.9-10.1c; SL.9-10.1d;
W.9-10.1; W.9-10.1a; W.9-10.1b; W.9-10.1e; L.9-10.1; L.9-10.2

Objective:
- Students will list and evaluate their favorite television programs.
- Students will do a quick-write persuasive essay using information from the class discussion.

Purposes:
The purposes of this lesson are:
- To get students to evaluate the kinds of television programs they regularly view
- To consider whether the most popular programming people watch is turning us into Mildreds
- To review and help retain the information discussed
- To practice writing a persuasive argument

Activity
Give students a few minutes to fill out the TV Favorites graphic organizer on the following page (also in the Student Workbook).

Discuss the responses in class together. Make a composite list of students' favorite TV shows on the board. Keep a tally to see which one is the most popular.

For each of the TV shows, discuss:
- What kind of a show is it (reality, sports, news, drama...)?
- What is the level of intellectual engagement or educational value of the show?
- What values does the show promote?
- What kind of language is used on the show (common, vulgar, intellectual)?
- Is the show purely "entertainment," or does it have other value?
- Would it fit in to programming on the Parlor Walls?
- Has this program become your "family"? Do you schedule your activities around seeing it?
- Why do you like this show so much? What about it appeals to you?

Look at the cumulative picture of the information you have discussed. Guide students to state and respond to the characteristics of the most popular TV shows, then put our popular programming in perspective with the programming of the Parlor Walls.

Follow-up
Have students do a Quick-Write exercise using the information gathered in this discussion as evidence that we either are or are not on our way to becoming Mildreds, watching mindless entertainment on our flat-screen TVs, our Parlor Walls (and other electronic devices!).

TV FAVORITES
Fahrenheit 451

List your three most favorite television shows below.

1. _____
2. _____
3. _____

For each of the TV shows you listed, answer these questions:
What kind of a show is it (reality, sports, news, drama...)?

1. _____ 2. _____ 3. _____

What is the level of intellectual engagement or educational value of the show (on a scale of 1 to 10 with 10 being the highest level of intellectual engagement or educational value)?

1. _____ 2. _____ 3. _____

What values does the show promote?

1. _____
2. _____
3. _____

What kind of language is used on the show (common, vulgar, intellectual)?

1. _____ 2. _____ 3. _____

Is the show purely "entertainment," or does it have other value (if so, what)?

1. _____ 2. _____ 3. _____

Would it fit well into programming on the Parlor Walls (yes or no)?
1. _____ 2. _____ 3. _____

Has this program become your "family"? Do you schedule your activities around seeing it and talk a lot about it?

1. _____ 2. _____ 3. _____

Why do you like this show so much? What about it appeals to you?

1. _____
2. _____
3. _____

JUDGING A CANDIDATE
ACTIVITY FOR READING ASSIGNMENT 3
Fahrenheit 451

CCSS: SL.9-10.1; SL.9-10.1b-d; SL.9-10.2; SL.9-10.3; SL.9.10-4; SL.9-10.5
W.9-10.7; W.9-10.8; W.9-10.10

Objective:
- Students will evaluate the criteria on which political candidates should be judged
- Students will participate in a follow-up activity related to this evaluation.

Purposes:
The purposes of this lesson are:
- To discuss the criteria on which political candidates should be judged
- To discuss the importance of carefully considering many facets of each candidate
- To actually evaluate a candidate on the criteria determined

Activity
Review the portion of the text in Reading Assignment 3 where the women talk about politics. (60th Anniversary edition, p.93)
Here are some discussion questions:
- On what kinds of things do the women compare and contrast the candidates?
- On what kinds of things should they compare and contrast the candidates?
- Do you listen to what the candidates say? Why or why not?
- What could happen if people would stop listening to what candidates say and would vote based on the criteria the women in the novel use?
- Does what the candidates say always match up with the actions they take?
- Why is it important to both listen to AND evaluate actions of a candidate?
- Does the moral character of a candidate make a difference? Why or why not?

The questions above are also on the student JUDGING A CANDIDATE page in the Student Workbook. You could have students answer these questions individually, in groups, or as a whole class activity. If done individually or in groups, be sure to bring everyone back together for a whole-class discussion of these points.

Follow-up
There are several possible follow-up activities to this discussion. Here are a few ideas:
- If you are in an election year, have each student evaluate one of the candidates running for office. An oral report or presentation (video or PowerPoint) to the class should follow.
- Whether it is an election year or not, have each student evaluate one politician currently in office, either on the local, state, or national level. Again, an oral report or presentation to the class should follow.
- Have different groups of students develop campaign materials (press release, banners, TV ads, etc.) for a candidate. Have the whole class compare and contrast the materials each group devises. Determine the strengths and weaknesses of each.
- Have each student write an article entitled "How To Determine Which Candidate To Vote For," and publish the best one in the school or local newspaper.

JUDGING A CANDIDATE
Fahrenheit 451

In Reading Assignment 3, Millie urges her friends to have a discussion about politics to please Guy. Review that section of the text and answer the following questions:

1. On what kinds of things do the women compare and contrast the candidates?

2. On what kinds of things should they compare and contrast the candidates?

3. Do you listen to what the candidates say? Why or why not?

4. What could happen if people would stop listening to what candidates say and would vote based on the criteria the women in the novel use?

5. Does what the candidates say always match up with the actions they take? Explain.

6. Why is it important to both listen to AND evaluate actions of a candidate?

7. Does the moral character of a candidate make a difference? Why or why not?

IF I WERE A BOOK
QUICK-WRITE ASSIGNMENT FOR READING ASSIGNMENT 4
Fahrenheit 451

CCSS: W.9-10.10; W.9-10.4; W.9-10.2b; W.9-10.2c; W.9-10.2e; W.9-10.2f; L.9-10.1; L.9-10.2

Objective:
- Students will do a quick-write assignment in which they choose a book that they would want to "become," or a book that best suits their personalities.

Purposes:
The purposes of this lesson are:
- To practice quick-writing skills
- To apply something from the book into students' own lives
- To get students to think about the books they have read in the past, analyze those books within the scope of the task at hand, to make decisions based on their analyses, and to be able to verbalize the reasons for their decisions

Activity
Have students orally brainstorm a list of books they have read in the past. Write the names of the books where students can see the list. Encourage students to make remarks about the books as the titles are given (good, bad, boring, exciting, funny, all-time favorite, etc.).

Transition: *Montag became the Book of Ecclesiastes. Other people in Fahrenheit 451 became books, too, to preserve the contents of the books.*

Have students do a quick-write completing one of the following statements:
- "If I were a book, I'd like to be..."
- "If I were a book, the title that would best suit my personality would be..."

Students should explain why they chose the book they did, and they should be as specific as possible using examples from the books they've chosen.

THE THINGS THAT MUST BE THOUGHT
GROUP ACTIVITY FOR READING ASSIGNMENT 4
Fahrenheit 451

CCSS: SL.9-10.1; SL.9-10.1c; SL.9-10.1d

Objectives:
- Students will participate in a small group discussion to create a list of "things that must be thought."
- Students will participate in a whole-class discussion of the list items all groups created and evaluate the relative importance of each item.

Purposes:
The purposes of this lesson are:
- Back in the beginning of the book, Montag asks Clarisse what she and her family talk about. Here near the end of the book, he wishes he had more time to think about everything; he has discovered what thinking people think and talk about and wants more time to do that. The purpose of this activity is to introduce students to things thinking people think and talk about, in case some students are more like Montag was at the beginning of the book.
- To give students food for thought and the opportunity to share ideas
- To relate the book to students' lives

Activity
- Convey to students that just before Montag steps from the river, he thinks of sleeping in fresh hay in a lonely barn away from the loud highways. The book says, "This was all he wanted now. Some sign that the immense world would accept him and give him the long time he needed to think all the things that must be thought."
- Briefly discuss what the quote means.
- Divide students into small groups, and have them create lists of "the things that must be thought." Tell students to consider:
    What categories of things would those thoughts include?
    What are a few items in each category?
- Come back together as a whole class to discuss the lists students have created. Examine why the items were included on the lists.
- Have students decide which things would be most important and/or least important to think about (and why).
- Hold a brief discussion about students' thoughts regarding a few of the most important list items.

Follow-up: Students could choose one topic from the list to research and report on what others have already thought about that topic.

ECCLESIASTES
READER RESPONSE ACTIVITY FOR READING ASSIGNMENT 4
Fahrenheit 451

CCSS: RL.9-10.9; RI.9-10.4; RI.9-10.10; W.9-10.2; W.9-10.2a-f; W.9-10.4; W.9-10.5

Objective:
- Students will read a passage from the beginning of the Book of Ecclesiastes.
- Students will reflect upon the verses presented.
- Students will respond to the verse of their choice from the passage.
- Students will participate in a class discussion of how this passage from Ecclesiastes relates to Fahrenheit 451.

Purposes:
The purposes of this lesson are:
- To familiarize students, at least a bit, with the Book of Ecclesiastes. Ecclesiastes is important in Fahrenheit 451. Of all the possible book titles, it was the one chosen by Mr. Bradbury for Montag to "become." Students should read at least a bit of it to see how it might relate to the novel.
- To get students to reflect on, evaluate, and respond to thought-provoking statements made in Ecclesiastes
- To have students verbalize their thoughts and put them down on paper in a coherent essay
- To discuss the importance of the ideas presented in Ecclesiastes as they relate to Fahrenheit 451

Activity
After students have finished reading the novel, discuss in detail the directions for the Ecclesiastes assignment on the following page. (The assignment page is also in the Student Workbook.) Include any additional requirements you might have as well as the date the assignment should be completed.

Follow-up: After students have completed this assignment, conduct a whole-class discussion of each verse, drawing on students' ideas. Follow that by tying the ideas presented in the passage to the ideas presented in Fahrenheit 451. Consider these discussion questions (by verse #):

- 3. What did Montag gain from his labor?

- 4. Where in the novel is an example of or allusion to the earth remaining forever, regardless of what people do? [A: the birds returning to the trees after the explosions in the city]

- 5, 6, 7, 9, 10. How do these passages relate to the Phoenix symbolism in the novel?

- 11. Montag thinks Mildred has probably already forgotten him. How many generations back in your family do you remember?

ECCLESIASTES
Fahrenheit 451

Montag "became" the Book of Ecclesiastes (from the Bible). Below is a passage from the beginning of the Book of Ecclesiastes (New International Version).

Your assignment is to read this passage and (in writing) respond to, discuss, or explain any one of the numbered verses.
- Several paragraphs would be an appropriate length for your written work.

3 What do people gain from all their labors
   at which they toil under the sun?
4 Generations come and generations go,
   but the earth remains forever.
5 The sun rises and the sun sets,
   and hurries back to where it rises.
6 The wind blows to the south
   and turns to the north;
   round and round it goes,
   ever returning on its course.
7 All streams flow into the sea,
   yet the sea is never full.
   To the place the streams come from,
   there they return again.
8 All things are wearisome,
   more than one can say.
   The eye never has enough of seeing,
   nor the ear its fill of hearing.
9 What has been will be again,
   what has been done will be done again;
   there is nothing new under the sun.
10 Is there anything of which one can say,
   "Look! This is something new"?
   It was here already, long ago;
   it was here before our time.
11 No one remembers the former generations,
   and even those yet to come
   will not be remembered
   by those who follow them.

One way to begin the writing portion of the assignment is to re-read each verse and see what ideas come to your mind. When you find one for which you have several ideas, focus on that one. Jot down your ideas. Expand upon them with additional notes. Begin to formulate them into complete thoughts and organize them so one idea will flow to the next. Use examples to help support and explain your statements.

NOTES
Fahrenheit 451

UNIT TESTS
Fahrenheit 451

INTERCHANGEABLE TEST PARTS:
MATCHING
SHORT ANSWER
EXTENDED ANSWER
QUOTATIONS
VOCABULARY

NOTES

- There are at least 3 different versions of each test part (3 Matching, 3 Short Answer, etc.)

- These are paginated so they can be mixed and matched however you want. Watch for duplicate questions in the Short Answer & Extended Short Answer if you choose more than one page of each to go into your test.

- Answer keys to the Matching and Vocabulary parts are at the end of the test section.

- The Short Answer questions are from the study questions, and answers are there.

- Quotations are from the quotation section of the study guide, and answers are there.

- Answers to Extended Answer (quasi "essay") questions need to be evaluated by you based on your own criteria and your class's discussions.

- Rather than taking up dozens of more pages with answer keys when the answers are already given elsewhere in the unit, it seemed a better value to include more new materials instead.

NOTES
Fahrenheit 451

Fahrenheit 451
Matching 1

Name _____

____ 1. Seashells   A. 2-way ear-radio

____ 2. Parlor Walls   B. Montag's means of escape from the Hound & his past

____ 3. Mechanical Hound   C. Tracks down and kills certain people

____ 4. Beetle   D. A show Millie and her friends watch on the parlor walls

____ 5. Books   E. The ____ And The Sand

____ 6. White Clown   F. They're hidden behind the ventilator grill.

____ 7. Sieve   G. Legendary bird that burns itself up and arises anew from the ashes

____ 8. Denham's   H. Introduces Montag to the possibility of a different lifestyle

____ 9. Green Bullet   I. Ear-sized music radios

____ 10. River   J. _____ Dental Detergent

____ 11. Phoenix   K. Claims not to worry about anything but cries at the poem

____ 12. Clarisse   L. The car; a means of escape

____ 13. Mrs. Bowles   M. Contain Mildred's "family"

____ 14. Mrs. Phelps   N. Has children but does not want anything to do with them

____ 15. Faber   O. Helps Montag from his old way of life to a new one

Fahrenheit 451 Name _____
Matching 2

____ 1. Seashells   A. What the No. Elm woman uses to start the fire at her own home, destroying her home, her books, and herself

____ 2. Parlor Walls   B. Sea of ___; poem excerpt Montag reads to Millie & friends

____ 3. Mechanical Hound   C. Introduces Montag to the possibility of a different lifestyle

____ 4. Kitchen Match   D. Literary hobo who accepts Montag

____ 5. Sickness   E. Montag's is a result of the realizations he is having about his society and his own life. It literally makes him sick, and he doesn't want to go to work and continue with his life the way it was.

____ 6. Sieve   F. Legendary bird who burns itself up and arises anew from the ashes

____ 7. Faith   G. Tracks down and kills certain people

____ 8. Railroad tracks   H. Helps Montag from his old way of life to a new one

____ 9. Phoenix   I. Sets herself and her own home on fire

____ 10. Beatty   J. Lead Montag to a new life with the literate hobos

____ 11. Clarisse   K. Montag's "wax doll" wife

____ 12. Granger   L. The ___ And The Sand

____ 13. Mildred   M. Ear-sized music radios

____ 14. No. Elm Woman   N. Montag's boss; represents the establishment/government

____ 15. Faber   O. Contain Mildred's "family"

Fahrenheit 451
Matching 3

Name _____

____ 1. Seashells   A. Helps Montag from his old way of life to a new one

____ 2. Parlor Walls   B. Literary hobo who accepts Montag

____ 3. Mechanical Hound   C. Montag's means of escape from the Hound & his past

____ 4. Beetle   D. Claims not to worry about anything but cries at the poem

____ 5. White Clown   E. The car; a means of escape

____ 6. Green Bullet   F. Montag's "wax doll" wife

____ 7. Faith   G. Legendary bird who burns itself up and arises anew from the ashes

____ 8. River   H. 2-way ear-radio

____ 9. Railroad tracks   I. Has children but does not want anything to do with them

____ 10. Ecclesiastes   J. Sea of ___; poem excerpt Montag reads to Millie & friends

____ 11. Phoenix   K. Introduces Montag to the possibility of a different lifestyle

____ 12. Protagonist   L. The book of the Bible that Montag "becomes"

____ 13. Faber   M. Tracks down and kills certain people

____ 14. Clarisse   N. Montag plants a book at his house.

____ 15. Granger   O. Ear-sized music radios

____ 16. Mildred   P. Contain Mildred's "family"

____ 17. No. Elm Woman   Q. Lead Montag to a new life with the literate hobos

____ 18. Mrs. Bowles   R. Sets herself and her own home on fire

____ 19. Mrs. Phelps   S. A show Millie and her friends watch on the parlor walls

____ 20. Black   T. Guy Montag

Fahrenheit 451 Name _____
Short Answer 1

1. One of the men who comes to pump Mildred's stomach says, "You don't need an M.D., case like this; all you need is two handymen, clean up the problem in half an hour." How does this statement aptly sum up the whole process described in the preceding paragraphs?

2. How is the world Clarisse and Montag live in similar to our world today?

3. When the firemen respond to the alarm at Mrs. Blake's house, she is still there. How does her presence "spoil the ritual" for the firemen?

4. What do you think Montag means when he says, "But that was another Mildred...so deep inside this one, and so bothered, really bothered, that the two women had never met." ?

5. Why is the event with the mechanical hound at the door significant?

6. From Mildred's point of view, explain why the parlor walls are better than books.

7. What is the difference between talking "things" and talking "the meaning of things"?

Fahrenheit 451　　　　　　　　Name _____
Short Answer 2

1. Faber says that there are three things missing from the world. What are they?

2. Chapter Two is entitled "The Sieve and the Sand." To what does this refer?

3. What motivates Montag to pull the trigger on the flame-thrower and set Beatty on fire?

4. Why does the search team find someone else to kill in place of Montag?

5. What is the one thing about Clarisse that most attracts Montag to her? Tell why it attracts Montag to her.

6. How are Mildred and her friends like a sieve?

7. List 5 things that are important images or symbols in Fahrenheit 451.

8. Why were the alarms to burn always at night?

Fahrenheit 451 Name _____
Short Answer 3

1. Why doesn't Mildred tell Beatty about the book she finds?

2. "Someone--the door--why doesn't the door-voice tell us---"
   "I shut it off."
   What do we learn about Montag and Mildred from these two lines?

3. Montag asks Millie "Does the White Clown love you . . . does your 'family' love you?"
   What is the significance of Montag's questions?

4. Montag and Faber hatch a plan to plant books in firemen's houses to help bring down the system, while also setting up clandestine reading rooms. Do you think this is a good plan? Evaluate their chances for success.

5. Why are Millie and her friends made so nervous when Montag turns the TV walls off?

6. Why does Mrs. Phelps start crying in response to the poem?

7. Montag believes Beatty wanted to die. Explain why you agree or disagree with him.

Fahrenheit 451 Name _____
Short Answer 4

1. Explain Granger's metaphor of the Phoenix.

2. Why did Ray Bradbury make Montag the Book of Ecclesiastes rather than some other book?

3. Is Beatty for or against Montag? Support your answer with evidence from the book.

4. Why does Mildred call in the alarm on her own house?

5. Faber is a relatively minor character in Fahrenheit 451, but he is important. What function does Faber's character have in the story?

6. Name three things or people that represent the establishment, those in control in Fahrenheit 451.

7. Why is Mildred incapable of sharing Montag's quest for a new lifestyle?

8. Write one phrase or sentence that best states the main theme of Fahrenheit 451.

Fahrenheit 451 Name _____
Short Answer 5

1. Of what is the number 451 on Montag's helmet symbolic?

2. Explain in what ways Clarisse and Mildred are different from each other.

3. What does the Hound's reaction to Montag at the firehouse tell us?

4. When Montag returns home after burning the No. Elm home, he describes his hands as "infected." What does he mean by this?

5. Beatty says, "We must all be alike. Not everyone born free and equal, but everyone made equal. Each man the image of every other; then all are happy, for there are no mountains to make them cower, to judge themselves against." Do you agree with Beatty's vision of happiness? Why or why not?

6. Why doesn't Mildred tell Beatty about the book she finds?

7. Summarize Beatty's explanation of how and why society changed in the 20th Century.

Fahrenheit 451
Short Answer 6

Name _____

1. "Someone--the door--why doesn't the door-voice tell us---"
   "I shut it off."
   What do we learn about Montag and Mildred from these two lines?

2. "The train radio vomited upon Montag, in retaliation, a great tonload of music made of tin, copper, silver, chromium, and brass." What type of figure of speech is exemplified in this sentence? The music is in retaliation of what? Why is the music described as being made of metals?

3. Why are Millie and her friends made so nervous when Montag turns the TV walls off?

4. Earlier in the book, Beatty says "If you don't want a man unhappy politically, don't give him two sides of a question to worry him; give him one. Better yet, give him none." On what criteria do Millie and her friends judge the political candidates, and how does their political conversation between Millie and her friends relate to Beatty's statement?

5. Beatty confesses that he sent the Hound to Montag's home. Why did he send it?

6. Montag wonders if the teenagers who almost ran him over just for fun were the ones who ran over Clarisse. Is there any evidence to support this thought? Based on evidence in the book, would you say Clarisse's death was likely a random or a premeditated act?

Fahrenheit 451
Short Answer 7

Name _____

1. The men in the countryside have a plan for saving books. What is it, and do you think it is a good plan?

2. Explain Granger's metaphor of the Phoenix.

3. Explain why Granger misses his grandfather but Montag won't miss Millie.

4. What is the single most important question Clarisse asks Montag? Why is that question important? What effect does it have on Montag?

5. List at least 3 important things Montag realizes in the course of the story.

6. What is the nature of humankind's relationship to the world in Fahrenheit 451?

7. Write one phrase or sentence that best states the main theme of Fahrenheit 451.

Fahrenheit 451　　　　　　　　Name _____
Extended Answer 1

1. Montag thinks Beatty wanted to die. Do you agree or disagree with him? Use evidence from the book to support your answer.

2. Explain why Clarisse's death is important in Fahrenheit 451.

Fahrenheit 451 Name _____
Extended Answer 2

1. A character who changes has to be motivated by something. What is Montag's motivation to change? What does he want more than anything else, enough to lose his home, his wife, and his job? Support your answer with textual evidence.

2. Explain the symbolic use of the Phoenix in Fahrenheit 451.

Fahrenheit 451
Extended Answer 3

Name _____

1. Is Beatty for or against Montag? Support your answer with evidence from the book.

2. Why is the salamander a good symbol for Montag?

Fahrenheit 451
Extended Answer 4

Name _____

1. Years after people read Fahrenheit 451, the thing they remember is that it is about book burning. What does the book burning actually symbolize?

2. Describe Montag's relationship with Mildred.

Fahrenheit 451 Name _____
Extended Answer 5

1. Montag thinks Beatty wanted to die. Do you agree or disagree with him? Use evidence from the book to support your answer.

2. What events would you characterize as turning points in Montag's development in the story? State each and explain why each was chosen.

Fahrenheit 451 Name _____
Extended Answer 6

1. Characterize Ray Bradbury's style of writing. How does it contribute to the value of the novel?

2. What is censorship, and how is it portrayed in Fahrenheit 451?

Fahrenheit 451　　　　　　Name _____
Quotations 1

1. "You laugh when I haven't been funny and you answer right off. You never stop to think what I've asked you."

2. "We burned a thousand books. We burned a woman."
   "Well?

3. "We are living in a time when flowers are trying to live on flowers, instead of growing on good rain and black loam."

4. "By the time the consequences catch up with you, it's too late, isn't it, Montag?"

5. Mrs. Black, are you asleep in there? . . . The house did not reply.

6. In the trees, the birds that had flown away quickly now came back and settled down.

Fahrenheit 451 Name _____
Quotations 2

1. They walked the rest of the way in silence, hers thoughtful, his a kind of clenching and uncomfortable silence in which he shot her accusing glances.

2. Go on, anyway, shove the bore down, slush up the emptiness, if such a thing could be brought out in the throb of the suction snake.

3. "What a shame," she said. "You're not in love with anyone."

4. "We need not to be let alone. We need to be really bothered once in a while."

5. Mildred kicked the book. "Books aren't people. You read and I look all around, but there isn't anybody!...my 'family' is people. They tell me things; I laugh, they laugh! and the colors!"

6. "I don't want to change sides and just be told what to do. There's no reason to change if I do that."

Fahrenheit 451 Name _____
Quotations 3

1. "...this fire'll last me the rest of my life. God! I've been trying to put it out, in my mind, all night..."
   "You should have thought of that before becoming a fireman."

2. "And don't look to be saved in any one thing, person, machine, or library. Do your own bit of saving, and if you drown, at least die knowing you were headed for shore."

3. "Now, Montag, you're a burden. And fire will lift you off of my shoulders, clean, quick, sure; nothing to rot later. Antibiotic, aesthetic, practical."

4. They would have killed me, thought Montag. . . . For no reason at all in the world they would have killed me.

5. . . . the river was mild and leisurely, going away from the people who ate shadows for breakfast and steam for lunch and vapors for supper.

6. Silently, Granger arose, felt of his arms and legs, swearing, swearing incessantly under his breath, tears dripping from his face.

Fahrenheit 451   Name _____
Vocabulary 1

____ 1. STOLID   A. Humiliating failure; fall on the buttocks

____ 2. REFRACTED   B. Described

____ 3. IMPERCEPTIBLY   C. The study of the dynamics of projectiles

____ 4. CAPILLARY   D. Having or revealing little emotion

____ 5. MULTIFACETED   E. Arousing dislike or displeasure

____ 6. BALLISTICS   F. Impossible to detect by ordinary senses

____ 7. ERECTED   G. Authoritative pronouncement

____ 8. PROCLIVITIES   H. Not able to make a decision

____ 9. ODIOUS   I. Does not burn easily

____ 10. RAVENOUS   J. Indian spice

____ 11. PRATFALL   K. Set up; established

____ 12. DICTUM   L. Predispositions; tendencies

____ 13. NONCOMBUSTIBLE   M. Showed; revealed

____ 14. RETALIATION   N. Deflected; avoided

____ 15. MANIFESTED   O. Returning like for like, especially evil

____ 16. PARRIED   P. Fine; small in diameter

____ 17. INDECISIVE   Q. A pile of combustible materials for burning a corpse

____ 18. LIMNED   R. Extremely hungry; greedy for gratification

____ 19. CARDAMON   S. Having many faces

____ 20. PYRE   T. Deflected from a straight path

Use ten of these words in a short composition related to Fahrenheit 451.
Write your short composition on the back of this page.

Fahrenheit 451
Vocabulary 2

Name _____

____ 1. IMPERCEPTIBLY   A. Relating to sense of touch

____ 2. PULVERIZED   B. With a rhythmic flow

____ 3. MELANCHOLY   C. Not readily noticed or seen; not commonly known

____ 4. MULTIFACETED   D. Overwhelming, advancing sight crushing all in its path

____ 5. ODIOUS   E. Authoritative pronouncement

____ 6. RAVENOUS   F. Wordiness

____ 7. PRATFALL   G. Having many faces

____ 8. DICTUM   H. Described

____ 9. TACTILE   I. Impossible to detect by ordinary senses

____ 10. CADENCED   J. Sadness; gloominess

____ 11. RECEPTACLE   K. Humiliating failure; fall on the buttocks

____ 12. COWARDICE   L. Bizarre; distorted

____ 13. SIMULTANEOUSLY   M. Having or revealing little emotion

____ 14. VERBIAGE   N. Happening at the same time

____ 15. STOLID   O. A container that holds matter

____ 16. OBSCURE   P. Those who flaunt their knowledge

____ 17. GROTESQUE   Q. Reduced to powder

____ 18. LIMNED   R. Extremely hungry; greedy for gratification

____ 19. JUGGERNAUT   S. Arousing dislike or displeasure

____ 20. PEDANTS   T. Lacks courage in the face of danger

Use ten of these words in a short composition related to Fahrenheit 451.
Write your short composition on the back of this page.

Fahrenheit 451 Name _____
Vocabulary 3

____ 1. STOLID   A. Arousing dislike or displeasure

____ 2. REFRACTED   B. A container that holds matter

____ 3. IMPERCEPTIBLY   C. Having many faces

____ 4. CAPILLARY   D. Fine; small in diameter

____ 5. MULTIFACETED   E. Wordiness

____ 6. BALLISTICS   F. A pile of combustible materials for burning a corpse

____ 7. ODIOUS   G. Deflected from a straight path

____ 8. RAVENOUS   H. Those who flaunt their knowledge

____ 9. PRATFALL   I. Bizarre; distorted

____ 10. DICTUM   J. Deflected; avoided

____ 11. NONCOMBUSTIBLE K. Set up; established

____ 12. RECEPTACLE   L. The study of the dynamics of projectiles

____ 13. COWARDICE   M. Lacks courage in the face of danger

____ 14. PARRIED   N. Described

____ 15. VERBIAGE   O. Does not burn easily

____ 16. ERECTED   P. Humiliating failure; fall on the buttocks

____ 17. GROTESQUE   Q. Extremely hungry; greedy for gratification

____ 18. LIMNED   R. Authoritative pronouncement

____ 19. PEDANTS   S. Impossible to detect by ordinary senses

____ 20. PYRE   T. Having or revealing little emotion

Use ten of these words in a short composition related to Fahrenheit 451.
Write your short composition on the back of this page.

Fahrenheit 451 Unit Tests
Matching Answer Keys

	Matching 1	Matching 2	Matching 3
1	I	M	O
2	M	O	P
3	C	G	M
4	L	A	E
5	F	E	S
6	D	L	H
7	E	B	J
8	J	J	C
9	A	F	Q
10	B	N	L
11	G	C	G
12	H	D	T
13	N	K	A
14	K	I	K
15	O	H	B
16			F
17			R
18			I
19			D
20			N

Fahrenheit 451 Unit Tests
Vocabulary Matching Answer Keys

	Vocabulary 1	Vocabulary 2	Vocabulary 3
1	D	I	T
2	T	Q	G
3	F	J	S
4	P	G	D
5	S	S	C
6	C	R	L
7	K	K	A
8	L	E	Q
9	E	A	P
10	R	B	R
11	A	O	O
12	G	T	B
13	I	N	M
14	O	F	J
15	M	M	E
16	N	C	K
17	H	L	I
18	B	H	N
19	J	D	H
20	Q	P	F

ADDITIONAL RESOURCES
Fahrenheit 451

BULLETIN BOARD IDEAS
MORE ACTIVITIES
QUIZ GAME BOARD

NOTES:
- The Student Workbook has many more activity worksheets and graphic organizers that are not duplicated in the teacher's manual. Become familiar with them and use them in any way you choose.

- For more puzzles, games, and worksheets, consider downloading our Puzzle Pack for Fahrenheit 451. It has crosswords, word searches, matching, fill-in-the-blanks, magic squares, bingo cards, and juggle letter puzzles for unit words as well as the vocabulary words, plus flash cards for vocabulary. These are useful for reinforcement, independent study, extra classwork for those who finish assignments early, and for substitute teacher days. http://www.tpet.com/product/puzzle-pack

NOTES
Fahrenheit 451

BULLETIN BOARD IDEAS
Fahrenheit 451

1. Save one corner of the board for the best of students' Fahrenheit 451 writing assignments.

2. Take one of the word search puzzles from the extra activities packet and with a marker copy it over in a large size on the bulletin board. Write the clue words to find to one side. Invite students prior to and after class to find the words and circle them on the bulletin board.

3. Write several of the most significant quotations from the book onto the board on brightly colored paper.

4. Make a bulletin board listing the vocabulary words for this unit. As you complete sections of the novel and discuss the vocabulary for each section, write the definitions on the bulletin board. (If your board is one students face frequently, it will help them learn the words.)

5. Title the board "IN THE YEAR 2525" and post the lyrics to this popular 1970's tune. Find pictures which relate to the lyrics. Take time to discuss the ideas presented by the song with your students.

6. Do a bulletin board about censorship, free speech, and the First Amendment.

7. Draw a big red thermometer with the red going up to 451 degrees Fahrenheit. Next to it, draw a big fire and have book covers appear to be going into it.

8. Do a bulletin board about fire prevention.

9. Make a bulletin board promoting reading. Make a title "PICK UP A BOOK OR MAGAZINE AND READ. YOUR BRAIN WILL THANK YOU." or "EXERCISE YOUR BRAIN: READ!" Post book jackets of books you think your students would enjoy, magazine covers, anything with printed material.

10. Do a bulletin board about the future of our planet, promoting recycling, conservation, responsible use of our resources, etc.

11. Title the board: WORKING FOR A BETTER TOMORROW. Post pictures of people doing things that are obviously intended to make our world a better place in which to live.

12. Title the board: MAKING OUR WORLD A BETTER PLACE. Have each student write up on the board something he/she can do (will do, should do) to make his/her neighborhood a better place to live.

MORE ACTIVITIES
Fahrenheit 451

1. Pick a chapter or scene with a great deal of dialogue and have the students act it out on a stage. (Perhaps you could assign various scenes to different groups of students so more than one scene could be acted and more students could participate.)

2. Use some of the related topics noted earlier as suggestions for an in-class library, as topics for research, reports, written papers, or topics for guest speakers.

3. Research what careers are currently available in journalism, fire prevention, library science, and technological sciences.

4. Have students design a book cover (front and back and inside flaps) for Fahrenheit 451.

5. Have students design a bulletin board (ready to be put up; not just sketched) for Fahrenheit 451.

6. Discuss advertising in detail. have students bring in examples of advertising. Discuss the things the ads have in common (how they are supposed to appeal to us) and what kinds of things people should beware of when they are reading advertising.

7. Have students plan and carry out a project which will improve your school or their neighborhoods.

8. Have a mini anti-drug unit. Spend some time getting your kids involved in a "Just Say No!" type of program. Provide information and help.

9. Discuss the effect of a society's use of drugs on that society. What do drugs do not only to the individual, but to society as a whole?

10. Discuss ways in which your community can combat drugs. What things have been done, what things are planned to be done, and what else can be done?

11. Have a read-a-thon during which students get pledges for every fifteen minutes (or however long) they read. Have students come in on a Saturday (or set aside two or three class periods) where students' time can be monitored and officially counted. Use the proceeds for your class's favorite charity or to buy more books for your English Department or library.

QUIZ GAME
Fahrenheit 451

RA 1	RA 2	RA 3	RA 4	QUOTATIONS
100	100	100	100	200
200	200	200	200	400
300	300	300	300	600
400	400	400	400	800
500	500	500	500	1000

Use the study & quiz questions from each reading assignment to play a game like Jeopardy.

VOCABULARY REVIEW ACTIVITIES
Fahrenheit 451

1. Divide your class into two teams and have an old-fashioned spelling or definition bee.

2. Give each of your students (or students in groups of two, three or four) a Fahrenheit 451 Vocabulary Word Search Puzzle. The person (group) to find all of the vocabulary words in the puzzle first wins.

3. Give students a Fahrenheit 451 Vocabulary Word Search Puzzle without the word list. The person or group to find the most vocabulary words in the puzzle wins.

4. Use a Fahrenheit 451 Vocabulary Crossword Puzzle. Display the puzzle so everyone can see it, and do the puzzle together as a class.

5. Give students a Fahrenheit 451 Vocabulary Matching Worksheet to do.

6. Divide your class into two teams. Use the Fahrenheit 451 vocabulary words with their letters jumbled as a word list. Student 1 from Team A faces off against Student 1 from Team B. You write the first jumbled word on the board. The first student (1A or 1B) to unscramble the word wins the chance for his/her team to score points. If 1A wins the jumble, go to student 2A and give him/her a definition. He/she must give you the correct spelling of the vocabulary word which fits that definition. If he/she does, Team A scores a point, and you give student 3A a definition for which you expect a correctly spelled matching vocabulary word. Continue giving Team A definitions until some team member makes an incorrect response. An incorrect response sends the game back to the jumbled-word face off, this time with students 2A and 2B. Instead of repeating giving definitions to the first few students of each team, continue with the student after the one who gave the last incorrect response on the team. For example, if Team B wins the jumbled-word face-off, and student 5B gave the last incorrect answer for Team B, you would start this round of definition questions with student 6B, and so on. The team with the most points wins!

7. Have students write a story in which they correctly use as many vocabulary words as possible. Have students read their compositions orally! Post the most original compositions on your bulletin board!

UNIT REVIEW ACTIVITIES
Fahrenheit 451

1. Ask the class to make up a unit test for Fahrenheit 451. The test should have 4 sections: matching, true/false, short answer, and essay. Students may use 1/2 period to make the test and then swap papers and use the other 1/2 class period to take a test a classmate has devised. (open book) You may want to use the unit test included in this packet or take questions from the students' unit tests to formulate your own test.

2. Take 1/2 period for students to make up true and false questions (including the answers). Collect the papers and divide the class into two teams. Draw a big tic-tac-toe board on the chalk board. Make one team X and one team O. Ask questions to each side, giving each student one turn. If the question is answered correctly, that students' team's letter (X or O) is placed in the box. If the answer is incorrect, no mark is placed in the box. The object is to get three marks in a row like tic-tac-toe. You may want to keep track of the number of games won for each team.

3. Take 1/2 period for students to make up questions (true/false and short answer). Collect the questions. Divide the class into two teams. You'll alternate asking questions to individual members of teams A & B (like in a spelling bee). The question keeps going from A to B until it is correctly answered, then a new question is asked. A correct answer does not allow the team to get another question. Correct answers are +2 points; incorrect answers are -1 point.

4. Have students pair up and quiz each other from their study guides and class notes.

5. Give students a Fahrenheit 451 crossword puzzle to complete.

6. Divide your class into two teams. Use the Fahrenheit 451 crossword words with their letters jumbled as a word list. Student 1 from Team A faces off against Student 1 from Team B. You write the first jumbled word on the board. The first student (1A or 1B) to unscramble the word wins the chance for his/her team to score points. If 1A wins the jumble, go to student 2A and give him/her a clue. He/she must give you the correct word which matches that clue. If he/she does, Team A scores a point, and you give student 3A a clue for which you expect another correct response. Continue giving Team A clues until some team member makes an incorrect response. An incorrect response sends the game back to the jumbled-word face off, this time with students 2A and 2B. Instead of repeating giving clues to the first few students of each team, continue with the student after the one who gave the last incorrect response on the team. For example, if Team B wins the jumbled-word face-off, and student 5B gave the last incorrect answer for Team B, you would start this round of clue questions with student 6B, and so on. The team with the most points wins!

UNIT CROSSWORD ANSWER KEY
Fahrenheit 451

VOCABULARY CROSSWORD ANSWER KEY
Fahrenheit 451

Across:
1. CADENCED
6. PYRE
7. BALLISTICS
12. ODIOUS
14. RETALIATION
17. MULTIFACETED
18. PEDANTS
19. MELANCHOLY

Down:
2. CAP
3. DIC
4. G
5. O
7. BSCURE
8. LIMNED
9. CARM / (SARCASM)
10. COWARD
11. CENTRIFUGE
13. S
14. (RETALIATION down continuation)
15. TACTILE
16. ERECTED

NOTES
Fahrenheit 451

www.ingramcontent.com/pod-product-compliance
Lightning Source LLC
Chambersburg PA
CBHW081438070526
44586CB00019B/2171